The Behavioral Study of Political Ideology and Public Policy Formation

Edited by
Carl Grafton and Anne Permaloff

University Press of America,® Inc.
Dallas · Lanham · Boulder · New York · Oxford

Contents

Acknowledgments

We thank the authors and journal publishers who allowed their articles to be reprinted in this volume. The works have been reformatted in order to establish a consistent style of presentation. The content itself has not been altered.

We also thank Mary Jane Hetrick, Anida Wishnietsky, and Janice Smith for their assistance and their professionalism and can-do attitudes.

Any errors found in this volume are our responsibility alone.

Introduction

This volume introduces a new area of inquiry, the behavioral study of political ideology and its connection to public policy formulation. A political ideology is an action-oriented model of people and society (Parsons 1951, 349), and outspoken advocates of a particular ideology are known as ideologues. In the United States the dominant political ideologies are liberalism and conservatism. Public policy is the set of decisions made by governmental officials including statutes, court decisions, executive orders, rules and regulations, and more.

There are four central themes covered in this book: how ideology is and can be studied empirically; why ideological change occurs; how ideology and ideological change affect public policy; and the dynamic relationships that exist between competing ideologies during policy formulation. Because the central focus is the relationship between ideology and public policy in the United States, liberalism and conservatism are the ideologies covered in the readings and discussion.

Political ideologies are usually studied in terms of the thoughts of theorists. The many textbooks on ideology often begin descriptions of liberalism with John Locke and move through history to examine the lives and works of such thinkers as Adam Smith, John Stuart Mill, T. H. Green, John Meynard Keynes, and John Rawls. The same textbooks will generally begin accounts of conservatism with Edmund Burke and then perhaps cover Benjamin Disraeli, Michael Oakeshott, and Russell Kirk among others. This is a perfectly reasonable way to approach the subject, but so much space is usually devoted to the subtleties of theorists' ideas that little room remains for the examination of the public policy prescriptions of an ideology or the role ideology plays in the formulation of public policy. Generally speaking, if a book title contains the words ideology, liberal, conservative, or any variation of them (e.g., ideological or liberalism), it will include little coverage of public policy except in the form of short examples.

The public policy implications of ideology, all but ignored by textbooks on ideology, have never been the purview of a single community of scholars. Instead, this area encompasses several specialties of political science, public administration, and economics. Across these disciplines the behavioral study of political ideology appears fragmented. This book is intended to pull these pieces together.

Negative Images of Ideology

The word ideology is often used in an unflattering manner. Ideology is said to produce bad public policy because ideologies fit true believers' preconceptions and not reality. Others believe ideology to be insignificant. In this view, ideology is not an independent cause of political behavior; ideology is merely an intermediate variable of little importance in explaining political behavior. Interest groups, political parties, or individuals are seen as using principled sounding ideological arguments to promote economic, social, sexual, racial, or other basic interests. Thus liberals are sometimes accused of advocating government expansion because it will add to the rolls of public-employee labor unions and result in more votes for liberal politicians. Similarly, conservatives are often criticized for promoting the interests of large corporations or wealthy individuals. Ideology in these examples is viewed as merely an instrument of combat or at most the grammar of dispute.

Definitions and characterizations of ideology often aim to discredit ideology. For example, Russell Kirk (1993, 5), a conservative, described ideology as:

> a dogmatic political theory which is an endeavor to substitute secular goals and doctrines for religious goals and doctrines; and which promises to overthrow present dominations so that the oppressed may be liberated.

He and many others of the right, center, and left along with some who claim to be above ideology come close to defining ideologies as the belief systems of rigid fanatics (McCarthy 1996, 7, 30). The definition used in this volume is neutral and assumes neither virtues nor defects in ideology.

Ideology as Bad Public Policy

Many, if not all, who seek to discredit the role of ideology in political thought are themselves ideologues. Indeed it seems that the more energetically an author denigrates ideology, the more vigorously he or she applies ideological thought. In doing so, supposed non-ideologues assert that the opinions being offered are based entirely on science or common sense guided by experience.

Ideology oversimplifies a complex world

In their advocacy of a federal technology policy Stephen J. Kline and Don E. Kash (1993) list ideology as inhibiting the creation of a comprehensive national program to assist or stimulate technological enterprises. Specifically, they target:

> an American ideology which celebrates the virtues of free markets, and thus suggests any government involvement in the market is inherently imprudent. The core theme of this ideology is that capitalist societies must be *laissez-faire* in structure and operation. This powerful value position places the burden of proof on those advocating government support of commercial technology. (368)

Kline and Kash describe this ideology and value position (another term used in a belittling manner) as based on "the neo-classical model of a free market."(368) They argue that this neo-classical free market model heavily influences the American public and has raised *laissez-faire* concepts to the status of an ideology.

Kline and Kash argue (369):

> the sociotechnical systems with which technology policy must deal place those systems well beyond the reach of any economic or other type of current, or foreseeable, predictive theory. In the absence of predictive theory . . . [we] see no alternative to careful empiricism, that is, looking at what has happened in the past over a wide range of experiences and summarizing the lessons those experiences teach us.

Accomplishing what Kline and Kash propose, that is, surveying past events and deducing prescriptions for technology policy, requires criteria by which to choose events to examine or ignore as well as standards by which to draw lessons from the selected events. Such criteria and standards constitute an ideology.

Ideology ignores real world experience

Derogatory references to ideology and ideologues are not new (Christenson, Engel, Jacobs, Rejai, and Waltzer 1975, 4). The first appearance of the term ideology is traced by historians to the radical French theorist Antoine Louis Claude Destutt de Tracy who used it in 1797 (Drucker 1974; Mannheim 1968, 55, 64). De Tracy believed that ideology was a new science that would permit him to discover the bases of a just and orderly society. He argued that reliance on science instead of metaphysical speculation and superstition would permit societies to avoid the many mistakes of the past (Kennedy 1978, 47). De Tracy maintained that the worst of these mistakes stemmed from the Roman Catholic Church's influence over education. The key to a good society was a scientifically based school system independent of Church influence.

Napoleon's increasing power and his alliance with the Church brought him into conflict with de Tracy. Napoleon gave the word ideologue its first negative connotation when he sarcastically called his opponents ideologues by which he meant society's intellectual elite devoid of experience and holding ideas that were not practically applicable (Boudon 1986, 25; Durant and Durant 1975, 266). Napoleon characterized ideology as a "cloudy metaphysics." He contrasted an ideology's attempt to establish laws based on theoretical searches for first causes with the much sounder approach of deriving "laws from knowledge of the human heart and from the lessons of history. . . ." (McLellan 1995, 5) A great variety of thinkers including Edmund Burke, Karl Marx, Michael Oakeshott, Edward Shils, and Talcott Parsons have shared Napoleon's criticism of ideology even though they have had little else in common with him or each other.

The Importance of Ideology

Political scientists and sociologists have examined many determinants of political behavior, most notably economic self-interest, race, religion, and geography. These factors are typically regarded as the bedrock of political behavior. For example, many congressional tariff votes can probably be explained rather fully by whether a member of Congress' constituents are economically dependent on exports or threatened by imports. And many votes on civil rights legislation are probably highly correlated to the percentage of racial minority voters in congressional districts and states.

Where does ideology fit into such explanations of political behavior? One theory is that ideology should be listed together with other bedrock independent variables. Operationally, this perspective holds that action oriented models of people and society are sometimes statistically separable from the other bedrock variables. This suggests that ideological thinking sometimes determines behavior in ways not predictable by those variables. For example, a conservative, free market oriented member of Congress who represents a rural district in which peanut farming is important could vote against subsidies for peanut farmers and against tariffs protecting domestic peanut markets. Or a liberal senator generally critical of defense spending on ideological grounds could refuse to defend a military base in her state scheduled for closure. The reader's sense of realism will correctly reject both of these extreme examples as fanciful. More realistically, a conservative member of Congress who represents a district not dependent on peanut farming will be seen voting against governmental support for peanut farming, and a liberal senator will refuse to defend a military base outside his or her state.

A theory that views ideologies as unimportant claims that ideologies merely reflect economic self-interest, race, and other bedrock variables (Downs 1957, 96-97). An example is a member of Congress who supports an increase in the minimum wage and affirmative action representing a low income district with a majority of African-Americans. However, John Kingdon reminds us that the "merely" in the first sentence in this paragraph may be inappropriate (1973, 246). Even if ideology can be explained or predicted by other factors, it remains the central language by which political actors communicate. For example, H. M. Drucker observed that ideologies are: "the only serious vessels in which political ideas are transmitted in our age." (1974, xi) This point is reinforced by the common use of ideological terminology by journalists and politicians including some of the most pragmatic of both breeds (Schneider 1979, 3-5). The widely respected and objective *Congressional Quarterly Weekly Report* regularly refers to members of Congress as occupying points on "the ideological spectrum," and members of Congress commonly characterize each other using similar terminology.

According to those who view ideologies merely as reflections of economic and other bedrock interests, the political actor is a thoughtless utility maximizer. Her or his decision is little more than the brain identifying the strongest interest (sometimes economic self-interest, sometimes race, sometimes sex, sometimes geography, and sometimes two or more simultaneously) and acting on it (them). Based on such a theory, a poor person favors a tax increase on the rich because it will result in more programs benefitting the poor. A wealthy individual favors regressive taxes because they lower his tax burden. A black favors affirmative action, and a white opposes it. That is the beginning and end of decision-making.

Ideology may serve the purely selfish decision-maker by allowing her or him to make more sophisticated choices than an automatic economic class, race, sex, or geographically based reaction would. Ideology can sometimes produce more complex causal analysis especially when it uses science. Science often generates unobvious and powerful theories. Phillip Converse saw ideology as fulfilling many of the same functions as science (1964, 206-261; 1975, 75-169). Ideology allows the user to understand the relationships among events, to facilitate the making of consistent judgments over time, and to process information more efficiently than a purely ad hoc approach would allow. David Apter saw ideology as improving a political actor's effectiveness: "Ideas help men to control and change their environment." (1964, 20)

Ideology can also protect an individual's or group's self esteem and fulfill other psychological and social functions. Erik H. Erikson saw involvement in ideology as one of many ways that adolescents resolve identity crises (1962, 14). Robert Lane (1972, 162-163) observed that:

> an *individual* must have a belief system to guide him in his daily tasks, to orient him towards others, to provide purposes and to give them sanction, to place himself in the ongoing stream of events. *Groups* must have belief systems to permit their members to work together and to provide their members with legitimate common goals. A political party, a union, or an ethnic association needs a rationale for its existence, a rationale that helps to define membership, moralize organizational claims on society, justify the sacrifices required of members, articulate some division of labor and role structures, and explain a mission to others.

The literature on the psychological functions of ideology makes clear that the connection, on a person by person basis, between bedrock variables and ideology is highly complex and subtle. The son or daughter of a family of conservative Republican party activists will probably become a conservative Republican, but he or she also might rebel and turn into a public interest lawyer. At an individual level the relationships between bedrock variables and ideology are so complex that they cannot be understood fully. This takes us back to the point made earlier that ideology becomes a sometimes observable phenomenon that summarizes a host of bedrock variables.

Liberalism and Conservatism

Most books on liberalism or conservatism pay little attention to public policy. One of the reasons is that both ideologies are almost impossible to define with any brevity. Both have histories spanning centuries, both have undergone substantial changes over these years, and both ideologies are fractured by internal conflict. This book concerns not the content of liberalism and conservatism, but how these ideologies affect the formulation of public policy, how they affect one another in the context of public policy formulation, and why they change over time. Because these topics concern the content of these ideologies, we need to define these terms at least to the degree that will allow the reader to determine whether our sense of them and the reader's are roughly the same.

Kenneth Janda, Jeffrey M. Berry, and Jerry Goldman (1992) present what may be the shortest comparison of liberalism and conservatism that can claim to encompass their long and complex histories. According to these scholars, liberals tend to value equality over freedom and freedom over order; conservatives tend to favor order over freedom and freedom over equality. It should be stressed that in some sense both liberals and conservatives value equality, freedom, and order. The difference lies in their priorities.

After devoting four chapters to a description of liberalism Vernon Van Dyke (1995, 101-102) concluded that liberalism is an ideology calling for:

> (1) public policies designed to enhance the worth of liberty and pro-
> mote fair equality of opportunity for all, (2) reliance on reason and the

market, (3) tolerance of diversity, and (4) concern for the common good; and it regards democratic government as a useful instrument in promoting its goals.

This characterization is roughly consistent with Janda, et al. to the degree that freedom and equality are emphasized over order which is not even mentioned. Van Dyke required even more space to describe conservatism than he did liberalism, and he failed to develop a comparable short definition. Most conservatives could probably accept a modified version of Van Dyke's definition of liberalism as a description of conservatism. Such a modification, written with Janda, et al. in mind, might read that conservatism is an ideology calling for: (1) public policies designed to enhance the maintenance of order, liberty, and promote equality of opportunity for all, (2) reliance on reason and the market with conservatives placing greater reliance on the market than liberals, (3) tolerance of diversity, and (4) less use of government than liberals except in the maintenance of order.

Ideology and Public Policy

This book is divided into three main sections and an appendix. The first section concentrates on public opinion, political parties, and interest groups which the editors view as the environment within which policy formulation occurs. Public opinion, parties, and interest groups influence the electoral process and the policies promoted by the president and Congress. The second section examines empirical studies that seek to measure the influence of ideology on congressional votes, and the third focuses on ideology and its relationship to problem definition and agenda setting in the policy formulation process. The Appendix presents a basic description of multiple regression, the major research tool used in many of the articles reprinted here. It is included to assist those readers who may be new to this technique.

Section 1. Public opinion, parties, and interest groups

Public opinion polls support a broad generalization that the American populace is not ideologically oriented nor are a majority of Americans interested in or knowledgeable about politics and government. However, the general public, the politically active public, and elites differ with regard to the degree to which ideology plays a part in their thinking and behavior just as they differ with regard to degrees of interest in and knowledge of government and politics. Phillip Converse (1964, 211) described ideological thought as an activity of a "minuscule proportion of any population." Once ideological ideas and related policy positions and electoral candidate endorsements are formulated by elites, they are marketed throughout society. As those ideas move from elite thinkers to the general public much of the logic of ideological thought is lost. What is left among the vast majority of the public are unconnected and often inconsistent ideas--disorganized fragments of ideology.

Converse presented survey data that show that a little over 10 percent of the American populace could be categorized as ideologues or near-ideologues. Ideologues relied:

> in some active way on a relatively abstract and far-reaching conceptual dimension as a yardstick against which political objects and their shifting policy significance over time were evaluated. . . . the liberal-conservative continuum . . . was almost the only dimension of the sort that occurred empirically. In a second stratum were placed those respondents [near-ideologues] who mentioned such a dimension in a peripheral way but did not appear to place much evaluative dependence upon it or who used such concepts in a fashion that raised doubt about the breadth of their understanding of the meaning of the term. (215-216)

With Converse we have only respondents' thought processes--not any consideration of how those processes relate to other variables such as socio-economic status, race, religion, or geography. He demonstrated only that a minority of the population think ideologically; the rest do so little or not at all. With Converse's data it would still be possible for elite members' ideological thinking to be socially and economically determined--in other words for ideology to be only an intermediate variable between political behavior and such factors as class, race, religion, and sex. It might also be possible for ideology to be an independent factor affecting political behavior along with class, race, and the rest.

Converse's work stimulated a blizzard of studies some of which contradicted his image of ideological inattention by most Americans while others supported it. Nearly 20 years of this effort is summarized by Donald R. Kinder and David O. Sears (1985, 670):

few Americans make sophisticated use of sweeping ideological ideas.
. . . . Innocence of ideology is revealed also in the political connections
Americans never make. Few Americans express consistently liberal,
conservative, or centrist positions on policy. . . .
    That the original [Converse] claim of ideological innocence is
largely sustained does not mean that the American mind is empty of
politics. Innocent though Americans may typically be of ideological
principles, they are hardly innocent of political ideas. Such ideas defy
parsimonious description, however. Some beliefs are classically
liberal, some classically conservative. . . . There are patches of knowledge and expanses of ignorance.

Warren E. Miller and J. Merrill Shanks (1996, 243) found evidence
in presidential elections of ideological thinking beyond an opinion-leading
elite. Presenting their findings very cautiously, they found evidence of
"persistent liberal/conservative disagreements over policy" with many
citizens "predisposed to take one side or the other whenever those conflicts become salient." These predispositions mediate "the influence of
social or economic characteristics on vote choice." (283) But these
predispositions also may have a "direct (or unmediated) impact on voters'
choice for President which is still visible after we control for all of the
other explanatory variables in our model. . . ." (293) Miller and Shanks
were not fully convinced of the direct impact of ideology, but their data
made it plausible. (294) They noted that their findings:

> should redress the tendency among many political scientists to underes-
> timate the electoral consequences of continuing social and economic
> conflicts and disagreements within the United States. We are im-
> pressed with the electoral consequences of controversies where individ-
> ual citizens hold quite different views concerning the most appropriate
> goals or priorities for the federal government. . . . (294)

Writing in 1995 William G. Jacoby, in the first article in Section 1 of
this volume, observed rudimentary ideological thinking among relatively
high percentages of the population. He found that more than half of the
population could correctly place the 1984 and 1988 presidential candidates and parties along the liberal-conservative continuum. Roughly one-
third also were consistent in the placement of themselves, candidates, and
parties along the ideological spectrum. Approximately one-quarter were
ideologically consistent regarding such matters as abortion, guaranteed
jobs, school prayer, and government spending. The mirror image of these

findings is that beyond locating presidential candidates and parties along the ideological spectrum, two-thirds to three-quarters of the populace could not make accurate and consistent judgments relating candidates, parties, and ideologies to the issues of abortion, guaranteed jobs, and the rest. In some issue areas such as government health insurance, school busing, and the status of women, 80 percent and more could not accurately and consistently place these issues on the ideological spectrum.

Until this point we have examined the degree to which public and elite opinions are structured ideologically. Political parties are another component of the policy formulation environment. The article by Jeffrey Levine, Edward G. Carmines, and Robert Huckfeldt (1997) inspects the structure of the post-New Deal Democratic party. The New Deal Democratic party was to a substantial degree an alliance of "Catholics, Jews, northern Blacks, industrial workers, White southerners, urban residents, and the poor." (Levine, et al. 1997, 20) This continued to be a valid description of Democratic party loyalists until the late 1940s or early 1950s, and it remains so to some degree. But, according to Levine, et al., since the early 1950s many members of these groups have slowly deserted the Democratic party.

As social group membership has been a progressively less reliable guide to Democratic party support, ideology has become a more reliable guide. Levine, et al. (1997, 23) note that this shift is consistent with claims made by scholars that: "during the late 1970s and 1980s, the ideological conflict between the Republicans and Democrats intensified and sharpened, cutting across the New Deal social group partisan coalitions."

Levine, et al.'s image of an increasingly liberal Democratic party and (by suggestion) an increasingly conservative Republican party is reinforced by the last article in this section, Jonathan Knuckey's (2001) description of ideological change in the South. Knuckey's objective is to explain the shift in the South from one-party dominance to two-party competition. In roughly the same time period covered by Levine, et al. the most puzzling aspect of southern politics was that conservative whites remained loyal to state Democratic parties when the national party was moving to the left. Most observers predicted that at some point ideology would trump party loyalty, and that enough whites would desert the Democrats for Republicans on ideological grounds to bring about two party competition in the South. Knuckey documents this movement.

Section 2. Policy formulation and congressional votes

In addition to the authors cited above, many writers such as McCann (1995), Eldersveld (1968), Fenno (1978, 143, 153), Langston (1992), and Kingdon (1973), have documented the presence of ideological thought among the politically active. A majority of these studies have focused on legislative bodies rather than the executive branch. The reason for this preference is the existence of recorded votes cast over time by representatives of districts and states of widely varying characteristics. In addition, members of the U.S. House of Representatives are relatively accessible for personal interviews which may be used in conjunction with roll call vote analysis or as the primary data source.

There is no doubt that government officials and opinion leaders employ ideological thought. Again, the question is whether ideology can be legitimately used as an independent variable. Figure 1 shows how these factors might relate for a member of Congress. On the far left are the bedrock variables affecting constituents' ideology, a legislator's ideology, and congressional roll call votes. In turn, constituents' ideology and a legislator's ideology also affect roll call votes. Constituents' ideology may also affect a legislator's ideology. Lines extending directly from the constituent economic self-interest and ideology boxes represent potential statistical relationships, but they do not portray authority-- constituents do not vote on the floor of the House or Senate. The same is true of the line extending from bedrock variables to roll call votes.

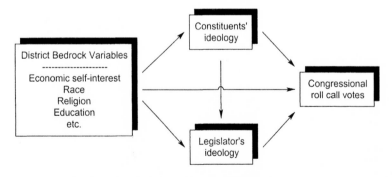

Figure 1. Bedrock Variables, Constituents' Ideology, Legislator's Ideology, and Roll Call Votes.

The Behavioral Study of Political Ideology

Studies show that the strength of these relationships varies widely from issue to issue, district to district (or state to state), and over time. Given the sophistication of the research methodologies often used, there should be no surprise that the strength of these relationships also appears to vary with those methodologies and among authors. The literature on congressional roll call voting is filled with complex methodological and statistical disputes. We will touch on a few below, but we will settle none. Instead, we try to describe some of the clearer and more recent research, and we attempt to represent a variety of approaches to this subject.

To a significant degree, most legislators vote in ways that reflect bedrock interests in their district or state as interpreted by constituent ideology. For example, Jeffrey A. Segal, Charles M. Cameron, and Albert D. Cover (1992) studied U.S. Senate voting on Supreme Court nominees. They found that such voting is "highly dependent on the ideological distance between a senator's constituents and the nominee" together with "the perceived qualifications of the nominee, and on the interaction between the two." (113; see also Kingdon 1973, 64) This tight relationship between constituent interests and congressional votes is consistent with democratic theory and common sense and is assumed, at least as a starting point, by most analysts who study legislative voting behavior. In some studies the question of the independent importance of ideology has centered on the relative importance of constituency pressure on a member of Congress versus the member's personal ideological views.

Lilliard E. Richardson and Michael E. Munger (1990) examined voting that occurred in 1983 on amendments to the Social Security Act. They distinguished among service to constituents, interest groups, and a legislator's own ideological preferences. Like many studies in this literature, Richardson and Munger used ratings of legislators issued by the liberal interest group Americans for Democratic Action (ADA). Despite the fact that their measures of constituent economic interests were especially detailed, they found that ideology was a statistically significant variable. They also found that senators gave greater weight to their own ideological preferences than did representatives. This is not surprising because senators, with six year terms, are expected to be more independent of constituents than are representatives. Other studies have shown that this independence tends to decline as a reelection year approaches; in this sense a senator behaves like a representative as both face reelection in less than two years. The finding of these differences and similarities between senators and representatives strengthens Richardson and Munger's findings. Nevertheless, the authors were cautious in interpreting their data. They concluded that their findings might mean that legislators were voting ideologically or they were voting according to ideological patterns to establish in voters' minds a "brand name" identification. They might also be representing or reflecting constituent ideology.

Joseph P. Kalt and Mark A. Zupan (1984) in the first article in Section 2 analyzed U.S. Senate votes on the Surface Mining Control and Reclamation Act which regulated strip-mining. Using measures of state coal oriented self-interest (relating to coal consumers and coal producers), environmental self-interest (relating to users of parks and hunting/fishing areas), environmental ideologues, and senatorial ideology (measured by senators' environmental rating on non-surface mining related votes), their analysis strongly suggests the influence of ideology in strip-mining votes. Perhaps their most notable finding is the high correlation between votes on strip-mining and votes on what they call social issues including: the death penalty; sex education; the neutron bomb; school desegregation; abortion; pregnancy disability; loans to communist countries; and the Panama Canal Treaty. Kalt and Zupan concluded: "For now, it appears that the economic theory of regulation will have to keep the door open to ideological behavior." (298)

Sam Peltzman (1985) examined which states gained and lost from federal taxation, tariff policies, and spending in the period 1910-1980. Wealthier areas (Peltzman labels the areas liberal) tended to favor redistributive policies, and poorer areas tended to oppose redistributive programs (an observation frequently made in the literature on the economic development of southern states). Northern urban liberal members of Congress tended to favor welfare, education, and other aid programs that redistributed wealth from their own districts and states to poorer, rural, southern districts and states whose representatives and senators tended to resist passage of such programs. Oddly, despite his use of the world "liberal" to describe the voting of legislators representing wealthier districts and states, Peltzman states that his findings support an economics-based interpretation of politics, i.e., wealthier states voted one way and poor states another. He fails to speculate about the altruistic (i.e., ideological) implications of his findings. Ordinarily, when the representative of a district or state votes for programs that economically benefit his or her district or state, such a vote is interpreted as motivated by economic self-interest. Deviations from this basic pattern, such as the ones detected by Peltzman, are viewed as requiring explanation and sometimes that explanation is the impact of ideology.

The methodological-statistical problem of separating ideological from economic interests virtually disappears when what Raymond Tatalovich and David Schier (1993) called symbolic-emotive policies or social regulations are considered. This policy category includes school prayer, pornography, gun control, capital punishment, and gay rights. The authors focused on votes in the 93rd, 94th, 96th, and 97th Congresses that sought to reverse the U.S. Supreme Court decision *Roe v. Wade* by modifying state restrictions on abortion. Tatalovich and Schier found that the effect of partisanship on these votes was not statistically significant and that constituency variables such as median family income, urbanism, and percent nonwhite were either statistically insignificant or minor factors. Religion (especially non-Catholic versus Catholic) was of some importance in the early years of these votes, but in the last three Congresses it became less important than ideology as measured by Americans for Democratic Action (ADA) scores. Tatalovich and Schier did not attempt to distinguish between constituent and legislator ideological beliefs.

The use of ADA scores as a measure of the ideologies of members of Congress has been the source of some debate. The basic argument as rendered by John E. Jackson and John W. Kingdon (1992, 809) is that ADA scores are based on roll call votes so that including ADA scores in a statistical analysis of roll call votes may be "tapping the same or related dimensions." This criticism is not entirely fair. ADA scores are not a random sample of congressional votes. The votes, usually numbering 20 per year, are carefully selected by the ADA and most seem accurate. For example, in 1999 Senators Ted Kennedy (D-MA) and Barbara Boxer (D-CA) received 95 and 100 respectively (out of a possible perfect score of 100), and Trent Lott (R-MS) and Jesse Helms (R-NC) both received zero. Probably none of these legislators would quarrel with their scores except that Kennedy might think of himself as just as liberal as Boxer.

Barry Burden, Gregory A. Caldeira, and Tim Groseclose's (2000) article in Section 2 compares ADA scores with eight other measurements including some that are not based on roll call votes. They conclude that the ADA scores are as valid as any and better than some noting: "roll-call measures tend to pick up confounding forces such as constituency and party, but find that the effects of these factors are overwhelmed by ideology." (250) Those unconvinced by the Burden, Caldeira, and Groseclose analysis can find a straightforward method for adjusting ADA scores in the next article included in this volume written by Mark J. Wattier and Raymond Tatalovich (1995) who address another controversy in this literature that concerns the relative importance of party and ideology as explanations of congressional votes.

In their literature review Wattier and Tatalovich (1995) found that many scholars including Tatalovich himself have concluded that ideology is a stronger explanatory factor than party. However, party is operationalized by these researchers as a dummy variable, e.g., Republican party membership symbolized as a zero and Democratic party membership as a one. Wattier and Tatalovich lodge theoretical and methodological complaints against this procedure. From a theoretical perspective it crams liberal and conservative Democrats together in one category and liberal and conservative Republicans in another. One could counter that it is exactly this kind of ideological heterogeneity that makes political parties what they are, especially in the United States, and suggests that dummy variables are an appropriate device for representing party.

The Wattier and Tatalovich methodological criticism of making party a dichotomous variable is that such variables included in the statistical technique utilized in these studies (multiple regression analysis) tend to lose predictive power when included with continuous variables such as the ADA ideology scale. Their solution is to generate a synthetic measure of party for each senator based on state ideology, state partisanship, state political culture, region, and personal ideology. Thus the measure of party rather than placing a senator in one category or another becomes somewhat like survey research questions that ask respondents to categorize themselves as strong Republicans, weak Republicans, independents, weak Democrats, or strong Democrats.

Wattier and Tatalovich use their measure of party membership, a modified ADA scale, and demographic factors of individual states to explain votes on abortion. Their measure of partisanship outperforms their modified ADA score. That their measure of partisanship provides stronger explanatory power than partisanship as a dichotomous variable is scarcely surprising. The authors themselves explain at several points that ideology is imbedded in their measure of partisanship.

Wattier and Tatalovich appear to be loading partisanship with greater ideological weight than it should be made to carry especially in the context of U.S. politics. A party's first purpose is to win elections and the second is to govern. To do either much less both they are often obliged to be ideologically inconsistent. Many scholars of ideology caution that there is often a substantial divide between practicing politicians and ideological purity. It might be more accurate to view the Republican and Democratic parties as imperfect conduits of ideology with politicians simply in one or the other. But the editors of this anthology are less interested in how partisanship is conceptualized than the fact that however it is conceptualized ideology must be included to even approach a full explanation of voting with regard to abortion.

The literature on congressional roll call voting is methodologically complex, but it firmly supports the conclusion that some members of Congress vote ideologically. The sources of ideological voting in Congress appear to be both constituents' ideology and the personal ideologies of members of Congress. Furthermore, we can say at least tentatively that congressional ideological voting is fairly completely describable by a standard left-right or liberal-conservative spectrum.

Section 3. Problem definition and redefinition, agenda setting, and public policy

It is clear that the most active members of the political community think ideologically some of the time while also acting on economic and racial interests among other bedrock factors. It is also clear that ideology also influences some roll call votes in Congress. But how does ideology influence policy formulation?

Public policy may be thought of as the decisions or nondecisions (inaction) of government. According to Stella Z. Theodoulou and Matthew A. Cahn, (1995, 2) public policy resolves conflicting claims on scarce resources, coordinates collective action, and regulates behavior collectively determined to be immoral. Wayne Parsons (1995, xv) says that public policy "is concerned with how issues and problems come to be defined and constructed and how they are placed on the political and policy agenda." Public policy often takes the form of legislation and executive branch regulations. As Parsons suggests, it is common to think of the process of policy formulation as a series of steps or stages beginning with the recognition of a problem requiring government action, the definition of the problem in a form that is widely understandable, placing the problem on the societal agenda (i.e., making the public aware of the problem and its dimensions and motivating significant numbers of the public to care about the problem's resolution), placing the problem on the governmental agenda (i.e., making government officials aware of the problem and its dimensions and motivating significant numbers of government officials to care about the problem's resolution), and policy formulation (i.e., passing legislation or enacting executive orders or regulations intended to resolve the problem).

David A. Rochefort and Roger W. Cobb (1993, 56) in the first article in this section observe that policy formulation is often depicted as a logical sequence:

> Through the accumulation of information, a troubling social condition comes to light and is documented. Next it is the job of public officials to assess that problem and its causes and to respond as efficiently as possible through such means as new legislative enactments.

But, they point out that reality is often not this simple and neat. A troubling social condition for some is to others a normal characteristic of life requiring no governmental intervention. For a problem to move through the stages from initial recognition to public policy depends not only on objective conditions but "the intensity of issue advocacy, leaders' openness to the issue, and the salience of competing problems." (56) Rochefort and Cobb's exploration of these topics is not intended to stress ideology, but ideology's importance is a continuing theme in their article. At the beginning they list issue areas including pollution, child abuse, AIDS, and illiteracy and note that: "there are divergent perceptions of any problem's origin, impact, and significance within the social context." (56) Such perceptions are ideological, and the divergent perceptions are the basis for ideological dispute (69).

Andrew S. McFarland (1990) distinguishes between two basic models of public policy formulation. One is represented by an arrow or series of arrows moving from a beginning to ending. The step or stages model of policy formulation with which Rochefort and Cobb are often associated is an example. But McFarland regards a circular or spiral model as more descriptive of most policy formulation cases. He places particular emphasis on cycles of interest group reform, counter-reform, counter-counter-reform, and so forth around and around over time.

In the next article in this volume Carl Grafton and Anne Permaloff (forthcoming) propose a device called a signed digraph as a framework for studying political ideology and public policy formulation. The models that Grafton and Permaloff develop are, like the models discussed by McFarland, circular. The difference between McFarland's circular models (together with most linear step or stages policy formulation models) and those of Grafton and Permaloff is that the latter are developed not from a theoretical conception of policy formulation stages but from events. One advantage of the Grafton and Permaloff approach is that various theories of ideological change, problem definition, and agenda setting can be plugged into it in a modular fashion giving it broad applicability.

In the next article Mark A. Zupan (1992) presents a methodology for using the ADA roll call vote scores discussed earlier to generate equivalent ratings of presidents. Grafton and Permaloff (2001) use Zupan's ingenious scoring system in the third article in this section. (An expansion of Zupan's scoring system is available at Grafton and Permaloff 2004.) They use newspaper and journal of opinion editorials to gauge the content of liberal and conservative thought regarding business and the economy from 1961-1998. Specifically, editorials of the *Washington Post* and *New York Times* represent liberalism and editorials of the *Wall Street Journal* and *National Review* represent conservatism. This technique provides an objectivity often lacking in scholarly discussions of ideology where authors choose definitions to support their personal definitions of liberalism or conservatism. Grafton and Permaloff present a theory of liberal and conservative consensus, conflict, and change regarding public policy for business and the economy.

John C. Whitaker (1996), in the last article in the volume, reviews the domestic policy of President Richard Nixon in ideological terms. The title characterizes Nixon's domestic policy as liberal and bold, a description that may surprise readers accustomed to thinking of Nixon as a conservative. This article is typical of many that frame descriptions of presidents and members of Congress in ideological terms. Again, this is not to suggest that politicians act exclusively in terms of ideological considerations. Their motives are usually mixed, but biographical accounts and case studies such as this one show that ideology is often an important factor in describing political decision-making.

An appendix completes the volume. It contains a basic explanation of multiple regression, the statistical technique used most often in the articles. The material is intended as a general introduction to the topic.

References

Apter, D. E. ed. 1964. Ideology and discontent. New York: Free Press.

Binder, L. 1964. Ideological foundations of Egyptian-Arab nationalism. In *Ideology and discontent*, ed. D. E. Apter, 128-154. New York: Free Press.

Boudon, R.1986. *The analysis of ideology*. Chicago: University of Chicago Press.

Burden, B. C., G. A. Caldeira, and T. Groseclose. 2000. Measuring the ideologies of U.S. senators: The song remains the same. *Legislative Studies Quarterly* 25:237-258.

Christenson, R. M., A. S. Engel, D. N. Jacobs, M. Rejai, and H. Waltzer. 1975. *Ideologies and modern politics*. New York: Dodd, Mead & Co.

Converse, P. 1964. The nature of belief systems in mass publics. In *Ideology and discontent,* ed. D. E. Apter, 206-261. New York: Free Press.

_____. 1975. Public opinion and voting behavior. In *Handbook of political science*, Vol. 4, eds. F. I. Greenstein and N. W. Polsby, 75-169. Reading, PA: Addison Wesley.

Downs, A. 1957. *An economic theory of democracy*. New York: Harper & Row.

Drucker, H. M. 1974. *The political uses of ideology*. New York: Harper and Row/Barnes and Noble Import Division.

Durant, W. and A. Durant. 1975. *The age of Napoleon*. New York: Simon and Schuster.

Eldersveld, S. J. 1968. The ideological structure of the party. In *Public opinion and public policy: Models of political linkage*, ed. N. R. Luttbeg, 334-355. Homewood, IL: Dorsey Press.

Erikson, E. H. 1962. *Young man Luther*. New York: W. W. Norton.

Fenno, R. E., Jr. 1978. *Home style: House members in their districts.* Boston: Little, Brown.

Grafton, C. and A. Permaloff. 2001. Public policy for business and the economy: Ideological dissensus, change and consensus. *Policy Sciences* 34:403-434.

_____. 2004. Supplementing Zupan's measurements of the ideological preferences of U.S. presidents. *Public Choice* 118:125-131.

_____. forthcoming. The behavioral study of political ideology and policy formulation. *Social Science Journal.*

Jackson, J. E. and J. W. Kingdon. 1992. Ideology, interest group scores, and legislative votes. *American Journal of Political Science* 36:805-823.

Jacoby, W. G. 1991. Ideological identification and issue attitudes. *American Journal of Political Science* 35:178-205.

_____. 1994. Public attitudes toward government spending. *American Journal of Political Science* 38:336-361.

_____. 1995. The structure of ideological thinking in the American electorate. *American Journal of Political Science* 39:314-335.

Janda, K., J. M. Berry, and J. Goldman. 1992. *The challenge of democracy*. Boston: Houghton Mifflin.

Kalt, J. P. and M. A. Zupan. 1984. Capture and ideology in the economic theory of politics. *American Economic Review* 74:279-300.

Kennedy, E. 1978. *A philosophe in the age of revolution: Destutt de Tracy and the origins of "ideology"*. Philadelphia: American Philosophical Society.

Kinder, D. R. and D. O. Sears. 1985. Public opinion and political action. In *Handbook of social psychology*, eds. G. Lindzey and E. Aronson, 659-741. New York: Random House.

Kingdon, J. 1973. *Congressmen's voting decisions*. New York: Harper & Row.

Kirk, R. 1993. *The politics of prudence*. Bryn Mawr, PA: Intercollegiate Studies Institute.

Kline, S. J. and D. E. Kash. 1993. Technology policy: What should it do? In *Technology and the future*, ed. A. H. Teich, 366-383. New York: St. Martin's Press.

Knuckey, J. 2001. Ideological realignment and partisan change in the American South, 1972-1996. *Politics & Policy* 29:337-358.

Lane, R. E. 1972. *Political man*. New York: Free Press.

Langston, T. S. 1992. Ideologues and presidents. Baltimore: Johns Hopkins University Press.

Levine, J., E. G. Carmines, and R. Huckfeldt. 1997. The rise of ideology in the post-New Deal party system, 1972-1992. *American Politics Quarterly* 25:19-34.

Mannheim, K. 1968. *Ideology and Utopia*. New York: Harcourt, Brace and World.

McArthur, J. and S. V. Marks. 1988. Constituent interest versus legislator ideology: The role of political opportunity cost. *Economic Inquiry* 26:461-470.

McCann, J. A. 1995. Nomination politics and ideological polarization: Assessing the attitudinal effects of campaign involvement. *Journal of Politics* 57:1-20.

McCarthy, E. D. 1996. *Knowledge as culture*. London/New York: Routledge.

McFarland, A. S. 1990. Interest groups and political time: Cycles in America. *British Journal of Political Science* 21:257-284.

McLellan, D. 1995. *Ideology*. Minneapolis: University of Minnesota Press.

Miller, W. E. and J. M. Shanks. 1996. *The new American voter*. Cambridge, MA: Harvard University Press.

Parsons, T. 1951. *The social system*. New York: Free Press.

Parsons, W. 1995. *Public policy*. Aldershot, UK: Edward Elgar.

Peltzman, S. 1985. An economic interpretation of the history of congressional voting in the Twentieth Century. *American Economic Review* 75:656-675.

Plamenatz, J. 1970. *Ideology*. New York: Praeger.

Richardson, L. E. and M. E. Munger. 1990. Shirking, representation, and congressional behavior: Voting on the 1983 amendments to the Social Security Act. *Public Choice* 67:11-33.

Rochefort, D. A. and R. W. Cobb. 1993. Problem definition, agenda access, and policy choice. *Policy Studies Journal* 21:56-71.

Scalapino, R. A. 1964. Ideology and modernization--The Japanese case. In *Ideology and discontent*, ed. D. E. Apter, 93-127. New York: Free Press.

Schneider, J. E. 1979. *Ideological coalitions in Congress*. Westport, CT: Greenwood Press.

Segal, J. A., C. M. Cameron, and A. D. Cover. 1992. A spatial model of roll call voting: Senators, constituents, presidents, and interest groups in Supreme Court confirmations. *American Journal of Political Science* 36:96-121.

Tatalovich, R. and D. Schier. 1993. The persistence of ideological cleavage in voting on abortion legislation in the House of Representatives, 1973-1988. *American Politics Quarterly* 21:125-139.

Theodoulou, S. Z. and M. A. Cahn. 1995. *Public policy: The essential readings*. Englewood Cliffs, NJ: Prentice Hall.

Van Dyke, V. 1995. *Ideology and political choice*. Chatham, NJ: Chatham House Publishers.

Wattier, M. J. and R. Tatalovich. 1995. Senate voting on abortion legislation over two decades: Testing a reconstructed partisanship variable. *American Review of Politics* 16:167-183.

Whitaker, J. C. 1996. Nixon's domestic policy: Both liberal and bold in retrospect. *Political Studies Quarterly* 26:131-153.

Zupan, M. A. 1992. Measuring the ideological preferences of U.S. presidents: A proposed (extremely simple) method. *Public Choice* 73:351-361.

Section 1

Empirical Studies of Ideology:
Public Opinion, Parties, and Interest Groups

Chapter 1

The Structure of Ideological Thinking in the American Electorate*

William G. Jacoby

This study examines the structure of ideological thinking across different political orientations. This approach allows for systematic differences in the ways that people apply liberal-conservative terms to candidates, parties, and their own political orientations. The assumption underlying this analysis is straightforward: ideological thinking is not a dichotomous characteristic, such that people either *do* or *do not* think about politics in ideological terms. Instead, ideological thinking is best viewed in continuous terms; that is, there are many gradations among individuals' abilities to apply the liberal-conservative continuum to specific political stimuli. Furthermore, there may well be systematic differences in the degree to which separate political stimuli are viewed in ideological terms by the American public. If this is the case, then it should be possible to measure both individual citizens and political objects in terms of a characteristic that we might loosely term their "ideological content." That is precisely the objective of the present analysis.

*Reprinted with permission from the *American Journal of Political Science* 39, 2 (1995):314-335.

More specifically, I use data from the CPS 1984 and 1988 National Election Studies to perform a scaling analysis on examples of liberal-conservative consistency in citizens' beliefs, attitudes, and behaviors. The latter are observable manifestations of a common underlying trait, which presumably corresponds to individual propensities to apply ideological abstractions to particular political stimuli. The results of the analysis show that there is a systematic, cumulative structure underlying liberal-conservative thinking in the American public. Stable over time, this structure has important implications for the ways that people employ ideological concepts in their political thinking.

Background

Mass-level ideological thinking is usually measured by the appearance of explicitly ideological themes in citizens' survey responses (Converse 1964) or by the degree to which people display ideologically "correct" political judgments (Hamill, Lodge, and Blake 1985; Jacoby 1989). Furthermore, political scientists typically rely on composite measures, which are created by combining (usually summing or averaging) individuals' responses on separate but related variables. Composite measures have been employed in the literature with important contributions to the study of mass-level ideology (Levitin and Miller 1979; Luskin 1987). But most measures have focused strictly on differences across individuals, rather than variability in ideologically oriented behaviors. The implicit assumption is that no type of ideological consistency is better or worse than any other as an indicator of the public's reliance on liberal-conservative terminology and ideas.

However, indirect evidence suggests sizable differences in the "ideological content" of different political stimulus objects. Many people place themselves along the liberal-conservative continuum, without showing any other evidence of ideologically oriented behavior (Stimson 1975; Jacoby 1991a). When survey respondents describe their likes and dislikes about political objects, they make ideological comments about political parties more frequently than they do about presidential candidates (Nie, Verba, and Petrocik 1979). But even among the latter, some candidates generate a larger number of ideological responses than others (Page 1978; Nie, Verba, and Petrocik 1979). Similarly, certain issues evoke a high proportion of ideologically consistent responses, while others do not (Carmines and Stimson 1980; Jacoby 1990). And finally, different manifestations of ideological thinking seem to exhibit varying patterns of temporal stability and change (Field and Anderson 1969; Pierce 1970).

All of the preceding results suggest that the nature of a political stimulus affects the extent to which citizens apply liberal-conservative ideas to that stimulus. If that is the case, variability in the ideological content of political stimuli and judgments is a distinct phenomenon from variability in individual levels of political sophistication and ideological awareness. It is important to take *both* types of variability into account, in order to obtain a complete, accurate empirical representation of liberal-conservative thinking within the American public.

If people and political objects both vary systematically in their ideological content, a recognizable structure among individuals' responses to questions about those political objects should emerge. But, what kind of structure underlies variability in different forms of ideological thinking? I believe that manifestations of individual-level ideological thinking conform to a cumulative pattern. According to this view, political orientations vary in terms of their "ideological difficulty." In some cases, the connections between liberal-conservative labels and political stimuli are well known and easily made. Ideologically consistent judgments about these stimuli occur relatively frequently within the mass public. In other cases, the relationship between ideology and a political stimulus will be less clearcut; accordingly, ideologically consistent reactions toward that stimulus are relatively difficult, and they should occur less frequently. If individuals exhibit an ideologically consistent response to a difficult stimulus, then they should also manifest ideologically consistent judgments for all "easier" political objects, as well.

The cumulative structure seems reasonable in substantive terms, and there is already some preliminary evidence that ideological thinking conforms to this type of pattern (Coveyou and Piereson 1977). If the cumulative model is supported empirically, then it will be possible to measure both individual people and political judgments along a common dimension of ideological capacity or difficulty. This is advantageous because it provides a more detailed view of the ways that people apply liberal-conservative terms to political objects than is possible with many other approaches.

Data and Scaling Procedure

Ideally, we would like to obtain information about *all* of the distinct elements within each person's political cognitive structure. But this is impossible, so we must settle for reactions toward some of the more prominent elements of the political environment confronting the public such as parties, candidates, and issues. With each separate response, we determine whether the individual is behaving in an ideologically consistent manner or not. For example, people are asked to place the two major parties along an ideological dimension. If an individual places the Democratic party at a more liberal position than the Republican party, it is counted as an ideologically consistent response. Alternatively, if the person places the parties at the same position, or locates the Democrats at a more conservative position than the Republicans, then the response is not considered to be ideologically consistent. This same kind of information is recorded across a variety of political judgments. It is the pattern of responses *across* the judgments that enables us to test for the presence of the hypothesized cumulative structure.

The data for this analysis are taken from the CPS 1984 and 1988 National Election Studies. Despite differences across the two years, most of the relevant survey items are asked at both time points. This is very useful because it enables two independent tests of the cumulative structure. The Appendix shows the complete set of political judgments that will be used in this analysis. For most of these items, the definition of what constitutes an ideologically consistent response is straightforward; complete explanations for each one are given in the table. In total, there are 21 items for the 1984 analysis, and 19 items for 1988.[1] It is important to reiterate that these variables by no means exhaust the possible manifestations of ideology in mass-level political thinking. Nevertheless, they do constitute a reasonable *sample* of each person's political orientations. Focusing on the respondents' ideological stances (as well as the degree of ideological consistency in their orientations toward parties, candidates, and issues) clarifies the ways that people apply liberal-conservative ideas to prominent political stimuli.

In order to fit the cumulative model to the data, I will employ a probabilistic version of the familiar Guttman scaling procedure, developed by Mokken (1970; also see Niemoller and van Schuur 1983). The Mokken procedure has several advantages over the traditional Guttman scalogram for assessing the presence of a common dimension underlying a set of empirical items (1970; Jacoby 1991b). The specific objectives of the scaling analysis are to determine whether a latent continuum of ideological difficulty exists (are the empirical data consistent with the hypothesized cumulative structure?) and to estimate the relative positions of the people and the stimuli along the underlying dimension (i.e., to measure the individuals and the judgments with respect to the scaled trait). As in a scalogram analysis, the scale scores are determined by the marginals of the responses toward the various stimuli. As more and more people display ideologically consistent judgments toward a particular stimulus, then the latter is located closer toward the easy side of the continuum and it receives a lower score. At the same time, as individuals display larger numbers of ideologically consistent judgments in their responses toward the stimuli, they are located closer toward the difficult side of the continuum, and they receive higher scores.

Content of the Empirical Scales

The Mokken scaling analysis indicates that the cumulative structure fits the data closely in both 1984 and 1988. The goodness-of-fit measure is a coefficient called Loevinger's H, which usually varies between zero and one. A value of 0 indicates that the results conform perfectly to a null model of statistical independence; in other words, there is *no* discernible common structure among the separate item responses. At the other extreme, a value of 1.0 means that there are no scaling errors at all in the data; the cumulative model fits perfectly, and all of the separate responses can be predicted from the structure of the empirical scale. The empirical *H* values are 0.60 for the 1984 scale, and 0.58 for the scale recovered from the 1988 data. Both of these values easily achieve statistical significance; that is, the probabilities that they are due to sampling errors are infinitesimal in each case. Furthermore, Mokken reports that a set of items with an *H* statistic greater than 0.50 constitutes a "strong scale"; the two empirical scales both surpass this criterion by wide margins. By any reasonable standard, variability in ideologically consistent political judgments corresponds closely to the hypothesized cumulative structure.

1984 scale content

Table 1 shows the array of items included in the 1984 scale. The ordering of the separate items is determined by the proportions of respondents who display ideologically consistent judgments about each stimulus; these proportions are also shown in the table. Clearly, this scale taps the respondents' willingness (or perhaps, abilities) to make ideological distinctions among political stimuli, including their own preferences and attitudes. Starting at the easy end of the scale, the first two items are the correct placements of the presidential candidates and parties along the liberal-conservative continuum. This is followed immediately by the respondents' willingness to place themselves at a nonneutral position along the same ideological dimension. Next come the four items that tap consistency between the respondents' personal ideological identifications, and their candidate evaluations, vote choices, party identifications, and

Table 1.   Scale Ordering of Items Included in Cumulative Scale
Obtained from the 1984 Data

Scale Position for Political Judgment	Political Judgment	Percent of Respondents Displaying Ideologically Consistent Behavior
19	Government health insurance, own attitude	10
18	School busing, own attitude	14
17	Status of women, own attitude	20
16	Central America, own attitude	20
15	Minority aid, own attitude	21
14	Defense spending, own attitude	22
13	Government spending, own attitude	22
12	Cooperation with Russia, own attitude	23
11	School prayer, own attitude	24
10	Feel close to ideological groups	24
9	Guaranteed jobs, own attitude	25
8	Abortion, own attitude	27
7	Feeling thermometers, ideological groups	29
6	Ideologically consistent party identification	33
5	Ideologically consistent vote choice	34
4	Ideologically consistent candidate evaluation	34
3	Identify with ideological group	48
2	Liberal-conservative, party placement	56
1	Liberal-conservative, candidate placement	56

Loevinger's H for Scale (Measure of Scalability) = 0.60   Reliability = 0.948
Total Number of observations is 1989
Source: 1984 CPS National Election Study

thermometer ratings of liberals and conservatives. Most of the remaining items in the scale assess consistency between ideological identifications and particular issue positions. The one exception is the tenth item in the scale, which determines whether the individual feels close to the appropriate ideological group. Thus, the trait that is measured by this scale apparently encompasses a fairly wide variety of political judgments. But, they are all joined by a common thread: the orientations included in this cumulative scale all seem to involve individuals' abilities to sort out political stimuli in liberal-conservative terms.

Note that two 1984 items are excluded because they do not meet the minimum criterion for scalability with the others. These items are the willingness to provide a definition for the terms liberal and conservative, and the ability to correctly specify which of the two parties is more conservative. The exclusion of these two items does not imply anything about the prevalence of these behaviors within the American electorate. Instead, responses to these items just do not conform to the cumulative structure that characterizes the other types of ideological thinking.[2] A person who can specify a definition for liberal-conservative labels (or one who can identify the Republican party as more conservative) is neither more nor less likely to manifest other kinds of ideologically consistent judgments.

1988 scale content

Table 2 shows the array of items in the scale obtained from the 1988 data. Once again, this continuum appears to measure the degree to which people orient their judgments about political objects along liberal-conservative lines; in this sense, the 1988 scale is virtually identical to the 1984 scale. But, there is also an interesting difference: Starting at the easier end of the scale the first two items are the ability to define ideological terms and to specify which of the parties is more conservative--precisely the two behaviors that did not scale with the others in the 1984 data. Apparently, the structure of mass-level ideological thinking changed by 1988, so that these two kinds of responses *do* conform to the common, underlying, cumulative structure.

Next in the scale come placements of candidates and parties along the liberal-conservative continuum, followed by nonneutral ideological identifications. After these items, the general pattern in the scale is that behaviors indicating consistency between personal ideology and other political preferences (e.g., party identification, vote choice, etc.) are followed by manifestations of ideological consistency in specific issue

Table 2. Scale Ordering of Items Included in Cumulative Scale
Obtained from the 1988 Data

Scale Position for Political Judgment	Political Judgment	Percent of Respondents Displaying Ideologically Consistent Behavior
19	Status of women, own attitude	19
18	Cooperation with Russia, own attitude	20
17	Defense spending, own attitude	21
16	Feel close to ideological groups	21
15	Government spending, own attitude	23
14	Government health insurance, own attitude	23
13	Minority aid, own attitude	25
12	Guaranteed jobs, own attitude	26
11	Abortion, own attitude	28
10	Feeling thermometers, ideological groups	32
9	Ideologically consistent candidate evaluation	33
8	School prayer, own attitude	34
7	Ideologically consistent vote choice	34
6	Ideologically consistent party identification	34
5	Identify with ideological group	50
4	Liberal-conservative, party placement	54
3	Liberal-conservative, candidate placement	56
2	Identify more conservative party	57
1	Define ideological terms	61

Loevinger's H for Scale (Measure of Scalability) = 0.58   Reliability = 0.944
Total Number of observations is 1775
Source: 1988 CPS National Election Study

attitudes. There are two exceptions to this overall pattern: consistency between ideological self-placement and attitudes toward school prayer occur at a relatively low scale position (eighth among the 19 scaled stimuli). And feelings of closeness to one's ideological group are relatively rare; this behavior is located at a high scale position (sixteenth out of 19).

Discussion of scale content

There are several interesting features of the empirical scales that deserve closer attention. First, many individuals apparently can place the parties and candidates along the liberal-conservative continuum, but still fail to orient their own attitudes and behaviors along the same lines. In each year's results, the ideological placements of the parties and candidates are among the most prevalent kinds of ideological judgments; they appear near the "easy" side of the 1984 and 1988 scales. This shows that people can recognize the ideological implications of political objects, even if they do not think of themselves in the same terms.

Second, liberals and conservatives do not serve as objects of personal attachment for most of the public. Very few people report feeling close to the ideological group with which they identify. Only 24% do so in 1984, placing this item at the precise middle of the scaled array of judgments (tenth out of 19). In 1988, only 21% do so, ranking this at the sixteenth position in the full scale of 19 judgments. Thus, feeling close to one's ideological group seems to be a relatively uncommon and hence, difficult form of liberal-conservative thinking. Note that this does not necessarily imply a lack of affective feelings toward ideological groups. To the contrary, consistent feeling-thermometer ratings of liberals and conservatives (i.e., self-identified liberals give liberals a warmer rating than conservatives and vice versa) are more widespread than feelings of closeness in both 1984 and 1988. Instead, these results merely confirm that liking or disliking an ideological group is psychologically easier than expressing a particularly strong personal involvement with the group itself.

Third, a comparison of the 1984 and 1988 scales reveals interesting insights about temporal change in the nature of the public's ideological thinking. The scale placement of two items--defining ideological terms, and identifying the Republican party as more conservative--changes markedly from 1984 to 1988. Both of these behaviors are relatively rare in the former dataset (34% and 26% of 1984 respondents, respectively), and they are not part of the common underlying structure with other kinds of liberal-conservative structuring in political preferences. By 1988, these two behaviors are much more prevalent (shown by 61% and 57% of the respondents), and they also become part of the cumulative pattern along with the other forms of ideological thinking. I contend that this change is due to the content of the political environment. In 1984, presidential campaign rhetoric was not particularly imbued with ideological content. Therefore, relatively direct questions about ideology ("can you define the terms liberal and conservative?" or "which party is more conservative?") require people to recognize and employ abstract terms on their own, without the assistance of external cues.

The situation was quite different four years later. Specifically, Bush made ideological terminology an integral component of the 1988 campaign rhetoric, in his efforts to discredit the Dukakis candidacy. This, in turn, made the terms liberal and conservative more accessible to many people within the general public. Essentially, the 1988 situation involved people responding to stimuli (the ideological labels) that were *presented* to them, rather than *retrieving* abstract objects from within their own cognitive structures. The ability to define and use ideological terminology in 1988 much more resembled other relatively easy forms of ideological thinking (i.e., locating the parties and candidates along the liberal-conservative continuum) than they did in 1984. Thus, the content of the political environment does have a noticeable effect on the very *ways* that citizens think about ideological terms, and not merely on the overall degree of ideological consistency within the American public.

A fourth feature is the general stability of the cumulative patterns across the four-year period separating the two elections. Even Bush's explicit efforts to promote the public's awareness of liberal and conservative terms had minor effects only on the overall structure or extent of American ideological thinking. The patterns of the items included in the 1984 scale and the 1988 scale are extremely similar to each other (except for the two exceptions discussed in the preceding paragraph). In each case, liberal-conservative placements of parties and candidates occur close to the easiest side of the array followed by nonneutral ideological identifications, ideological consistency in several political choices, and finally, ideological consistency in various issue attitudes.

The temporal consistency in scale content can be easily demonstrated by correlating the items' scale positions across the two time points. Seventeen ideological judgments appear in both of the cumulative scales. For these items, the correlation between their respective 1984 and 1988 scale scores is very strong, at 0.842. Thus, the details differ somewhat across the two years, but the general similarity in scale content is immediately obvious. This result is very important, because it indicates that the *structure* of liberal-conservative thinking--that is, application of ideological concepts to political stimuli--constitutes a stable and lasting component of American public opinion

Distributions of Individual Scale Scores

A cumulative scale measures individuals, as well as stimuli, with respect to the common underlying trait. These scales measure the degree to which the public is ideologically oriented, that is, the extent to which citizens' political judgments are organized in ways that are consistent with the usual interpretations of liberal and conservative political stances. Therefore, the distributions of individual scores are important in their own right, separately from the item-content of the scales.

Figure 1 shows the frequency polygon for the individual scores on the scale obtained from the 1984 data; Figure 2 shows the same information for 1988. The reliability coefficients for the individual scale scores are extremely high, at 0.95 and 0.94 for the 1984 and 1988 scales, respectively. This indicates accurate, as well as detailed, views of ideological thinking within the American public.

In both years, the score distributions are highly skewed, with the vast majority of respondents falling in the lower half of their respective scales. In each case, the modal score is 0: 28.5% of the 1984 respondents and 16.3% of the 1988 respondents display *no* ideologically consistent judgments across *any* of the 19 behaviors that are included in their scales. The remainder of the respondents are scattered throughout the higher scale scores.

Both years show a slight bump in the upper segment of the distribution: about 20% of the 1984 respondents and 22% of the 1988 respondents display scale scores between 11 and 15. These people do, in fact, display a fairly wide range of ideological judgments. They can identify the ideological positions of political actors; they take on nonneutral ideological positions themselves, which are also consistent with their other choices between candidates, parties, etc.; and they also display ideological consistency on some issues. Thus, in both years, there is a sizable minority of people who do appear to use liberal-conservative ideas to most of their political orientations.

The median score is two in 1984, and four in 1988. But, this difference is more apparent than real. In both years, the most difficult ideological behaviors manifested by the median person are the successful place-

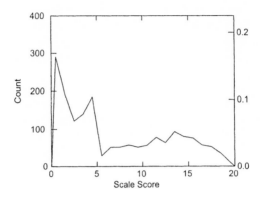

Figure 1. Frequency Polygon for Individual Scale Scores on 1984 Cumulative
Scale of Liberal-Conservative Consistency in Political Perceptions and Choices
Source: Mokken Scale Analysis of Data from the 1984 CPS National Election
Study

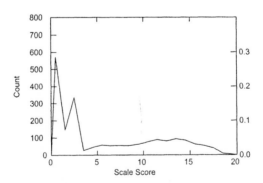

Figure 2. Frequency Polygon for Individual Scale Scores on 1988 Cumulative
Scale of Liberal-Conservative Consistency in Political Perceptions and Choices
Source: Mokken Scale Analysis of Data from the 1988 CPS National Election
Study

ment of the parties and candidates along the liberal-conservative structure continuum. The higher scale score for the 1988 median actually results from the fact that two relatively "easy" items are added at the lowest extreme of the scaled continuum. And, this temporal change is due more to differences in the external political environment (again, Bush's explicit use of ideological terminology in his 1988 campaign rhetoric) than to an upward shift in the public's capacity for liberal-conservative thinking. Ideological structuring appears to be a highly stable component of American public opinion.

Determinants of Individual Scale Positions

The scales obtained in this analysis summarize the extent to which people manifest political judgments that are based upon or consistent with these liberal-conservative labels. But what determines the placements of the people themselves along these scales? This question is important because the scales only tap overt ideological *consistency* and not actual ideological *thinking* per se. The problem is that ideologically consistent behaviors could occur for reasons that have nothing to do with an individual's reliance on the liberal-conservative continuum. If this is the case, then the scales are only spurious and invalid measures of ideological thinking. Therefore, it is important to determine whether the scales found in this analysis are related to other variables that are known to affect ideological thinking and political sophistication within the American electorate.

The respondents' scale scores can be used as dependent variables in regression analyses.[3] The independent variables consist of several factors that are identified in the literature as potential influences on ideological thinking, two directly related to individuals' cognitive capacities. The levels of conceptualization tap the structuring principles that people employ to organize their political thinking (Hagner, Pierce, and Knight 1990). The levels are operationalized as three dummy variables ("nature of the times," "group benefits" and "ideologue") leaving the lowest level ("no issue content") as the omitted category. Next, years of education is included to tap each person's level of formal training, and presumably, attendant capacity to think about politics in abstract terms. The next four variables measure various aspects of political involvement. Political participation, political knowledge, and reliance on the mass media are all operationalized using standard items from the 1984 and 1988 NES data.[4] Psychological involvement is defined as a combination of each person's reported interest in politics and level of concern over the election outcome.[5]

There are three other independent variables included in each of the regression equations. Two dummy variables are used to represent liberal and conservative self-identifications, leaving moderate self-identification as the omitted category. And, there is an opinion-holding variable, which simply counts the number of issues on which each person takes a nonneutral stance. These three variables are probably more important as controlling factors, rather than causal influences on ideological thinking. We can only exhibit an ideologically consistent political preference (in candidate evaluations, voting choices, or whatever) from an ideological position. Similarly, an individual cannot display an ideologically consistent issue stand unless he or she maintains a nonneutral issue attitude. These preconditions must be met before scoring highly on the scales. These three variables should all show strong positive influences on the dependent variables and the effects of the other variables are only meaningful *after* these characteristics are taken into account.

The two regression equations are estimated using ordinary least squares, and the results are shown in Table 3 and Table 4.[6] In each table, the left-hand column gives the nonstandardized regression coefficients and the standard errors. Standardized regression coefficients are shown in the rightmost columns.

There are striking similarities in the regression results for the two years. The R^2 values are both extremely high, at 0.806 and 0.826, respectively. However, these values are misleading, because a large part of the variance that is apparently explained by the independent variables is actually due to the presence of the three control variables described above. Precisely as expected, placements as well as opinion holding all have strong positive effects--in fact they have the largest impacts of any of the independent variables, in both years. While this is not particularly interesting in substantive terms, it is still important; the other variables' influences can only be meaningfully interpreted after these variables are taken into account.

Almost all of the remaining independent variables have an impact on ideological consistency in 1984 and 1988 political judgments. In both years, only three coefficients fail to achieve statistical significance at the 0.05 level: nature-of-the-times and group-benefits levels, and the measure of media use in the campaign.

The specific patterns of influence are also virtually identical across the two years. Although it is clearly inappropriate to compare the magnitudes of the standardized coefficients across the two years, it is possible to make comparisons of their relative sizes *within* each of the equations.

Table 3. Regression Analysis of Influences on Individual Scale Scores from 1984 Data

Independent Variables	Coefficient Estimates	Standard Errors	Standardized Coefficients
Control variables			
Liberal Identifier	**8.272**	0.166	0.568
Conservative Identifier	**8.597**	0.143	0.695
Opinion Holding	**0.297**	0.028	0.115
Levels of conceptualization			
Nature of the Times	0.100	0.172	0.008
Group benefits	0.031	0.187	0.002
Ideologue	**1.500**	0.216	0.107
Cognitive capacity measures			
Education	**0.117**	0.022	0.060
Political Knowledge	**0.242**	0.047	0.061
Political involvement measures			
Psychological Involvement	**0.102**	0.024	0.049
Political Participation	**0.176**	0.051	0.039
Media Use	-0.003	0.044	-0.001
Intercept	-3.669		
R^2	0.806		
Adjusted R^2	0.805		
Number of Observations	1923		

Bold coefficients statistically significant at the 0.05 level.
Source: 1984 CPS National Election Study

Table 4. Regression Analysis of Influences on Individual Scale Scores
from 1988 Data

Independent Variables	Coefficient Estimates	Standard Errors	Standardized Coefficients
Control variables			
Liberal Identifier	**8.424**	0.170	0.548
Conservative Identifier	**8.185**	0.143	0.666
Opinion Holding	**0.350**	0.035	0.106
Levels of conceptualization			
Nature of the Times	0.173	0.189	0.013
Group benefits	0.162	0.183	0.014
Ideologue	**2.039**	0.230	0.137
Cognitive capacity measures			
Education	**0.119**	0.023	0.060
Political Knowledge	**0.288**	0.030	0.127
Political involvement measures			
Psychological Involvement	**0.139**	0.025	0.068
Political Participation	**0.171**	0.052	0.037
Media Use	0.028	0.041	0.008
Intercept	-4.157		
R^2	0.826		
Adjusted R^2	0.825		
Number of Observations	1738		

Bold statistically significant at the 0.05 level.
Source: 1988 CPS National Election Study

In both years, the variable for ideologue-level conceptualization stands out for its strong effects. The highest conceptual level contains people who actively think about the political world in abstract, ideological terms. Therefore it is not at all surprising that these people show a particularly marked tendency to display liberal-conservative consistency in their political judgments. Political knowledge shows the next-strongest effects in both years. This is followed by formal education and psychological involvement, although the order of these variables' effects reverses from 1984 to 1988. Finally, overt political participation shows a relatively small, but nontrivial impact in both years.

The results in this section show that temporal stability extends to the factors that influence the degree of liberal-conservative thinking manifested by individual citizens. These results also show that there are, in effect, two different avenues to ideological consistency in political orientations and judgments. On the one hand, maintaining abstract political conceptualizations and possessing higher cognitive capacities have clear effects. But, since these characteristics are somewhat limited in the general public, they probably only generate a minority of citizens who are strongly attuned to the ideological lines of American politics. At the same time, many people can arrive at ideologically consistent judgments through a combination of political involvement and intensity of feelings toward political issues. The latter characteristics are not necessarily constrained cognitive limitations, so they probably result in a fairly sizable set of people with some ability to think and act consistent with an underlying ideological dimension.

Conclusions

The most general finding from the analysis is that a discernible structure does, in fact, exist. There is systematic variability in the *ways* that people manifest ideological awareness, which exists separately from individual *abilities* to engage in ideological reasoning.

The results obtained in this study provide useful information about the nature of variability in mass-level ideology. Perhaps most important, the strong fit of the empirical-cumulative scales says a great deal about what *kind* of differences in liberal-conservative orientations exist in the first place. The different ideological judgments vary according to their difficulty; that is, the level of ideological awareness required for a person to exhibit each kind of behavior. In some cases, it is a relatively straightforward task to establish the appropriate linkages between abstract symbols and political objects--hence, many people can locate candidates and parties along the liberal-conservative continuum. But, there are other forms of behavior where ideological connections are not so clear-cut-- relatively few people report feeling close to liberals or conservatives as social groups. And, those individuals who engage in the more difficult forms of ideological thinking tend to exhibit all of the easier forms of ideological judgment and behavior. Thus, the cumulative structure successfully accounts for the wide variability in the application of liberal-conservative labels to different political stimuli.

The cumulative scales also provide information about precisely which behaviors are subsumed within a common structure, and this has important substantive ramifications. Several researchers have distinguished between *active use* of, and *recognition and understanding* of ideological abstractions (Converse 1964; Luskin 1987). But, the results obtained in this study suggest that this distinction is largely unnecessary, because it does not really correspond to *qualitative* differences in the public's use of liberal-conservative concepts. The items contained in the 1984 and 1988 empirical scales combine recognition-understanding and active use of ideological terminology. The former is something of a precondition for the latter in the sense that the items tapping recognition-understanding fall at lower scale positions than those that imply active use. But this type of variation represents more of a difference in the *degree* of ideological thinking, rather than a difference in kind. Recognition-understanding and active use merely occupy different positions along a common dimension of liberal-conservative thinking.

Second, the results from this study illuminate the relationship between individuals' willingness to structure their political judgments along liberal-conservative lines and the ideological content of the external political environment. There appears to be very little change over time in the overall structure of mass-level ideological thinking. And, that change which does occur seems to take place at the margin, rather than as a fundamental shift in the ways that people think about liberal-conservative terms.

The primary evidence for this conclusion is, of course, the strong similarity in the content of the 1984 and 1988 scales. In both years, the scaled array of judgments progresses from liberal-conservative placements of parties and candidates, to ideological consistency in political choices, followed by ideological consistency in issue-attitudes and feelings of attachment to ideological groups. The parallels are all the more striking because of the vastly different winning political campaigns conducted in the two years: the 1984 Republican campaign emphasized unification in order to reelect a popular incumbent; the 1988 effort explicitly used ideological terminology (e.g., "The L Word") to denigrate the Democratic candidate. And yet, the latter had hardly any effect on the structure of ideological thinking in the electorate. The general structure of ideological judgments seems to be largely impervious to influences from the external political environment. This is an important interpretation because it may contradict widely cited conclusions from other studies. Although their arguments are based on very different premises, Nie, Verba, and Petrocik (1979) and Smith (1989) argue that the public's ideological awareness can vary sharply, along with the salient content of the existing political environment. But once again, such interpretations would lead us to expect much more variability in the structure of ideological thinking than actually occurs between the 1984 and 1988 data. The ways that people apply liberal-conservative terms to their own political perceptions, attitudes, and choices seems to stand as a highly stable characteristic of American public opinion.

Finally, the cumulative scales obtained from this analysis are important because they can be used as empirical variables in subsequent analyses of ideological thinking. Most previous composite measures of political sophistication score individuals according to the number of ideologically consistent behaviors they exhibit, neglecting precise behavioral differences between people who receive different scores. Thus, we could conclude that one person is more or less ideological than another, but we could not say what makes them different. Here, if an individual displays a given level of ideological thinking (i.e., receives a given scale score), then it is immediately possible to state exactly *which* kinds of ideologically consistent judgments this person has given. I contend that this is a more satisfactory interpretation of the empirical evidence. With other measures, survey respondents are merely assessed according to the extent that they matched the researchers' definition of a complete set of ideological behaviors. With the cumulative scales, there is an immediate behavioral referent for each person's empirical score. This, in turn, enhances the validity of this scaling approach as a strategy for measuring the degree to which individuals employ ideological concepts in their political thinking.

Appendix
Definitions of Ideologically Consistent Responses
for Items in Scaling Analysis

All items included in both the 1984 and 1988 National Election Studies unless otherwise noted.

Identify with ideological group?
Respondent places self at nonneutral position along 7-point liberal-conservative continuum (note that this self-placement defines "own ideological group" in all other items described below and used in the analysis).

Feel close to ideological groups?
Respondent reports feeling close to own ideological group, and not close to opposing ideological group.

Identify more conservative party.
Respondent identifies the Republican party as the more conservative of the two parties.

Define ideological terms?
Respondent supplies at least one definition each for terms "liberal" and "conservative."

Ideologically consistent vote choice.
Liberals voting for Mondale (1984) or Dukakis (1988), conservatives voting for Reagan (1984) or Bush (1988).

Ideologically consistent party identification.
Liberals identifying with the Democratic party and conservatives identifying with the Republican party (includes leaners).

Ideologically consistent candidate evaluations.
Liberals give Mondale (or Dukakis) a warmer rating than Reagan (or Bush),and vice versa for conservatives.

Feeling thermometers, ideological groups.
Respondent gives own ideological group a warmer rating than the opposing ideological group.

Liberal-conservative candidate placement.
Respondent places Mondale closer than Reagan to liberal extreme on 7-point liberal-conservative continuum.

Liberal-conservative, party placement.
Respondent places Democrats closer than Republicans to liberal extreme on 7-point liberal-conservative continuum.

Government services, own attitude.
Liberals support services, spending and conservatives do not.

Guaranteed jobs, own attitude.

Liberals support guaranteed jobs, conservatives do not.
Government health insurance, own attitude.
Liberals support government health insurance, conservatives prefer private insurance plans.
Abortion, own attitude.
Liberals support choice on abortion. conservatives support restrictions.
School prayer, own attitude.
Liberals oppose school prayer, conservatives support it.
Status of women, own attitude.
Liberals support equal role for women, conservatives prefer womens' place in the home.
Negotiations with Russia, own attitude.
Liberals support cooperation with Russia, conservatives prefer to get tougher with Russia.
Defense spending, own attitude.
Liberals prefer to decrease defense spending, conservatives prefer to increase defense spending.
Minority aid, own attitude.
Liberals support government aid to minorities, conservatives say that minorities should get ahead on their own.
Central America, own attitude. *
Liberals support reduced U.S. involvement, conservatives support increased U.S. involvement.
*Busing, own attitude.**
Liberals support busing, conservatives prefer neighborhood schools.

*This item is only included in the 1984 National Election Study.

Notes

1. The scaling analysis could be limited to include only those items that appeared in both the 1984 and 1988 NES interview schedules. However, I argue that such a limitation would be substantively unrealistic, because the content of the political environment can, itself, change over time. For example, old issues fade from public attention (busing and Central America), while newer social problems and political stimuli replace them on the public agenda. The content of the empirical scales must reflect this kind of temporal variability. Furthermore, even if the item pools were the same in both years, the content of the scales could still differ. As we will see below, this does take place in the present study and this kind of variation is substantively interesting on its own merits. A few differences in the item-pools across the two years do not pose any problems at all for the analysis.

2. These two items do show a cumulative pattern with each other. How-

ever, a two-item scale does not have much substantive relevance or methodological utility, so it is not reported here. Further analyses of the 1984 NES data also
revealed that these items seemed to form a common scale with respondents'
abilities to place liberals and conservatives on specific issues. This scale is
problematic on several grounds: the scale's meaning is unclear; the degree of
external validity is questionable; and the relevant items are not included in the
1988 data. For these reasons, this scale is not reported in the present study. Full
details on this scale are available from the author, upon request.

    3. Strictly speaking, the Mokken procedure generates scales that are
measured at the ordinal level. However, the scales in the present study can
legitimately be treated as interval-level variables. First, the distinction between
the ordinal and interval levels becomes less important as the number of scale
categories increases. And, the 20 distinct scores that occur in each of these scales
certainly constitute a large number of categories. Second, the high reliabilities
for the scales indicate that the empirical variables are linear functions of their
underlying latent traits; this is simply a restatement of the definition of an
interval-level variable. Third, the regression analyses were replicated using an
estimation procedure (alternating least squares, optimal scaling, or ALSOS; for
details see Jacoby 1991b) that treated the dependent variables as ordinal-level
measures; the empirical results were identical to those reported here. Evidence
suggests that the scales can be regarded as accurate, interval-level measures of the
respondents' degrees of ideological thinking.

    4. While the exact survey questions differ somewhat from 1984 to 1988,
the procedures for operationalizing these variables are basically identical.
Political participation is defined by counting up the number of political activities
that the respondent has engaged in during the current campaign. Similarly, media
reliance is an additive index, based upon the *number* of media to which the
respondent pays attention, along with the *amount* of attention paid to the campaign on television, in newspapers, and in weekly newsmagazines. The measurement of political knowledge varies a bit more across the two years. In 1984, it is
an index based upon the respondents' abilities to identify the majority parties in
the House of Representatives and the Senate, both before and after the election.
In 1988, the knowledge variable is based upon the respondents' abilities to
correctly identify each of seven public figures, as well as their ability to specify
the majority party in the House and the Senate.

    5. In both 1984 and 1988, the NES asked people whether they were
interested in the campaign, and whether they cared which party won the presidential election. Responses to these questions were recoded to common ranges
(ranging from a score of one for least interest and not caring very much to five for
very interested or cared very much). The recoded responses were then summed
to produce the psychological involvement variable.

    6. Luskin (1990) has recently argued that a more complicated model,
involving nonlinear and nonadditive effects, is required in order to adequately
explain political sophistication. This appears to be unnecessary in the present
study. I conducted extensive analyses of diagnostic statistics, residuals, and

alternative specifications for the models employed in this analysis. In every case, the linear, additive functional form of the standard regression model proves to be perfectly adequate.

References

Carmines, E. G. and J. A. Stimson. 1980. The two faces of issue voting. *American Political Science Review* 74:78-91.

Converse, P. E. 1964. The nature of belief systems in mass publics. In *Ideology and discontent*, ed. D. E. Apter, 206-261. New York: Free Press.

Coveyou, M. R. and J. Piereson. 1977. Ideological perceptions and political judgment: Some problems of concept and method. *Political Methodology* 4:77-102.

Field, J. O. and R. Anderson. 1969. Ideology in the public's conceptualization of the 1964 election. *Public Opinion Quarterly* 33:380-398.

Hagner. P. R., J. C. Pierce, and K. Knight. 1990. *Content coding of levels of political conceptualization*. Ann Arbor, MI: Inter-University Consortium for Political and Social Research.

Hamill, R. C., M. Lodge, and F. Blake. 1985. The breadth, depth, and utility of class, partisan, and ideological schemata. *American Journal of Political Science* 29:850-870.

Jacoby, W. G. 1989. The sources of liberal-conservative thinking: Education and conceptualization. *Political Behavior* 10:316-332.

_____. 1990. Variability in issue alternatives and American public opinion. *Journal of Politics* 52:579-606.

_____. 1991a. Ideological identification and issue attitudes. *American Journal of Political Science* 35:178-205.

_____. 1991b. *Data theory and dimensional analysis*. Newbury Park, CA: Sage Publications.

Levitin, T. E. and W. E. Miller. 1979. Ideological interpretations of presidential elections. *American Political Science Review* 73:751-771.

Luskin, R. C. 1987. Measuring political sophistication. *American Journal of Political Science* 31:856-899.

_____. 1990. Explaining political sophistication. *American Journal of Political Science.* 12:331-361.

Mokken. R. J. 1971. *A theory and procedure of scale analysis*. The Hague: Mouton.

Nie, N. H., S. Verba, and J. Petrocik. 1979. *The changing American voter.* Cambridge, MA: Harvard University Press.

Niemoller, K. and W. van Schuur. 1983. Stochastic models for unidimensional scaling: Mokken and Rasch. In *Data analysis and the social sciences*, ed. D. McKay, N. Schofield, and P. Whitely. London: Frances Pinter Publishers.

Page, B. I. 1978. *Choices and echoes in presidential elections.* Chicago: University of Chicago Press.

Pierce, J. C. 1970. Party identification and the changing role of ideology in American politics. *Midwest Journal of Political Science* 14:25-42.

Smith, E. R. A. N. 1989. *The unchanging American voter.* Berkeley: University of California Press.

Stimson, J. A. 1975. Belief systems: Constraint, complexity, and the 1972 election. *American Journal of Political Science* 19:393-418.

Acknowledgments

I am very grateful to Saundra K. Schneider for her advice and assistance; this article could not have been completed without her help. I would also like to thank Carolyn Lewis for comments and suggestions on earlier drafts of this paper. All data used are available from the ICPSR. Documentation for replication purposes can be obtained from the author.

Chapter 2

The Rise of Ideology in the Post-New Deal Party System, 1972-1992*

Jeffrey Levine, Edward G. Carmines, and Robert Huckfeldt

It is now widely presumed that the social structural basis of the party system in the United States developed during the New Deal era has weakened. Since World War II, researchers have consistently found that membership in New Deal social groups has exerted only a weak influence on the parties' long-term bases of support (Dalton and Wattenberg 1993, 199). The inability of the core groups of the New Deal coalition to condition partisanship as strongly as in earlier eras raises a fundamental question: If New Deal social groups have declined as determinants of partisanship, what, if anything, has taken their place?

A persistent theme in recent writings concerning Western party systems has centered on the notion that the weakness of social structural loyalties has resulted in an increasing tendency for political beliefs to shape partisan support. Scholars argue that instead of making decisions about partisanship chiefly on the basis of traditional social group membership, citizens today are increasingly reacting to politics as individuals by

*Reprinted with permission from *American Politics Quarterly* 25, 1 (1997):19-34.

employing their own political beliefs--beliefs that cut across rather than reinforce membership in traditional social groups (Mackie and Franklin 1987, 574). Some American scholars have readily adopted this hypothesis, asserting that ideology plays an increasing role in shaping partisanship in the post-New Deal era--a role that is distinct from that played by membership in traditional New Deal social groups (Carmines and Stanley 1992, 218).

The goal of this article is to provide a test of this proposition by examining the role of ideology in the formation of partisanship in the United States over the last two decades. We seek to answer two main questions. First, does ideology play an increasing role in shaping partisanship over the last two decades? Second, is the role of ideology one that increasingly cuts across New Deal social cleavages? To address these questions, we use data from the American National Election Studies (ANES) for the six presidential elections between 1972 and 1992.

The Decline of the New Deal Coalition and the Rise of Ideology

One of the most popular approaches for explaining the origins and dynamics of partisan coalitions in the United States focuses on their social group composition (Carmines and Stanley 1992, 216-217). Scholars using this approach view political parties as a combination of various overlapping demographic groups (e.g., Axelrod 1972; Stanley, Bianco, and Niemi 1986; Stanley and Niemi 1991, 1995).[1] For example, during the New Deal, the Democratic party was said to be composed of a majority of Catholics, Jews, northern Blacks, industrial workers, White southerners, urban residents, and the poor.

Despite the widespread adoption of this approach, recent evidence suggests that such an approach is limited. Researchers have found evidence to suggest that New Deal social groups are of decreasing relevance to contemporary American politics. Indeed, since the early 1950s the core groups of the New Deal coalition have collectively done a poor job of explaining partisanship (Miller and Lockerbie 1992, 369). In addition, New Deal social groups, when considered individually, have had an inconsistent and often declining impact on partisanship since the New Deal era (Miller and Lockerbie 1992; Stanley and Niemi 1995). The weak link between social group membership and partisanship since the New Deal era has been linked to a variety of factors, including the successful resolution of deep-seated social conflict, fundamental changes in the social structure, generational turnover, and technological advances (Dalton and Wattenberg 1993, 198-202). Whatever the causes of the decline, its existence naturally prompts us to consider what sorts of factors, if any, have superseded New Deal social groups as determinants of partisanship. Although recent research suggests several possibilities, most notably alternative social groupings (Goldthorpe 1980; Heath et al. 1991), issues (Franklin 1985; Mackie and Franklin 1987), and candidates (Wattenberg 1991), we confine our attention here to another hypothesis, one that has never been subjected to comprehensive empirical testing.

As noted, scholars concerned with Western party systems argue that the decline in the extent to which traditional social structure influences partisanship has led to an increasing tendency for political beliefs--beliefs that cut across membership in traditional social groups--to shape partisan support (Mackie and Franklin 1987, 574). In the context of American politics, some scholars have made a similar argument, asserting that the inability of New Deal social groups to condition partisanship has resulted in an increasing tendency for ideological beliefs to shape partisan support (Carmines and Stanley 1992, 218). They argue that ideology can be expected to exert an increasing impact on partisanship in the post-New Deal era, one that is distinct from membership in New Deal social groups (Carmines and Stanley 1992, 218).

Although this hypothesis is plausible, supporting empirical evidence is incomplete. First and most fundamentally, researchers have not constructed a multivariate model of the relationship between New Deal social groups, ideology, and partisanship. Instead, bivariate analyses have typified the study of American partisan coalitions (e.g., Carmines and Stanley 1990, 1992). As a result, it is still not clear what sort of influence ideology has on partisanship after controlling for New Deal social group membership.

Second, even the most comprehensive studies of ideology and partisanship (Carmines and Stanley 1990, 1992; Miller and Lockerbie 1992) do not thoroughly examine the role that ideology plays in shaping partisanship over an extended period of time. These studies also typically focus only on theoretically interesting subsets of the population (e.g., White southerners), thus making it difficult to determine whether their findings can be applied to the population as a whole.

In short, previous studies do not provide a comprehensive examination of the role of ideology in shaping partisanship over an extended period of time, thus preventing a more definitive test of the hypothesis that the decline of New Deal social groups has led to an increasing tendency for ideological beliefs--beliefs that cut across New Deal social group membership--to shape partisan support. By examining the impact of ideology and New Deal social group membership on partisanship over the last twenty years, we can test this hypothesis more completely. We begin with an examination of whether ideology plays an increasing role in shaping partisanship over the last two decades.

Ideology and Partisanship

To test the proposition that partisanship has been increasingly dependent on ideological beliefs, we examine the impact of ideology on partisanship between 1972 and 1992 to assess whether ideology plays an increasing role in shaping partisanship during this period. Accordingly, we estimate a set of simple (bivariate) regression models using ordinary least squares. In order to facilitate comparison across the years, the wording and coding of the variables in the models are identical in each year.[2] The dependent variable in the models is self-reported partisanship,[3] and self-reported political ideology is the independent variable.[4]

As we demonstrate in Table 1, ideology exerts an increasing impact on partisanship between 1972 and 1992. The unstandardized regression coefficient for ideology exhibits a general upward trend, rising from 0.79 in 1972 to 1.09 in 1992. In addition, the R^2 increases during this period such that, by 1992, ideology explains 18% of the variation in partisanship, close to twice the amount it explains in 1972.[5] Although the findings presented here are only for the full sample of respondents, it is important to note that, consistent with previous research (Carmines and Stanley 1990, 1992), the results hold for several important subsets of the population, most notably southern Whites and northern Whites.[6] The findings, then, indicate that the increasing role of ideology not only occurs among the electorate as a whole but also among various racial and regional subsets of the population.

An explanation for why ideological concerns have become increasingly salient is beyond the scope of this article, but it is interesting to note that the rise of ideology makes considerable sense if one considers the behavior of elites during this period. Scholars have claimed that during the late 1970s and 1980s, the ideological conflict between the Republicans and Democrats intensified and sharpened, cutting across the New Deal social group partisan coalitions (Carmines and Stanley 1990, 23-24). Indeed, there is evidence to suggest that Reagan's strong conservative rhetoric and his aggressive pursuit of conservative policies increased the ideological content of political debate at the national level and caused the parties to take more distinct ideological positions (Carmines and Stanley 1990, 23-24; Stone, Rapoport, and Abramowitz 1990, 69-70). Because visible changes in the behavior of party elites have been shown to be a strong force in the public's orientation toward the parties (Carmines and Stimson 1989), it is reasonable to infer that an explanation for the development of ideology and its impact on partisanship may at least partially rest on the behavior of political elites during this period.

Table 1. Regression Estimates of Partisanship as a Function of Ideology, 1972-1992

Variable	1972	1976	1980	1984	1988	1992
Constant	2.08	1.63	1.61	1.64	1.69	1.52
t-score	14.92	11.62	9.52	11.61	11.06	12.35
Ideology	0.79	1.00	0.95	1.05	1.04	1.09
t-score	12.77	16.29	13.09	17.13	16.10	20.27
R^2	0.10	0.15	0.15	0.16	0.16	0.18
N	1,536	1,496	993	1,537	1,408	1,814

Source: ANES cumulative data file 1952-1992.
Note: Analysis done with full sample of respondents.

Ideology, New Deal Social Groups, and Partisanship

The discovery that ideology has an increasing impact on partisanship lends support to part of our hypothesis. It is still necessary, however, to examine the second part of the hypothesis--that is, that ideology exerts an impact on partisanship that is distinct from membership in New Deal social groups.

To determine whether ideology plays a significant role in shaping partisanship above and beyond that of New Deal social groups, we estimate two sets of regression models in each of the years between 1972 and 1992. In the first, we regress partisanship on traditional New Deal social group variables (model 1).[7] We then estimate a second set of models, identical to the first except for the addition of the ideology variable (model 2). If ideology makes a distinct and increasing impact on partisan coalitions, then the magnitude of the coefficient for ideology should increase significantly over the years. In addition, the amount of variation in partisanship explained by ideology, after controlling for social groups, should be significant and increasingly large over the years.

These expectations are strongly supported by the data. As Table 2 demonstrates, the coefficient for ideology, after controlling for membership in New Deal social groups, displays a general upward trend, rising from 0.70 in 1972 to 1.02 in 1992. In addition, the amount of variation explained by ideology (R^2), above and beyond that of social groups, is statistically significant in each of the six years and is increasingly large over the years. In fact, ideology explains more than twice the amount of variation in partisanship in 1992 (15%) than in 1972 (7%).[8] Again, it is important to note that these results also hold among various important racial and regional subsets of the population, including White southerners and White nonsoutherners.[9] Clearly, there is strong empirical evidence to support the contention that ideology not only exerts an increasing impact on partisanship over the last two decades but one that is increasingly distinct from membership in New Deal social groups.

It is also important to make a few observations concerning the role of New Deal social groups during this period. Consistent with previous research (Miller and Lockerbie 1992; Stanley and Niemi 1995), our analysis thus far indicates that the impact of individual New Deal social groups on partisanship tends to rise and fall without a clear pattern between 1972 and 1992. Indeed, as both the models in Table 2 illustrate, the impact of most of the social groups on partisanship fluctuates slightly from year to year, exhibiting no strong tendency to either rise or decline steadily between 1972 and 1992.

To explore further the role of social groups during this period, we estimate another regression model, this time pooling each of the years from 1972 to 1992. By interacting each of the social group and ideology variables with a year counter[10] variable, we can determine whether the social group and ideology variables exert an impact on partisanship that significantly changes over time.

The results conform to those presented in Table 2. As Table 3 demonstrates, the impact of most of the social group variables changes only slightly from year to year. Indeed, only three social group variables exert a significantly different impact by year on partisanship; urbanization exerts a significantly greater impact on partisanship from year to year, and both region and Catholic have a significantly smaller influence on partisanship in each succeeding year (Table 3).

Two other points are worthy of note. First, although the findings presented in Tables 2 and 3 are consistent with previous work done concerning the role of New Deal social groups in shaping partisanship between 1972 and 1992 (Miller and Lockerbie 1992; Stanley and Niemi 1995), the results do not suggest that the impact of most of the New Deal social groups has either rapidly or consistently declined during this period. Because our analysis covers only a small portion of the period

Table 2. Regression Estimates of Partisanship as a Function of New Deal Social Groups (Model 1) and New Deal Social Groups/Ideology (Model 2), 1972-1992

Variable	1972	1976	1980	1984	1988	1992
MODEL 1						
Constant	**2.14**	**2.20**	**1.90**	**2.51**	**2.69**	**1.70**
t-score	7.49	7.73	5.02	8.12	8.53	6.18
Education	0.12	**0.22**	0.12	0.05	**0.18**	**0.27**
t-score	1.81	3.15	1.31	0.62	2.09	3.50
Income	**0.19**	**0.15**	**0.29**	**0.35**	0.15	**0.28**
t-score	2.75	2.24	3.16	4.61	1.87	4.12
Region	**-0.62**	**-0.70**	-0.25	**-0.37**	-0.25	-0.04
t-score	-5.49	-6.16	-1.79	-2.99	-1.94	-0.37
Race	**1.69**	**1.70**	**1.64**	**1.34**	**1.46**	**1.56**
t-score	8.50	8.82	6.42	6.51	7.40	9.11
Class	-0.07	**-0.33**	-0.19	**-0.29**	**-0.66**	-0.10
t-score	-0.60	-3.01	-1.38	-2.56	-5.45	-0.95
Union	**-0.50**	**-0.82**	**-0.65**	**-0.74**	**-0.64**	**-0.70**
t-score	-4.18	-6.93	-4.29	-5.63	-4.31	-5.12
Urban	-0.04	-0.02	**-0.31**	**-0.37**	**-0.32**	**-0.65**
t-score	-0.38	-0.20	-2.06	-2.77	-2.24	-5.59
Jewish	**-1.73**	**-1.90**	**-1.99**	**-1.62**	**-1.43**	**-1.77**
t-score	-5.03	-6.62	-6.17	-5.10	-3.24	-5.55
Catholic	**-0.92**	**-0.84**	**-0.33**	**-0.61**	**-0.36**	**-0.63**
t-score	-7.77	-7.09	-2.16	-4.87	-2.61	-5.20
$R^2(1)$	.14	.19	.15	.13	.15	.16
N	1,434	1,334	853	1,340	1,211	1,474
MODEL 2						
Constant	**0.99**	**0.98**	0.21	0.60	**0.87**	-0.31
t-score	3.37	3.44	0.54	1.90	2.71	-1.14

Table 2. Continued

Variable		1972	1976	1980	1984	1988	1992
Ideology		**0.70**	**0.84**	**0.82**	**0.94**	**0.94**	**1.02**
	t-score	11.17	13.26	10.87	14.96	13.96	18.08
Education		**0.20**	**0.27**	**0.21**	0.10	0.10	**0.34**
	t-score	3.00	3.99	2.34	1.32	1.24	4.79
Income		0.12	0.08	**0.21**	**0.27**	0.10	**0.23**
	t-score	1.79	1.19	2.43	3.82	1.33	3.68
Region		**-0.69**	**-0.75**	**-0.34**	**-0.41**	**-0.30**	-0.15
	t-score	-6.40	-6.96	-2.57	-3.61	-2.50	-1.49
Race		**1.31**	**1.09**	**1.39**	**1.16**	**1.33**	**1.29**
	t-score	6.72	5.81	5.80	6.06	7.25	8.30
Class		-0.07	**-0.35**	-0.12	**-0.22**	**-0.56**	-0.10
	t-score	-0.68	-3.41	-0.95	-2.09	-4.97	-1.04
Union		**-0.45**	**-0.64**	**-0.60**	**-0.65**	**-0.58**	**-0.67**
	t-score	-3.93	-5.66	-4.21	-5.41	-4.26	-5.43
Urban		0.05	-0.06	-.021	-0.21	-0.05	**-0.40**
	t-score	0.44	-0.56	-1.50	-1.65	-0.37	-3.77
Jewish		**-1.31**	**-1.27**	**-1.53**	**-1.34**	**-0.99**	**-1.26**
	t-score	-3.95	-4.64	-5.02	-4.54	-2.42	-4.34
Catholic		**-0.88**	**-0.75**	-0.23	**-0.54**	-0.25	**-0.60**
	t-score	-7.77	-6.71	-1.59	-4.63	-1.95	-5.55
$R^2(1)$		.21	.29	.26	.25	.27	.31
N		1,434	1,334	853	1,340	1,211	1,474
$R^2(2)-R^2(1)$		**.07**	**.10**	**.11**	**.12**	**.12**	**.15**

Source: ANES cumulative data file 1952-1992.
Note: Analysis done with full sample of respondents. The statistical significance of the R^2 change ($R^2(2)-R^2(1)$) is calculated using the F test under the null hypothesis that the change in R^2 is equal to 0.
Bold = statistically significant at p <=.05.

Table 3. Regression Estimates of Partisanship as a Function of New Deal Social Groups and Ideology: Pooled Cross Sections, 1972-1992.

Variable	b	t
Constant	**1.26**	4.60
Ideology x Year	**0.06**	4.04
Education x Year	0.00	0.27
Income x Year	0.02	1.20
Region x Year	**0.11**	4.43
Race x Year	0.01	0.33
Class x Year	-0.02	-0.85
Union x Year	-0.02	-0.82
Urban x Year	**-0.07**	-2.55
Jewish x Year	0.03	0.38
Catholic x Year	**0.08**	2.83
Ideology	**0.67**	11.37
Education	**0.19**	3.01
Income	0.10	1.55
Region	**-0.84**	-8.25
Race	**1.20**	6.71
Class	**-0.16**	-1.66
Union	**-0.52**	-4.69
Urban	0.09	0.81
Jewish	**-1.43**	-4.95
Catholic	**-0.84**	-7.82
Year	**-0.20**	-2.85

$R^2 = .26$

$N = 7,684$

Source: ANES cumulative data file, 1952-1992.
Note: Analysis done with full sample of respondents.
Bold coefficients statistically significant at p <= .05.

since the New Deal era, however, these findings do not seriously challenge the assumption made throughout this article that New Deal social groups have had a weak and often declining impact on partisanship since the New Deal era. Indeed, as noted, research that does estimate the role of New Deal social groups since the New Deal period has found strong evidence to suggest that many such social groups are of decreasing relevance to partisanship (Miller and Lockerbie 1992; Stanley and Niemi 1995).

Second, and more central to the purpose of this article, the results presented in Table 3 lend further support to our contention that ideology has had a strong, increasing impact on partisanship between 1972 and 1992. Indeed, ideology exerts a significantly greater impact on partisanship in each succeeding year between 1972 and 1992. What is more, the increasing influence of ideology on partisanship occurs even after controlling for membership in New Deal social groups.

Caveats

We have shown that ideology exerts an increasing and distinct impact on partisanship over the past two decades. Before concluding, however, it is important to emphasize several points concerning the findings and their implications.

First, the purpose of this article is tightly defined: We aim to test the hypothesis that ideology plays an increasing role in shaping partisanship, even after controlling for membership in traditional social groups (i.e., New Deal social groups). As such, our analysis deals only with New Deal social groupings. We cannot comment, therefore, on the role of alternative social groupings in determining partisanship during this period. (For such a discussion, see Stanley, Bianco, and Niemi 1986; Stanley and Niemi 1991, 1995.)

Second, although our findings show that ideology exerts an impact on partisanship that is increasingly distinct from that of membership in New Deal social groups, we nevertheless accept the notion that ideological beliefs reflect some sort of social group location. It seems likely that ideology is not only rooted in new, more complex social cleavages (Zuckerman 1982; van der Eijk et al. 1992) but is also still partially rooted in New Deal social groups. Indeed, New Deal social groups explain about 5% of the variation in ideology in 1992. Our only argument here is that ideology plays a role in shaping partisanship that is increasingly, but not entirely, distinct from New Deal social groups over the last two decades.

Third, although the results presented here imply that citizens are increasingly using their political beliefs to make partisan choices, we do not claim that citizens are becoming increasingly sophisticated and thoughtful when making political decisions. Indeed, it is entirely possible that, as Sniderman, Brody, and Tetlock (1991) suggest, many individuals use heuristics such as ideology to make political choices without spending a great deal of time and energy making their decisions. Thus the fact that people increasingly use their ideological labels to make decisions does not imply that individuals are thinking more carefully about politics than they used to; citizens may merely be using different cues to make decisions.

Finally, throughout the article we assume that the weakness of New Deal social groups and the increasing strength of ideology are related trends; they act on each other and influence each other's development. The causal nature of this relationship, however, is not clear. Indeed, researchers are still debating whether the rise of political beliefs has caused a decline in the importance of social structure or whether the aging of social structure has made room for political beliefs (Mackie and Franklin 1987, 574; Franklin, Mackie, and Valen 1992, 55).

Conclusion

It is now widely recognized that the social structural basis of the New Deal party system has weakened since the New Deal era. Some argue that the decline of such traditional social groups will result in an increasing tendency for ideological beliefs--beliefs that cut across rather than reinforce membership in traditional New Deal social groups--to shape partisan coalitions (Carmines and Stanley 1992). This article provides a test of this proposition by examining the role of ideology in the formation of partisanship in the United States over the last two decades. We discover, as hypothesized, that ideology not only exerts an increasing impact on partisanship over the last two decades, but one that is increasingly distinct from membership in New Deal social groups.

These findings naturally raise important questions about the future of electoral coalitions in the United States. One wonders, for example, whether ideology will continue to play an increasing role in shaping partisanship and eventually replace traditional New Deal social groups as determinants of partisanship. Before this sort of question can be answered empirically, however, more work must be done on the process and dynamics underlying the development of political cleavages. Specifically, the forces driving the rise of ideology must be empirically examined in order to gain a more complete understanding of the trends discovered here and whether they can be expected to continue in the future. The contribution of this article has been to provide a starting point for such an analysis by examining the role of ideology in shaping partisanship over the last two decades.

Appendix A
Coding and Question Wording of Variables

Dependent Variable: Partisanship [a]

Independent variables
Ideology	1 = *liberal*, 2 = *moderate*, 3 = *conservative*
Education	1 = *less than high school*, 2 = *high school graduate*, 3 = *some college*
Income	1 = *0 to 30 percentile*, 2 = *31 to 60 percentile*, 3 = *61 to 100 percentile*
Region	1 = South, 0 = non-South
Race	1 = White, 0 = Black
Class	1 = working class, 0 = not working class
Union	1 = union member, 0 = not a union member
Urban	1 = urban resident (50,000+), 0 = not an urban resident
Jewish	1 = Jewish, 0 = not Jewish
Catholic	1 = Catholic, 0 = not Catholic
Year	1 = *interviewed in 1972*, 2 = *interviewed in 1976*, 3 = *interviewed in 1980*, 4 = *interviewed in 1984*, 5 = *interviewed in 1988*, 6 = *interviewed in 1992*

---

[a] *1 = strong Democrat, 2 = weak Democrat, 3 = independent Democrat, 4 = independent, 5 = independent Republican, 6 = weak Republican, 7 = strong Republican*

Appendix B
Means and Standard Deviations of
Partisanship and Ideology, 1972-1992

	Partisanship		Ideology	
Year	Mean	SD	Mean	SD
1972	3.61	1.98	2.11	.78
1976	3.61	1.97	2.16	.78
1980	3.52	1.98	2.19	.81
1984	3.77	2.07	2.15	.80
1988	3.82	2.09	2.22	.80
1992	3.71	2.03	2.13	.82

Source: ANES cumulative data file 1952-1992.
Note: Analysis done with full sample of respondents.

Notes

1. It is important to note that social group membership can also be thought of as psychological reference identification and not merely membership in demographic groups (Miller and Wlezien 1993). We treat social groups in the latter and more traditional sense--as demographic descriptors.

2. For coding of variables see Appendix A.

3. Partisanship is treated here as a continuous variable and coded on a 7-point scale. Although there is some debate about whether partisanship measured on a 7-point scale is indeed continuous (Asher 1983; Niemi and Weisberg 1993), preliminary analyses revealed that treating partisanship as a dichotomous variable (e.g., 1 = Democrat, 0 = Republican) yields similar results. Therefore, ordinary least squares (OLS) models with the continuous partisanship variable are reported because such models are more easily interpreted and provide statistics appropriate to the purpose of the article.

4. Political ideology is assessed using responses to the question, "We hear a lot of talk these days about liberals and conservatives. Here is a 7-point scale on which the political views that people might hold are arranged from extremely liberal to extremely conservative. Where would you place yourself on this scale, or haven't you thought much about this?" Preliminary analyses revealed that the full 7-point scale and two collapsed versions of the scale (5-point and 3-point) generate virtually the same pattern of results. The results also remain essentially unchanged when those who lie off the scale (i.e., those who say they haven't thought much about it) are treated as moderates. Thus, rather than reporting the

results produced with each coding method, we present only those generated by the 3-point version of the scale, where those who lie off the scale are treated as missing data (1 = *extremely liberal, liberal, and slightly liberal*, 2 = *moderate*, 3 = *extremely conservative, conservative, and slightly conservative*).

5. As King (1986) and others have pointed out, the R^2 is dependent on the beta coefficient and the standard deviations of the independent variables and the dependent variable:

$$R^2 = (\text{beta [standard deviation of } x/\text{standard deviation of } y])^2.$$

Thus it is possible that the rising R^2 may also be due to an increase in the standard deviation of the independent variable and/or a substantial decrease in the standard deviation of the dependent variable. As Appendix B suggests, however, the standard deviation of the independent variable, ideology, stays relatively constant during this period, rising only slightly between 1972 and 1992. In addition, the standard deviation of the dependent variable, partisanship, is actually larger in 1992 than in 1972. Thus it is clearly the stronger structural relationship between ideology and partisanship (i.e., the beta coefficient of ideology) that accounts for the higher R^2, not the change in standard deviations.

6. The results also hold for southerners, northerners, and Whites. Separate analysis could not be done for Blacks because of the small size of the Black sample (approximately 200).

7. To capture the traditional social group composition of the electorate beginning in the New Deal, we included education, income, union membership, class, religion, place of residency, region, and race as the independent variables in these models (Carmines and Stanley 1990, 1992; Stanley and Niemi 1991, 1995). For coding of the variables see Appendix A.

8. In order to calculate the amount of variation in partisanship accounted for by ideology above and beyond that explained by social groups, we subtract the R^2 of model 1 from the R^2 of model 2. To do this correctly, we make sure each of the models was drawn from the same sample of respondents (King 1986). Thus we do not include respondents who had missing values on any of the social group variables or the ideology variable in the analyses (i.e., listwise deletion of missing values). It is important to note that when the models are reestimated using less exclusive procedures of dealing with missing values (i.e., pairwise deletion; setting missing values to the mean), the results are similar to those presented in Table 2.

9. The findings also hold among southerners, northerners, and Whites.

10. For coding of the variables see Appendix A.

References

Asher, H. B. 1983. Voting behavior research in the 1980s: An examination of some old and new problem areas. In *Political science: The state of the discipline*, ed. A. Finifter, 339-381. Washington, DC: American Political Science Association.

Axelrod, R. 1972. Where votes come from: An analysis of electoral coalitions, 1952-1968. *American Political Science Review* 66:11-20.

Carmines, E. G. and H. W. Stanley. 1990. Ideological realignment in the contemporary South: Where have all the conservatives gone? In *The disappearing South? Studies in regional change and continuity,* ed. R. P. Steed, L. W. Moreland, and T. A. Baker, 21-33. Tuscaloosa: University of Alabama Press.

_____. 1992. The transformation of the New Deal party system: Social groups, political ideology, and changing partisanship among northern whites, 1972-1988. *Political Behavior* 14:213-237.

Carmines, E. G., and J. A. Stimson. 1989. *Issue evolution: Race and the transformation of American politics.* Princeton, NJ: Princeton University Press.

Dalton, R. J., and M. P. Wattenberg. 1993. The not so simple act of voting. In *Political science: The state of the discipline II,* ed. A. W. Finifter, 193-218. Washington, DC: American Political Science Association.

Franklin, M. N. 1985. *The decline of class voting in Britain: Changes in the basis of electoral choice, 1964-1983.* Oxford: Clarendon.

Franklin, M. N., T. T. Mackie, and H. Valen, eds. 1992. *Electoral change.* New York: Cambridge University Press.

Goldthorpe, J. 1980. *Social mobility and class structure in modem Britain.* Oxford: Clarendon.

Heath, A., R. Jowell, J. Curtice, G. Evans, J. Field, and S. Witherspoon. 1991. *Understanding political change: The British voter 1964-1987.* Oxford: Pergamon.

King, G. 1986. How not to lie with statistics: Avoiding common mistakes in quantitative political science. *American Journal of Political Science* 30:666-687.

Mackie, T. T. and M. N. Franklin. 1987. Social structure and party alignments in Western countries. In *The Blackwell encyclopedia of political institutions,* ed. V. Bogdanor, 571-574. New York: Basil Blackwell.

Miller, A. H. and B. Lockerbie. 1992. The United States of America. In *Electoral Change,* ed. M. N. Franklin, T. T. Mackie, and H. Valen, 362-380. New York: Cambridge University Press.

Miller, A. H. and C. Wlezien. 1993. The social group dynamics of partisan evaluations. *Electoral Studies* 12:5-22.

Niemi, R. G. and H. F. Weisberg, eds. 1993. *Controversies in voting behavior.* Washington, DC: Congressional Quarterly Press.

Sniderman, P. M., R. A. Brody, and P. E. Tetlock, eds. 1991. *Reasoning and choice: Explorations in political psychology.* New York: Cambridge University Press.

Stanley, H. W., W. T. Bianco, and R. G. Niemi. 1986. Partisanship and group support over time: A multivariate analysis. *American Political Science Review* 80:969-976.

Stanley, H. W. and R. G. Niemi. 1991. Partisanship and group support, 1952-1988. *American Politics Quarterly* 19:189-210.

_____. 1995. The demise of the New Deal coalition partisanship and group support, 1952-92. In *Democracy's feast: Elections in America,* ed. H. Weisberg, 220-240. Chatham, NJ: Chatham House.

Stone, W. J., R. B. Rapoport, and A. I. Abramowitz. 1990. Party polarization: The Reagan revolution and beyond. In *The parties respond: Changes in American parties and campaigns,* ed. L. S. Maisel, 69-99. Boulder, CO: Westview.

van der Eijk, C., M. N. Franklin, T. T. Mackie, and H. Valen. 1992. Cleavages, conflict resolution and democracy. In *Electoral Change,* ed. M. N. Franklin, T. T. Mackie, and H. Valen, 383-405. New York: Cambridge University Press.

Wattenberg, M. T. 1991. *The rise of candidate-centered politics: Presidential elections of the 1980's.* Cambridge, MA: Harvard University Press.

Zuckerman, A. S. 1982. New approaches to political cleavage. *Comparative Political Studies* 15:131-144.

Acknowledgments

This is a revised version of a paper presented at the annual meeting of the Midwest Political Science Association, Chicago, April 6-8, 1995. The data used here were collected by the National Election Study, which is supported by the National Science Foundation. The data were supplied by the Inter-University Consortium for Political and Social Research. The authors are solely responsible for the analysis and interpretations. The authors are grateful to the editor and the anonymous referees for their detailed comments and thank Don Farole, Brandon Haller, and Will Morgan for their advice on earlier versions of the article.

Chapter 3

Ideological Realignment and Partisan Change in the American South, 1972-1996*

Jonathan Knuckey

The Democratic "Solid South" (Key 1949) has been transformed into a region characterized by a vigorous two-party competition and, arguably, Republican ascendancy (Black and Black 1992, 1987; Lamis 1999, 1990). This change is one of the most intriguing and certainly one of the most important developments in contemporary American politics. Despite the fact that scholars of southern politics have documented this monumental partisan change, they disagree over its precise cause. Specifically, debate has centered upon whether "realignment"--meaning an enduring shift in partisan identifications--or "dealignment"--meaning a loosening of voter ties to political parties--is the most appropriate description of this change (Swansbrough and Brodsky 1988; Stanley 1988; Black and Black 1987).

This paper examines one important explanation of partisan change in the southern electorate: *ideological realignment*.[1] The partisan-ideological mismatch of Democratic partisan identification and voting behavior of white southern conservatives has been one of the greatest anomalies in American politics. Since the New Deal era, the potential for a regional realignment along ideological lines has been a recurring theme in the

*Reprinted with permission from *Politics & Policy* 29, 2 (2001):337-358.

examination of southern partisan change. For example, Key (1955b), Heard (1952) and Sundquist (1983) made similar arguments, stating that as the national Democratic party became solidly identified as the liberal party, white southern conservatives would increasingly become alienated from their ancestral party and would find the Republican party (GOP) to be a more viable political home.

The ideological realignment of southern political parties has progressed in glacial fashion. For example, Philip Converse wrote at a time *before* the Great Society and both the Civil Rights and Voting Rights Acts had transformed the Democratic party into one of economic and racial liberalism. He argued that "the historical link between the South and the Democratic Party has become implausible from the ideological point of view" (Converse 1963, 196). However, in 1968, the Democratic presidential nominee Hubert Humphrey, carrying but one southern state, Texas, placed third in the popular vote behind Richard M. Nixon and George C. Wallace. Yet half of white southern conservatives still held a Democratic partisan identification (Black and Black 1987, 252). There was clearly some "white flight" from the Democratic to Republican partisan identifications and especially *presidential-level* voting among southern conservatives in the 1950s and 1960s. But, the continuing allegiance of a majority of white conservatives to the Democratic party is a testimony to the inertial quality of partisan identification and to the strength of social-group ties to the Democratic party in the South.

Since 1968, the pace of the "ideological sorting" of the mass electorate in the South has hastened as demonstrated by the findings of Black and Black (1987) and Carmines and Stanley (1990). Both of these analyses demonstrated how conservatives were becoming a larger group within the Republican party at the same time that they were becoming a less dominant faction within the Democratic party. It should be noted that both of these analyses of ideological realignment in the South ended with 1984 as a final data point. This paper extends the time series beyond 1984.

Exploration of ideological realignment among white southerners beyond 1984 is appropriate because the Reagan presidency was a great stimulus for further partisan changes among white conservatives (Stanley 1991). Under Reagan, the Republican party became a coherent conservative party as social and cultural conservatism reinforced the existing economic and racial conservative appeal of the GOP to white southerners, thus accelerating the ideological realignment of partisan identifications.

A second reason to examine ideological realignment in the South is the stunning improvement in the electoral success of Republican candidates in the region's subpresidential elections in the 1990s (Rohde 1996;

Hadley 1993). The 1998 elections were viewed as a setback for the Republican party in the South because of some high-profile defeats.[2] However, southern Republicans continued to enjoy an advantage in U.S. Senate seats (14-8), U.S. House seats (71-54) and governorships (7-4). Only in the state legislatures did the last vestiges of Democratic dominance remain. The Democratic party controlled fifteen of the lower and upper houses in the region. Yet even at this level, significant Republican gains have been registered in the 1990s (see McGlennon 1996).

A variety of factors have been offered to explain the surge in southern subpresidential Republicanism: the "nationalization" of elections in the region (Beachler 1998), the negative evaluations of the Clinton presidency by white southerners (Aistrup 1996), and the effects of the creation "majority-minority" congressional districts after the 1990 round of redistricting (Hill 1995; Petrocik and Desposato 1998; Engstrom 1995). However, an important hypothesis to test is whether southern Republican gains in the 1990s are the consequence of the ideological realignment that has been underway for decades. White conservatives are now voting for Republican candidates in *subpresidential* contests at the same level that they have for Republican *presidential* candidates since 1972 (Black and Black 1992).

Overall, updating the topic of ideological realignment in the South will provide valuable insights into recent partisan change in the South, and it will suggest some future trends in party and electoral competition in the region. At the same time, focusing upon the case of the South will reveal a more general understanding of the dynamics of both partisan and electoral realignment.

Data and Methods

Data for this analysis are taken from the American National Election Study (NES) Cumulative File (Sapiro et al. 1998). The analysis must begin in 1972 because it was the first year that NES asked the ideological identification item. The focus is on the partisan change among *white* southerners because black southerners, like blacks in every other region of the nation, held an almost monolithic identification with the Democratic party and have supported its candidates in overwhelming numbers since 1964 (Kinder and Sanders 1996).

Two dependent variables are used to measure partisan change. Following Carmines and Stanley (1990), one focus is partisan identification. This is an appropriate index of partisan change because durable partisan change will result in a change in the underlying distribution of partisan identification (Campbell et al. 1960; 1966). However, an exclusive focus on changes in partisan identification is not satisfactory because Republican candidates in the South, especially those at the presidential level, have achieved electoral support far exceeding what would be expected given the distribution of partisan identification in the region. More generally, as Ladd and Hadley (1975) and Bullock (1988a, 1988b) argue, changes in partisan identification may lag behind changes in voting behavior. Thus, in addition to partisan identification, the voting behavior of white southerners will be examined. Because white conservatives consistently have voted for Republican presidential nominees since 1972, the main focus in this paper is vote choice in *U.S. House elections*. This is an important level of party competition to explore given the success of Republican U.S. House candidates in the 1990s. At the same time, the advantage of focusing on U.S. House elections is that all districts are contested every two years, hence one does not have to pool data across years as if examining U.S. Senate or gubernatorial contests.

Ideological Realignment and Changing Partisan Identification

The distribution of ideological identification

An important preliminary to an examination of ideological realignment is to simply plot the distribution of ideological identification among white southerners. Figure 1 presents the percentage of conservative, moderate and liberal ideological identifiers among white southerners since 1972.[3] Conservatives remain the single largest group, constituting either a majority or a plurality of ideological identifiers in each year. Figure 1 also shows that if an ideological realignment has occurred among white southern conservatives, it should have profound consequences on the region's political parties and elections given the numerical superiority of conservatives. At the same time, Figure 1 also updates and confirms the assertion that "increasing conservatism cannot account for growing Republicanism in the white South since 1972 *because there has been no increase in conservatism*" (Carmines and Stanley 1990, 23 emphasis added).

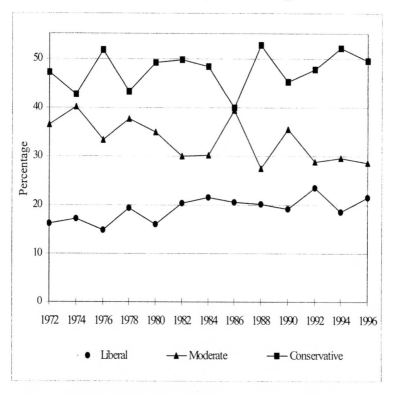

Figure 1. Ideological Identification of White Southerners, 1972-1996
Source: American National Election Studies, 1972-1996

Partisan identification and ideology

The first step in examining ideological realignment among white southern conservatives is to examine their partisan identifications over time.[4] Figure 2 shows clear evidence of the ideological realignment that has taken place among white conservatives in the South since 1972.[5] For example, in 1972, a majority (51.0 percent) of white conservatives still held Democratic partisan identification. As noted above, this represents a decline from the 1950s and 1960s. Yet it is still a remarkable finding given that the Great Society legislation and the passage of both the Civil Rights and Voting Rights Acts had clearly cast the Democrats as the party of economic *and* racial justice. At the same time, the presidential candidacy of Democratic U.S. Senator George McGovern in 1972 portrayed

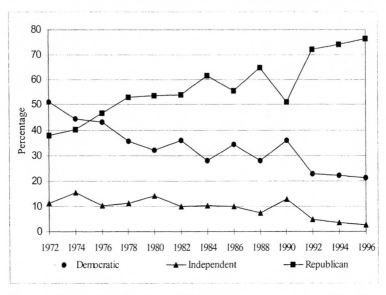

Figure 2. Partisan Identifications of White Southern Conservatives, 1972-1996
Source: American National Election Studies, 1972-1996

the Democrats as the party of "cultural" or "lifestyle" liberalism.

However, since 1972, white conservatives have clearly eschewed a Democratic partisan identification. In their analysis, Black and Black (1987, 251) described this partisan change as "secular realignment." This was the concept introduced by Key to describe "a movement of members of [a] population category from party to party that extends over several presidential elections and appears to be independent of the peculiar factors influencing the vote at the individual elections" (Key 1959,199). Clearly, prior to the 1990s, the changes in the partisan identifications of white conservatives did not take place over one or more "critical elections" (Key 1955a). However, in 1992, a dramatic jump in the time series is evident with 72.4 percent of white conservatives now identified as Republicans. Moreover, data for 1994 and 1996 suggest that the 1992 partisan changes were durable. Thus, by 1996, 76.4 percent of white conservatives identified themselves as Republicans in contrast to only 21.1 percent who identified themselves as Democrats.

Ideological realignment and changing party composition

The change in the partisan identification of white conservatives also has affected the ideological *composition* of the Democratic and Republican parties-in-the-electorate. Figures 3 and 4 respectively show the ideological composition of Democratic and Republican partisan identifiers. Figure 3 shows that conservative Democrats are now a minority faction within the party. Of particular importance is how the position of white *liberals,* as well as white moderates, within the Democratic party has been strengthened since the mid-1980s. In 1984, liberals (33.3 percent) were more numerous than conservatives were (31.6 percent). By 1996, the proportion of white Democrats who were liberals stood at an all time high of 43.2 percent, with just 24.5 percent considering themselves conservatives. Of course, it should be noted that the position of liberals within the Democratic party-in-the-electorate is further strengthened by the addition of black Democrats, who, at least on economic and racial issues, share positions consistent with white liberal Democrats.

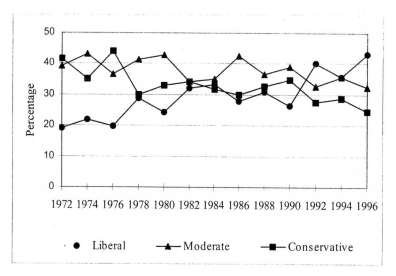

Figure 3. Ideological Identification of White Democratic Partisan Identifiers, 1972-1996
Source: American National Election Studies, 1972-1996

The ideological composition of the Republican party-in-the-electorate did not experience the same change as that found within the Democratic party. As Figure 4 shows, in 1972, the Republican party already was a much more ideologically homogeneous one, with conservatives comprising a majority (59.3 percent) of partisan identifiers. Moderate and liberal Republicans were a sizeable minority (40.7 percent) within the party which explains why many white conservatives were still reluctant to identify themselves as Republicans in 1972. It was not yet a party *dominated* by conservatives. Over the next decade, however, conservatives became more numerous within the party, and the exodus from the Democratic party of white conservatives in the 1990s has made the Republican party the natural political home for white conservatives in the contemporary South. Consequently, this weakened the moderate/liberal wing of the Republican party so that by 1996, only 23.1 percent of Republicans considered themselves moderates or liberals compared to 76.9 percent conservative.

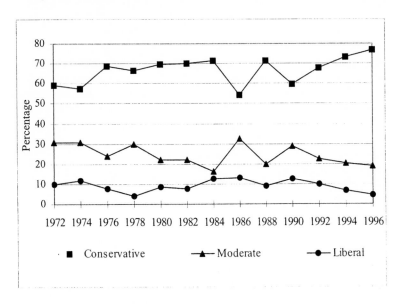

Figure 4. Ideological Identification of White Republican Partisan Identifiers, 1972-1996
Source: American National Election Studies, 1972-1996

The changes in the ideological composition of the Democratic and Republican parties-in-the electorate further contributed to the ideological realignment of white southerners. For example, Sundquist (1983) noted that as more conservatives move into the Republican party, the Democratic party they leave behind will increasingly come under the influence of moderates and liberals. These party members will, in turn, be more prone to select moderate-to-liberal candidates for political office and, in so doing, will further alienate conservatives who remain Democrats. By the 1990s, although the Democratic party-in-the-electorate was not dominated by liberals to the same extent that the Republicans were dominated by conservatives, there was, nonetheless, a clear sharpening along partisan-ideological lines as predicted by Sundquist. Consequently, this has generated more coherent party images and formed the basis for a more "rational" regional party system.

The issue context of ideological realignment

The scope and nature of the ideological realignment in the South is apparent. To further demonstrate its breadth, the approach of Carmines and Stanley (1990) is followed to determine whether the realignment also is manifest among *issue-conservatives*. Carmines and Stanley (1990, 27) found that "there had been a marked reduction in Democratic support and a corresponding increase in Republican support among issue-defined southern conservatives" across ten issue areas. To what extent has this pattern persisted into the 1990s? Figures 5 through 8 show the partisan identification of whites holding conservative issue preference on four policy items that have been asked consistently since 1972: federal government spending on minorities, federal guarantee of jobs and standards of living, defense expenditure, and attitudes on a women's right to choose to have an abortion.[6]

Figures 5 through 7 show a similar pattern of realignment among issue-conservatives to that found for general political ideology, the Democratic advantage eroding through the 1970s, Republican and Democratic partisan identifications at near parity in the early 1980s, and a slight advantage in Republican partisanship emerging in 1984. However, not until the 1990s did a solid and durable Republican advantage among issue-conservatives become apparent, demonstrating again that the early 1990s was a critical period in the ideological realignment of the South.

The one issue that does not fit this pattern is that of abortion. For example, Figure 8 shows that the gap between Democratic and Republican identifications among white southerners holding pro-life views did not diminish in the same way as with the other three issues until 1984. By the 1990s, a partisan gap had emerged that paralleled the one found for the other issues for a majority of those with a pro-life position and with Republican partisan identification. Arguably, the movement of religious conservatives into the Republican party that took place in the mid-1980s (see Baker 1990) and their rise to prominence within state and

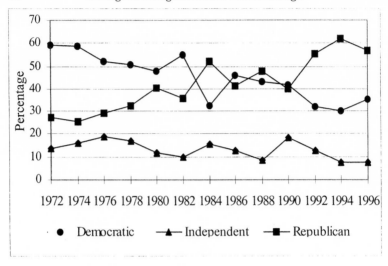

Figure 5. Partisan Identifications of White Southerners Opposed to Government
Aid to Minorities, 1972-1996
Source: American National Election Studies, 1972-1996

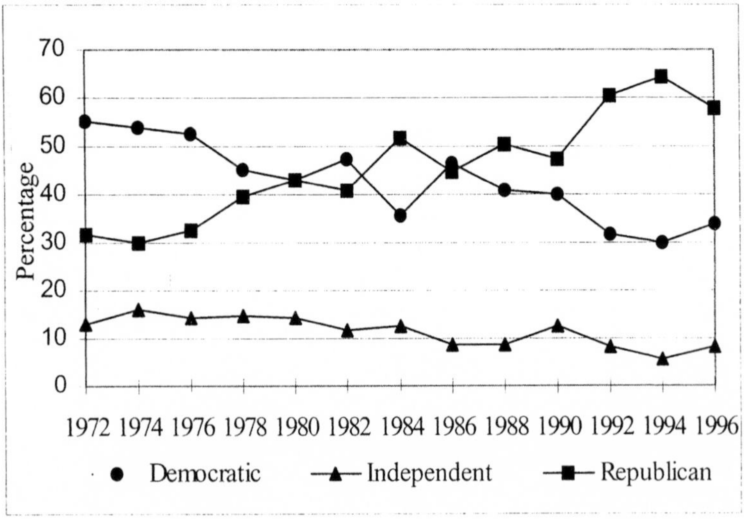

Figure 6. Partisan Identifications of White Southerners Opposed to Government
Guarantee of a Job, 1972-1996
Source: American National Election Studies, 1972-1996

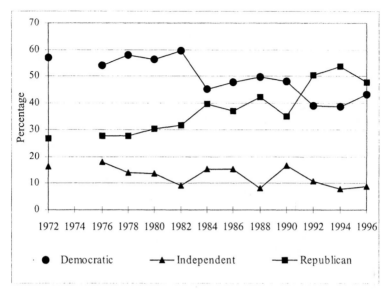

Figure 7. Partisan Identifications of White Southerners Opposed to Freedom of Choice on Abortion, 1972-1996
Source: American National Election Studies, 1972-1996

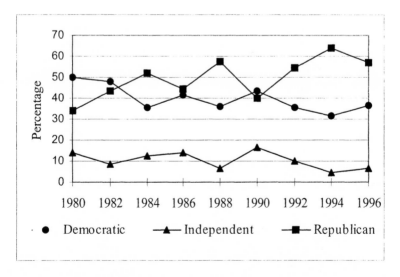

Figure 8. Partisan Identifications of White Southerners Favoring Increased Defense Expenditure, 1980-1996
Source: American National Election Studies, 1980-1996

local Republican parties in the South (Oldfield 1996) may have sharpened partisan lines on the abortion issue.

Overall, by the 1990s, one finds an ideological realignment of partisan identifications that extends beyond general ideological identification. This produced a process of partisan sorting whereby white southern conservatives increasingly have found a suitable political home in the Republican party. In turn, this made the Democratic party a far more liberal one than two decades or even one decade ago. In this transformed partisan environment, the Republican party and its candidates stand to reap considerable electoral success, as evidenced by an examination of how the culmination of ideological realignment in the South has produced unprecedented Republican gains in elections for the U.S. House of Representatives in the 1990s.

Realignment and Republican House Gains

Perhaps one of the most significant developments in the recent politics of the South was the stunning gains made by the Republican party in U.S. House elections in the 1990s. The Republican gains should be set in context with the lack of success by GOP House candidates prior to the 1990s (see Glaser 1996). For example, although Republican presidential candidates swept the South in the 1980s, Republicans held just 39 U.S. House seats (33.6 percent) by the end of that decade. At the same time, when one examines the aggregate vote for all Republican candidates in the 1980s, it never exceeded 45 percent.

Since then, the growth of Republican voting in U.S. House elections has been nothing short of spectacular. In 1992, the Republicans made a net gain of nine U.S. House seats in the South, and the aggregate GOP vote stood at the then record high of 47.6 percent. The 1992 electoral tremor was apparently the precursor to the 1994 electoral earthquake, as the Republican party gained 16 seats in the South, giving the party a majority of U.S. House seats in the region for the first time since Reconstruction.[7] These gains were a result of a surge in the aggregate Republican vote to 56.5 percent, an increase of 8.9 percent from just two years earlier and the largest election-to-election increase in the Republican vote since 1962. Balloting in the 1996 and 1998 elections reflect the durability of these 1992 and 1994 gains. In 1996, Republicans had a net gain of six seats and an aggregate majority of the two-party vote (52.3 percent). Although the 1998 elections in the South were considered to have stalled Republican growth, there was no change in the overall distribution of seats between the parties,[8] and Republican candidates still garnered a majority of the aggregate two-party vote (53.2 percent). Does the ideological realignment of the South explain this growth of congressional Republicanism in the 1990s? Figure 9 shows the vote percentages among conservatives, liberals and moderates for Republican U.S. House candidates. Moderates and liberals were combined because of the small number of white liberals in any year. Clearly, the lack of electoral success by Republican candidates in U.S. House elections in the 1970s and 1980s was a consequence of their failure to win the support of white conservatives. In 1972 and 1974, the level of support among conservatives for Republican candidates (29.3 percent and 29.2 percent) was almost identical to that found among moderates and liberals (28.2 percent and 29.6 percent). Increases in support for Republican candidates among conservatives is apparent beginning in 1976 and lasting through the early 1980s when the Republicans were finally able to attract a majority of votes from white conservatives. However, it was only a slender majority. For example, the average Republican vote among white conservatives over all U.S. House elections in the 1980s was 54.7 percent. To put this in perspective, Ronald Reagan and George Bush in the 1980, 1984 and 1988 presidential elections received, on average, 82.2 percent of the votes from white conservatives. Despite the increase in support from conservatives in the 1980s, it was not sufficient to offset the continuing Democratic advantage among white liberals and moderates coupled with the overwhelming support of blacks. Consequently, the Republican party remained a regional minority in balloting for U.S. House elections.

The change in the voting behavior of conservatives in the 1990s is evident from Figure 9. The vote received by Republican U.S. House candidates from white conservatives increased from 57.1 percent in 1990 to 70.3 percent in 1992. It then increased to 80.3 percent in 1994, the year of the Republican's subpresidential breakthrough in the South. Moreover, the support in 1994 was not an aberration. Republican candidates in 1996 received 82.6 percent of the vote from white conservatives. Perhaps the most important point to note from Figure 9 is that the surge in the aggregate Republican vote in the 1990s was entirely due to changes in the voting behavior of white conservatives, while the vote cast by white liberals and moderates remained constant through the 1990s. Thus, it would be reasonable to conclude that ideological realignment played a major role in the Republicans capturing southern seats in the 1990s and, ultimately, in helping the GOP to attain majority status in the U.S. House for the first time in forty years.[9]

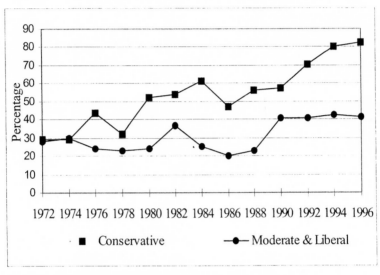

Figure 9. Percentage of White Southerners Voting for Republican U.S. House
Candidates by Ideological Identification, 1972-1996
Source: American National Election Studies, 1972-1996 .

Consequences of Ideological Realignment

A major ideological realignment has taken place among white
southern conservatives, and it appears to have culminated in the 1990s.
It is worth noting that the realignment took place over many decades and
was slow to evolve. Since 1972, however, two "critical" periods of the
realignment are salient. The first was in the early-to-mid 1980s, especially
1984, and the second occurred in the 1990s. In both periods, there was
sharp movement among white conservatives to assume Republican
partisan identification. In the 1990s, this was also true with regard to
GOP *voting* in U.S. House elections. While this conclusion helps in
understanding partisan change in the South, more generally, it suggests
that scholars who study partisan change along with the realignment
paradigm should not view the critical election and secular realignment
routes to partisan change as mutually exclusive.

A final question to consider is whether the ideological realignment in
the South has made the Republicans a regional majority party. In considering this question with respect to southern partisan change in the 1980s,
Carmines and Stanley (1990, 33) argue that while the position of the
Republican party was strengthened by the ideological realignment, it was
not yet a majority. Further realignment together with the electoral success

of the Republican party in the 1990s has prompted a discussion of whether a Republican "Solid South" finally arrived (see Rohde 1996; Hadley 1993). Although Republican gains among conservatives were considerable, it would appear rash to discuss a new Republican "Solid South," given the continuing Democratic edge in partisan identification among both white moderates and liberals and its definite presence among black southerners.[10] At the same time, a Republican strategy that relies exclusively on the support of white conservatives is exceedingly risky, because the support of *some* white moderates in most elections will be necessary for victory. Republican strategists need only look to the 1998 elections where GOP incumbent governors lost in Alabama and South Carolina, losses primarily attributed to a poor showing among white moderates and liberals.

A further reason why the Democratic party may remain in a competitive electoral position is that the movement of white conservatives into the Republican party has been something of a mixed blessing. Many of the new Republicans are social conservatives who are sympathetic with the agenda of the "Religious Right." Although religious conservatives have become active within the Republican party by helping to revitalize grassroots state and local party organizations that had previously stymied Republican growth (Hadley and Bowman 1995), their rise to prominence within the party has increased ideological and issue tensions within both southern Republican state and local parties. If southern Republican parties continue to be captive of religious conservative activists, they run the risk of alienating many moderates, independents, and even some *Republican* partisan identifiers. Again, the defeat of Republican governors in Alabama and South Carolina in 1998, where both GOP incumbents opposed state lotteries to shore up support among religious conservatives, demonstrates the problem faced by the Republican party as it grows.

With all of these caveats noted, the ideological realignment that took place in the South provides the southern Republican party and its candidates with a major electoral advantage that is unlikely to erode in the foreseeable future. White conservatives who now *identify* with the Republican party can be expected to continue to *vote* for GOP candidates at higher rates similar to those found in the 1990s. Hence the Republican party should retain the U.S. House seats which were gained in the 1990s. Indeed, further Republican gains are likely (see Black 1998; Burnham 1996; Hadley 1993) as the Democrats find themselves confronting the problem once faced by the GOP in the region: recruitment of quality candidates and attraction of campaign funds. Democratic candidates can still win elections in the South, but their electoral prospects increasingly seem to rely more either on divisions within the Republican party or on the nomination of ideologically extreme GOP candidates.

Overall, ideological realignment in the South has reshaped the terrain of both southern party and electoral politics, a reshaping that now advantages the Republican party and its candidates. The acceleration of ideological realignment in the South has generated an electoral environment for the twenty-first century where contests will be for the Republicans to lose rather than for the Democrats to win.

Notes

1. For a more general treatment of ideological realignment from a national perspective, see Abramowitz and Saunders (1998).
2. Two incumbent Republican governors Fob James (AL) and David Beasley (SC) were defeated as was one-term U.S. Senator Lauch Faircloth (NC). Additionally, the Democrats kept control of the governor's mansion in Georgia where Roy Barnes defeated Republican nominee Guy Millner in a contest that many commentators predicted a Republican victory.
3. The NES ideological identification item was measured on a seven-point scale, ranging from extremely liberal to extremely conservative. Respondents placing themselves at points 1, 2 or 3 were classified as liberal, those placing themselves at point 4 as moderate and those placing themselves at points 5, 6 or 7 as conservative.
4. Following Keith et al. (1992), both Democratic and Republican identifiers include strong, weak and independent-leaning partisans. Independents are "pure" independents only.
5. Examination of the partisan identification of white liberals and moderates revealed that, while there had been some movement toward Republican partisan identifications, mainly among moderates, it was not of the same magnitude as that found among white conservatives.
6. On the racial, social-welfare and defense expenditure items, a conservative position represented a score of four or higher on a seven-point scale. The abortion item was not measured on a seven-point scale. Following Carmines and Stanley (1990, 29), conservatives on this issue were those who were not pro-choice, e.g., those who did not believe that by law a woman should always be able to obtain an abortion as a matter of personal choice.
7. Following the 1994 elections this majority was further bolstered by the defection of five conservative Democrats: Nathan Deal (GA-9), Greg Laughlin (TX-14), W. J. "Billy" Tauzin (LA-3), Jimmy Hayes (LA-7) and Mike Parker (MS-5).
8. The Republicans gained one southern seat in the 1998 midterm elections (NC-8), but also lost one (MS-5), the latter being the district represented by Mike Parker, one of the Democrats who has switched parties after the 1994 elections.
9. Of course a multivariate analysis would be required to specify more fully the causal link between ideological realignment and Republican congressional success in the 1990s. The evidence presented here, however, strongly suggests that such a hypothesis should be further explored.

10. For the 1992-1996 period there was a Democratic advantage among white moderates, 47.6 percent of whom held a Democratic partisan identification compared to 36.3 percent holding a Republican partisan identification, with 16.1 percent identifying as Independents. Among white liberals, 77.9 percent held a Democratic partisan identification, compared to 16.8 percent holding a Republican identification, and 6.5 percent identifying as Independents. Finally, among blacks, 77.9 percent held a Democratic identification, compared to 9.3 percent holding a Republican partisan identification, with 10.7 percent identifying as Independents.

References

Abramowitz, A. I. and K. L. Saunders. 1998. Ideological realignment in the U.S. electorate. *Journal of Politics* 60:634-652.

Aistrup, J. A. 1996. *The southern strategy revisited: Republican top-down advancement in the South.* Lexington: University Press of Kentucky.

Baker, T. A. 1990. The emergence of the religious right and the development of the two-party system in the South. In *Political parties in the southern states—party activists in party coalitions*, ed. T. A. Baker, C. D. Hadley, R. P. Steed, and L. W. Moreland. New York: Praeger.

Beachler, D. W. 1998. A tale of two decades: Southern House elections in the 1980s and 1990s. Paper presented at the annual meeting of the Southern Political Science Association, Atlanta.

Black, E. 1998. The newest southern politics. *Journal of Politics* 60:591-612.

Black, E. and M. Black. 1987. *Politics and society in the South.* Cambridge, MA: Harvard University Press.

_____. 1992. *The vital South.* Cambridge, MA: Harvard University Press.

Bullock, C. S., III. 1988a. Regional realignment from an officeholding perspective. *Journal of Politics* 50:553-574.

_____. 1988b. Creeping realignment in the South. In *The South's new politics: Realignment and dealignment*, ed. R. H. Swansbrough and D. M. Brodsky. Columbia: University of South Carolina Press.

Burnham, W. D. 1996. Realignment lives: The 1994 earthquake and its implications. In *The Clinton presidency: First appraisals,* ed. C. Campbell and B. A. Rockman. Chatham, NJ: Chatham House.

Campbell, A., P. E. Converse, W. E. Miller, and D. E. Stokes. 1960. *The American voter.* New York: John Wiley and Sons.

_____. 1966. *Elections and the political order.* New York: John Wiley and Sons.

Carmines, E. G. and H. W. Stanley. 1990. Ideological realignment in the contemporary South: Where have all the conservatives gone? In *The disappearing South: Studies in regional change and continuity*, ed. R. P. Steed, L. W. Moreland, and T. A. Baker. Tuscaloosa: University of Alabama Press.

Converse, P. E. 1963. A major political realignment in the South? In *Change in the contemporary South*, ed. A. P. Sindler. Durham, NC: Duke University Press

Engstrom, R. L. 1995. Voting rights districts: Debunking the myths. *Campaigns and Elections* 16:24-46

Glaser, J. M. 1996. *Race, campaign politics, and the realignment in the South.*. New Haven, CT: Yale University Press.

Hadley, C. D. 1993. Southern politics after the election of President Clinton: Continued transformation toward the Republican party. *American Review of Politics* 14:197-212.

Hadley, C. D. and L. Bowman. 1995. *Southern state party organizations and activists*. Westport, CT: Praeger.

Heard, A. 1952. *A two-party South?* Chapel Hill: University of North Carolina Press.

Hill, K. A. 1995. Does the creation of majority black districts aid Republicans? An analysis of the 1992 congressional elections in eight southern states. *Journal of Politics* 57:384-401.

Keith, B. E., D. B. Magleby, C. J. Nelson, E. Orr, M. C. Westyle, and R. E. Wolfinger. 1992. *The myth of the independent voter.* Berkeley: University of California Press.

Key, V.O., Jr. 1949. *Southern politics in state and nation.* New York: Alfred A. Knopf.

_____. 1955a. A theory of critical elections. *Journal of Politics* 17:3-18.

_____. 1955b. The erosion of sectionalism. *Virginia Quarterly Review* 31:161-179

_____. 1959. Secular realignment and the party system. *Journal of Politics* 21:198-210.

Kinder, D. R. and L. M. Sanders. 1996. *Divided by color: Racial politics and democratic ideals.* Chicago: University of Chicago Press.

Ladd, E. C. and C. D. Hadley. 1975. *Transformations of the American party system.* New York: W.W. Norton.

Lamis, A. P. 1990. *The two-party South.* Rev. ed. New York: Oxford University Press.

_____. 1999. *Southern politics in the 1990s.* Baton Rouge: Louisiana State University Press.

McGlennon, J. J. 1996. Party competition in southern legislatures, 1976-96: The last block of the solid South crumbles. *American Review of Politics* 17:213-224.

Oldfield, D. M. 1996. The Christian right in the presidential nominating process. In *In pursuit of the White House—How we choose our presidential nominees*, ed. W. G. Mayer. Chatham, NJ: Chatham House.

Petrocik, J. R. and S. W. Desposato. 1998. The partisan consequences of majority-minority redistricting in the South, 1992 and 1994. *Journal of Politics* 60:613-633.

Rohde, D. W. 1996. The inevitability and solidity of the "Republican solid South." *American Review of Politics* 17:23-46.

Sapiro, V., S. J. Rosenstone, W. E. Miller, and the National Election Studies. 1998. *American National Election Studies, 1948-1997* (CD-ROM). ICPSR ed. Ann Arbor, MI: Inter-University Consortium for Political and Social Research (producer and distributor).

Stanley, H. W. 1988. Southern partisan changes: Dealignment, realignment or both? *Journal of Politics* 50:65-88.

_____. 1991. The Reagan legacy and party politics in the South. In *The 1988 presidential election in the South: Continuity amidst change in southern party politics*, ed. L. W. Moreland, R. P. Steed, and T. A. Baker. New York: Praeger.

Sundquist, J. L. 1983. *Dynamics of the party system: Alignment and realignment of political parties in the United States*, rev. ed. Washington, DC: Brookings Institution.

Swansbrough, R. H. and D. M. Brodsky. 1988. *The South's new politics: Realignment and dealignment.* Columbia: University of South Carolina Press.

Acknowledgments

The author would like to thank Charles D. Hadley and the four anonymous reviewers for their helpful comments and suggestions. Data used in this paper are taken from the American National Election Studies, 1972-1996. Data were collected by the Center for Political Studies of the Institute for Social Research at the University of Michigan. Responsibility for the analyses and interpretations presented here are those of the author alone.

Section 2

Empirical Studies of Ideology:
Policy Formulation and Congressional Votes

Chapter 4

Capture and Ideology in
the Economic Theory of Politics*

Joseph P. Kalt and Mark A. Zupan

The economic theory of regulation long ago put public interest theories of politics to rest. These theories have correctly been viewed as normative wishings, rather than explanations of real world phenomena. They have been replaced by models of political behavior that are consistent with the rest of microeconomics (Downs 1957; Buchanan and Tullock 1965; Stigler 1971; Peltzman 1976). Recently, however, debate has arisen over whether some version of a public interest theory of regulation will have to be readmitted to our thinking about actions and results in the political arena. What is at issue is the empirical importance of the altruistic, publicly interested goals of rational actors in determining legislative and regulatory outcomes (Kau and Rubin 1979; Kalt 1981; Peltzman 1982).

This study assesses the nature and significance of publicly interested objectives in a particular instance of economic policymaking: U.S. Senate voting on coal strip-mining regulations. The existence of such objectives is, of course, no contradiction of the economic view of human

*Reprinted with permission from *American Economic Review* 74, 3 (1984):279-300.

behavior (Arrow 1972; Becker 1974); and may well be rooted in genetic-biological history (Becker 1976; Hirshleifer 1978). Generally, however, individuals' altruistic, publicly interested goals have been given little attention. This reflects the judgment that such goals are so empirically unimportant as to allow the use of Occam's razor in positive models, or well-founded apprehensions that these goals are unusually difficult to identify, measure, and analyze. Notwithstanding the latter problem, we find that approaches which confine themselves to a view of political actors as narrowly egocentric maximizers explain and predict legislative outcomes poorly. The tracking and dissecting of the determinants of voting on coal strip-mining policy suggest that the economic theory of politics has been prematurely closed to a broader conception of political behavior.

Interests and Ideology in the Economics of Politics

The setting: Coal strip-mining regulation

The Surface Mining Control and Reclamation Act (SMCRA) was the product of a protracted political struggle. Congress twice passed versions of SMCRA--in 1974 and 1975--only to have them vetoed by President Ford. SMCRA was finally signed into law by President Carter on August 3, 1977. The Act requires the restoration of strip mined land to its premining state. In addition, the Act established an Abandoned Mine Reclamation Fund and clarified previously indefinite property rights to water and land in areas underlain by strippable coal.

The Act reduces the use of environmental inputs and raises the costs of strip mining. This tends to raise the price of coal and generates income transfers *from* surface coal producers and coal consumers *to* underground producers and the consumers of environmental amenities. The combined losses of surface producers and coal consumers appear to be on the order of $1.4 billion per year (split approximately 70/30, respectively; Kalt 1983). After accounting for a small deadweight loss, the annual gains of noncoal environmental users and under ground producers are in the range of $1.3 billion (split roughly 90/10).

While incidence analysis can produce more or less precise estimates of particular market participants' gains or losses from SMCRA, there is clearly no reason to expect these economic stakes to translate one-for-one into political clout (Olson 1971; Stigler 1971). Indeed, one of the tasks of the economic theory of regulation and the research below is to describe how economic stakes map into political influence. For our purposes, incidence analysis indicates the *direction* of relevant parties' interests in SMCRA: the regulation of the environmental damage attendant to strip mining should be expected to be opposed by surface coal producers and coal consumers; underground coal producers and consumers of affected environmental amenities should support SMCRA.

Related research

The tenor of economic ("capture") theories of regulation, when applied to a specific case such as SMCRA, might suggest that the incidence of the legislation summarizes not only the economics, but also the politics of the issue: narrowly self-interested underground coal producers and environmental consumers captured policymakers at the expense of narrowly self-interested coal consumers and surface coal producers. This line of reasoning, however, cannot be disproved. Since every economic policy decision produces transfers of wealth, it is always possible to infallibly relate political outcomes to distributional impacts. This approach, in fact, leaves open the question of whether the behavior and results we observe in the political arena are the product of something more than the parochial pecuniary interests of affected parties.

Probably the most basic proposition of economic, capture models of regulation is the (sometimes implicit) assertion that the altruistic, publicly interested goals of individuals are such insignificant factors in political processes that they are empirically uninteresting and dispensable. Stigler (1972) has noted the possibility of altruistic motives in political action. These might take the form of a sense of "civic duty," that is, a duty to serve the interests of the public. Pursuit of such a duty is a consumption activity that yields utility in the form of the warm glow of moral rectitude. Classifying this type of argument in the utility function as a "consumption motive" (as distinguished from the self-interested "investment motive" of increasing one's own wealth), Stigler asserts with respect to economic theories of politics: "The investment motive is rich in empirical implications, and the consumption motive is less well-endowed, so we should see how far we can carry the former analysis before we add the latter." (104)

The sentiment of this assertion may yet prove to be supportable. A number of recent investigations, however, have suggested that policymakers' self-defined notions of the "public interest" are dominant explanatory factors in congressional voting behavior (Mitchell 1979; Kau and Rubin 1979; Kalt 1981). These studies have attempted to explain voting records on specific issues (for example, oil price controls) as functions of relevant economic interest variables *plus* some measure of the "ideological" orientation of congressmen. The latter is typically based on rating scales provided by ideological watchdog organizations such as the Americans for Democratic Action (ADA) or the Americans for Constitutional Action (ACA). The consistent findings are that economic interest variables play surprisingly weak roles in legislative outcomes, while the hypothesis of no ideological effect is quite easily rejected. Peltzman (1982) has taken a critical look at these findings. The interests of constituents and the ideological "preferences" of their representatives are plausibly interrelated--perhaps with causation running from the former to the latter. The apparent importance of ideology may, therefore, be due to left-out economic interest variables. By examining Senate voting across a broad sample of issues, Peltzman is able to "explain away" most of the importance of ideological preferences with an extended array of constituent interest measures (for example, demographic characteristics). The research strategy behind these results, however, differs in a fundamental way from the approach taken in the research it critiques. Specifically, Peltzman examines a sample covering essentially the entire package of votes offered by senators to their constituents, rather than voting on a specific issue. The query remains whether conclusions reached at such a high level of bundling can safely be applied to the specific case. The economic theory of regulation has generally been put forth and applied as an issue-specific theory (Stigler 1971; Peltzman 1976; Abrams and Settle 1978).

Possible sources of ideological voting

In the jargon of recent research, the purported social objectives of political actors have been termed "ideology." Political ideologies are more or less consistent sets of normative statements as to best or preferred states of the world. Such statements are moralistic and altruistic in the sense that they are held as applicable to everyone, rather than merely to the actor making the statements. Accordingly, political ideologies are taken here to be statements about how government can best serve their proponents' conceptions of the public interest. Behavior in accord with such statements has two possible sources: 1) the direct appearance of altruism in actors' preference functions (termed "pure" ideology); and 2) a convenient signaling mechanism when information on political decisions is otherwise costly.[1]

Pure ideology in voters and their representatives

Pure ideology, if it exists at all, is the manifestation of altruism in the political sector. The returns from the furtherance of an ideology appear to come in at least two forms. First, the successful promotion of an ideology may give individuals the satisfaction of knowing that they have concretely improved the lot of others. Second, even if the pursuit of ideology has no effect on others, individuals may derive satisfaction from "having done the right thing" (Stigler's consumption motive).[2] Do individuals really get utility from these sources? It is not our intention here to dispute tastes. We take the presence of ideological tastes as given by introspection and observation. Following Becker (1974), we also take the pursuit of such tastes to be rational--to be responsive, that is, to opportunity costs. This contrasts with the unfortunate terminology which characterizes altruistic-ideological behavior as "non-economic" (Peltzman 1982) and/or "irrational" (Barzel and Silberberg 1973). The rationality of ideological behavior is tested below.

Political behavior based on pure ideology may arise from either the publicly interested objectives of constituents or the independent publicly interested objectives of their representatives.

Constituents: Voters' ideological goals might include, for example, anticommunism, communism, Jeffersonian agrarianism, Rawlsian egalitarianism, and so on.[3] The presence of such goals poses no problems for the economic theory of politics. Publicly interested ideologues are just another special interest capable of capturing the political process, subject to the comparative statics of organizational costs and benefits as modeled by Peltzman (1976). We suspect, however, that most economists would conclude that the pursuit of ideological objectives is not an important phenomenon. At least on the basis of behavior observed in the market sector, this would appear to be well-founded. Is there any reason to expect pure ideological actions to be relatively more common in the political arena? Several factors suggest the answer may be affirmative.

First, altruistic ideological interests that depend upon actually improving the welfare of others have clear collective good attributes. The apparatus of government provides the classic Samuelsonian (1954) means (i.e., coercive power) for overcoming the free-rider problems that can plague a marketplace. Indeed, this apparatus may be made comparatively inexpensive for the representative altruist to the extent it can be hijacked and used to require outsiders to finance the benefits delivered to the altruist's targeted group.

Second, in much political activity, the individual has no meaningful prospect of influencing outcomes. In the case of large-number majoritarian elections, for example, the individual voter is generally incapable of promoting his or her investment interests. This observation has led to the recognition that altruistic-ideological preferences play central roles in motivating the act of voting. Nevertheless, it has typically been assumed that, once the decision to vote has been made, we can explain the ballot cast by reference to the voter's economic interests. As Geoffrey Brennan and Buchanan (1982) have pointed out, however, this is a *non sequitur*: if the decision to vote is based on consumption motives, it does not follow that these motives are set aside upon entering the voting booth. Comparing the consumption choices made in voting with invest-ment decisions in the marketplace (emphasis in original):

> . . . we may presume that the individual *cares* as to which outcome emerges from the voting process. But this does not permit us to pre-sume that his choice in the polling booth *reflects* or corresponds with his preferences over outcomes. For the voter is not *choosing* between outcomes. . . . When the voter pulls a particular lever, the opportunity cost of doing so is not a particular policy forgone. . . . (14-15)

> [Thus] . . . the choice of candidate. . .depends overwhelmingly on tastes for showing "preferences" as such--and hardly at all on the evaluation of outcomes. Voting behavior is then to be understood perhaps as "symbolic" or "liturgical". . . and [is] hardly at all like the choice among alternative investments.(18)

Third, even when political participation is motivated by the prospect of pecuniary gains, such gains are often subject to substantial public goods problems. Pecuniary political gains commonly must be shared with large numbers of congruent parties (for example, all coal consumers or all environmental users). While private sector investments can be accompa-nied by free-rider problems, such problems are virtually the rule at the legislative level in U.S.-style democracy (the Chrysler and Lockheed cases notwithstanding). In contrast, at least that part of ideology based on individuals' tastes for the warm glow of moral rectitude is a strict private good in both the public and private sectors. Thus the opportunity cost (i.e., forgone pecuniary return) of ideology might be expected to be generally lower in the political arena than in the marketplace. Accord-ingly, the rational actor in the political sector would be expected to reveal behavior tilted relatively more toward altruistic-ideological objectives.

Representatives: Institutional attributes of the political sector may allow pure ideological action by representatives themselves. This oppor-tunity could arise because, analogous to the case of management in the private corporation, there may be some separation of "ownership" by constituents and "control" by policymakers. Any such slack in the principal-agent relationship can be expected to result in policymaker independence or "shirking"--as Armen Alchian and Harold Demsetz (1972) call it. Models of the specific-issue legislative process that have grown out of the economic theory of regulation (Peltzman 1976) seldom leave room for policymaker shirking.[4] By endowing legislators with goals such as vote maximization, rather than own-utility maximization, such models preclude behavior that is not directly controlled by constituents. This conception of the strength of the principal-agent bond in the legislative process, however, does not seem to be in line with the conception of this bond that comes out of the property rights theory of institutions (Alchian and Demsetz 1972; Jensen and Meckling 1976) and the bulk of associated empirical evidence (see the summary by Louis De Alessi 1982). Conditions under which the market system's invisible hand is likely to encounter difficulty in narrowing the separation of ownership and control would appear to be especially prevalent in the legislative context.[5]

First, the "market for control" (Manne 1965) is characterized by significant indivisibilities that impair adjustment at the margin by constituents. The typical constituent is presented with all-or-nothing choices between a small number of large bundles of issues to be addressed by policymakers over their tenure; *and* the market meets only infrequently-- every six years in the case of the U.S. Senate. Second, as "hirers" of political representation, voter-owners have poor incentives to be well-informed. As Olson (1971) has stressed, collective decisions are subject to classic free-rider problems that affect participants' willingness to invest in the acquisition of information. Third, these free-rider problems are exacerbated by the fact that "ownership" by constituents is held under attenuated property titles. Political ownership is nontransferable, and, as residual claimants to the net benefits of correct decisions, constituent-owners promoting such decisions cannot easily capture resulting gains (see Alchian and Demsetz 1972). Fourth, the political market is apparently subject to less than perfect competition (Ferejohn 1977). The provision of representation services in the U.S. political system takes place under conditions of effective duopoly; barriers to entry are significant (Abrams and Settle 1978); elements of natural monopoly are present (Stigler 1971); and collusion to prevent Tiebout-type (1956) competition is officially sanctioned. Finally, these attributes of the market for legislative seats create conditions conducive to "opportunism" in Oliver Williamson's (1975) sense; and the range of enforceable contractual agreements of the type examined by Benjamin Klein, Robert Crawford, and Alchian (1978) that might be struck to minimize opportunism is notably limited (for example, to the verbal agreement that "I will keep my campaign promises").

It must be stressed that none of this implies that shirking is costless to legislative representatives. Analogous to the position of shirking private sector managers vis-a-vis shareholders, representatives face some control through the voting booth, as well as more continuous pressure from constituents who have some ability to affect the pleasantness of the policymaker's working day, future employment opportunities, and other aspects of the returns to positions of policy responsibility. Nevertheless, legislative institutions such as the U.S. Senate would appear to be archetypical Alchian-Demsetz organizations in which agents are imperfectly policed by their principals--where "imperfectly" is defined relative to a nirvana world of zero policing costs. The implied result is some amount of own-welfare maximization by representatives at the expense of their constituents--an amount that may be optimal for constituents given the real world policing costs they face.

Any shirking by imperfectly policed representatives can be expected to center around those activities that have low opportunity costs (for example, in terms of reelection prospects) and/or poor substitutes off the job. Paralleling Becker's (1957) analysis of private managers' on-the-job consumption and Alchian and Reuben Kessel's (1962) examination of nonprofit institutions, shirking by legislators may focus on nonpecuniary perquisites of office holding--although opportunities for personal pecuniary gain are certainly available. The perquisites of political office range from "fact finding" junkets and postservice employment connections with rent-seeking interest groups to public notoriety, prestige, and the ability to use the power of government to impose one's own pet theories of the "good" society. The last of these emoluments is almost uniquely available in the political sector and is what we have termed ideological consumption.

For a number of reasons, shirking in an activity such as Senate voting might be expected to have an ideological component. Morris Fiorina and Roger Noll (1978) have noted, for instance, that legislators' fates depend heavily on the provision to constituents of so-called "facilitation services" (for example, supportive intervention at other levels of government), as distinguished from their provision of floor votes. This is complemented by the fact that nonideological shirking on floor votes (for example, taking bribes, failing to be informed, or missing roll calls in favor of office parties) is comparatively costly as a result of institutional penalties, while a legislator does not face expulsion or censure for voting his or her "conscience" (i.e., ideology).[6] Furthermore, to the extent the individual legislator can rationally take the fate on the floor of any particular piece of legislation as given, that legislator's vote becomes valueless to any constituent--that vote, that is, has no impact on the economic well-being of constituents since it does not affect outcomes.[7] The only remaining value of the vote to the legislator, then, would be its consumption value-- no constituent would be willing to pay anything for it. This is, of course, the legislative-floor analogue to Brennan and Buchanan's (1982) analysis (noted above) of voting booth behavior by citizens, although it would be inappropriate to conclude that the investment value of a vote in a place like the U.S. Senate is typically nil as it is in the very large-number-majoritarian voting booth. Lastly, the governmental apparatus is the preeminent mechanism for affecting broad social change. The opportunities this creates, if coupled with comparatively low costs to ideological shirking, would imply a self-selection process that attracts individuals with relatively intense demands for ideology to the political sector.

Impure ideology and costly information

It is certainly possible that policymakers base their decisions on consultation with the precepts of an ideology when nothing more than narrow self-interest is being served. In a world in which information on the concordance between constituent interests and the consequences of policy proposals is scarce, political representatives may serve their investment motives (for example, the desire to get reelected) by relying on the dictates of an ideology as a shortcut to the service of their constituents' goals (Downs 1957; Buchanan and Tullock 1965). In this view, ideology plays the same role in the economic theory of the political process that managerial rules of thumb play in the theory of the profit-maximizing firm. The implication that the apparent ideologies of representatives are in fact proxies for constituents' interests suggests collinearity between measures of ideology and those interests. This implication has not received support in studies of voting on individual issues, but has been borne out in Peltzman's (1982) examination of voting on the aggregated bundle of issues addressed by senators. These apparently conflicting results are analyzed below within the context of a Downsian view of representative democracy.

Downs' (1957) seminal look at representative democracy suggests an important implication of ideology as a device for economizing on information: if legislators are not perfectly policed on every vote, the rational constituent could be expected to support representatives whose demands for pure ideology are intense relative to other motives for shirking. To be sure, as each specific issue arises between elections, the constituent prefers that representatives vote the constituent's interests on that issue, not their own ideologies. But the constituent faced with 1) an uncertain bundle of issues to be decided by representatives over their terms of office, 2) uncertainty about the effects of policy decisions, and 3) positive policing costs and hence shirking, can attempt to wind up on net on the winning sides of issues (in a pecuniary *or* nonpecuniary sense) by supporting candidates with appropriate ideologies. Upon election, such candidates will engage in pure ideological shirking on particular issues rather than permit themselves to be captured by the issue-specific interests that organize and present themselves at any particular moment; an economic incidence approach to issue-specific political economy will be inadequate. Over the full slate of issues, however, representatives' voting should fall in line with general indicators of their constituents' ideological and investment interests--as Peltzman (1982) finds. We now examine these Downsian implications in the context of the specific issue of SMCRA.

Senate Voting on SMCRA

Study design

Our objective is to untangle the causal forces behind Senate voting on strip-mining controls. We seek to separate the effects of constituents' interests (economic and ideological) and senators' ideology. In addition, we would like to be able to uncover that part, if any, of senators' ideology which is purely publicly interested shirking and that part of ideology which merely stands in for otherwise difficult to identify constituent interests.

Voting on strip-mining legislation is observed as either a "yea" or a "nay." To measure senators' positions, a variable *ANTISTRIP* is constructed to reflect the frequency, f_i, with which the ith senator casts a vote unfavorable to strip mining. A senator voting an anti-strip position on r_i out of n_i opportunities has $f_i = r_i/n_i$. This frequency is bounded by zero and unity. Adjusting for $r_i = 0$, $r_i = n_i$, and heteroskedasticity (Gart and Zweifel 1967), the weighted logit technique of Arnold Zellner and Tong Lee (1965) is employed in our econometric analysis. Thus

(1) $ANTISTRIP_i = \ln[(r_i + .5)/(n_i - r_i + .5)]$; and has variance estimator:

(2) $\text{Var}_i = 1/(r_i + .5) + 1/(n_i - r_i + .5)$;

The variable *ANTISTRIP* is based on the voting of the 100 senators that served in the 95th Congress (1977-78); and is derived from 21 roll call votes in which the interests of surface coal producers, underground producers, coal consumers, and the consumers of environmental amenities were clearly delineated. These votes deal with either SMCRA or its vetoed predecessors.[8] Measures that would have raised the costs of surface mining were taken to be detrimental to surface mining--and conversely. Selected votes and their economic implications are not identical; and Charles Phelps (1982) suggests the possibility of aggregation problems in *ANTISTRIP*. In this case, however, results are unaffected when individual votes are used as dependent variables (see our earlier paper).

Interests and their influence

The economic theory of regulation provides the basis for measures of constituents' interests and influence. Specifically, the *interests* constituents have in capturing the political process are their prospective gains or losses from any policy proposal. The *ability* constituents have to capture the political process depends critically on their ability to overcome the free-rider effects inherent in collective decisions. Any group's influence will depend positively on members' per capita stakes and the concentration of their interests; and negatively on the heterogeneity of members' objectives and group size. Where data permit, we employ variables reflecting determinants of group effectiveness, as well as the magnitude of groups' interests in SMCRA.

Turning first to the magnitude of groups' interests, we introduce variables reflecting the stakes of surface coal producers, underground coal producers, coal consumers, and consumers of affected environmental amenities.

Coal Producers: The variables *SURFRES* and *UNDERRES* measure each state's reserves (in Btus) in 1977 of surface and underground coal, respectively; and are expressed as fractions of state personal income to scale for the relative importance of coal production to states' economies. Reserve-based measures are used to proxy for the present value of SMCRA's impacts on coal resources. Particularly in many western states where strip mining was in its infancy in 1977, current production figures inadequately capture the present-valued importance of the industry to states' economies. Results of most interest, namely the relative roles of economic and ideological variables, are not affected by switching to production- or employment-based measures (see our earlier paper).[9]

There are significant differences across states in SMCRA's impact on strip mining costs. The variable *MC* measures the regulation-induced increase in the long-run average cost of surface mining in each state, as derived by ICF, Inc. (1977). Because surface mining interests were adversely affected by SMCRA, *MC* as well as *SURFRES* are expected to be negatively related to *ANTISTRIP*. The variable *UNDERRES* is expected to have a positive impact on *ANTISTRIP*.

Coal Consumers: The variable *CONSUME* is employed to represent the importance of coal consumption in each state. Electric power generation accounts for 78 percent of U.S. coal demand and *CONSUME* is the share of state electricity generated from coal in 1977.[10] It is preferred to other measures such as total coal Btus consumed per capita if it is primarily electric utilities, small in number and large in size, who overcome the free-rider problems that plague political lobbying.[11] The organizational effectiveness of the electric power industry is examined below. Reflecting the effect of SMCRA on coal prices, *CONSUME* is expected to be negatively related to *ANTISTRIP*.

Environmental Consumers: Environmental interests may be classed into two broad types: environmental users in the literal sense; and those for whom environmental protection represents an ideological cause. Empirical evidence on the existence of the latter is provided by William Schulze et al. (1981). They find that, based on willingness to pay, the most significant value of an undeveloped environment is derived from individuals' demands for just knowing that an area is used "properly," independent of whether such individuals ever visit or even plan to visit the area themselves. These values are notably altruistic-ideological. They arise from prescriptive opinions about what environmental uses are consistent with self-defined standards of ethical propriety and the public interest. These standards include the view of wilderness as an antidote for purported psychological costs of urbanization; the conception of the American West as a peculiar cultural and natural history lesson; the quasi-religious question of the propriety of appropriating of environmental resources for human ends; the social desirability of rapid economic growth; and the appropriate beneficiaries of public lands. Moreover, the results of Schulze et al. suggest that people's willingness to pay to uphold these precepts has standard comparative static properties--ideological environmentalism is just another economic good.

To capture the ideological interests that constituents have in SMCRA, we employ a variable *ENVIROS*. This is defined as state membership in the six largest environmental groups (as a fraction of voting-age population). Interestingly, the correlation between *ENVIROS* and measures of actual recreational use of the environment (for example, hunting and fishing, budgets for parks and recreation, visits to parklands) is quite low.[12] If senators' voting has been captured by ideological environmentalists, *ENVIROS* should have a positive effect on *ANTISTRIP*.

The interests of actual nonmining consumers of the environment threatened by strip mining are represented by three variables: *HUNTFISH, SPLITRIGHTS,* and *UNRECLAIMED.* The variable *HUNT-FISH* is defined as the number of hunting and fishing licenses as a percentage of state population. It is highly correlated with other measures of outdoor recreational activity. The analysis in Kalt (1983) indicates that outdoor recreation is little threatened by strip mining; and *HUNTFISH* is consistently insignificant in the econometric analysis. Since results of interest are invariant with respect to the inclusion of *HUNTFISH,* the variable is excluded here (see our earlier paper). The variable *SPLIT-RIGHTS* captures the support of ranchers, farmers, lumberers, and other noncoal business interests for legislation that preserved their preferential rights to the large land areas underlaid by federally controlled strippable coal. The economic values at stake are measured by the agriculture/timber revenue yield of the disputed surface acres, expressed as a percentage of state personal income. Similarly, *UNRECLAIMED* measures the prospective value of already stripped but unrestored acres to noncoal interests who stood to benefit from the Abandoned Mine Reclamation Funds' subsidies. The variables *SPLITRIGHTS* and *UNRECLAIM-ED* should be positively related to *ANTISTRIP.*[13]

Group Influence: The magnitude of a group's interests, even when scaled by state size, does not account fully for that group's ability to overcome the free-rider problems associated with political lobbying. These sorts of problems have been incorporated into empirical research on nonpolitical collective action, most notably in dealing with joint maximization in oligopolistic markets. Available data permit us to address this issue in the political context. To reflect the likelihood that a group can surmount free-rider difficulties, we introduce Herfindahl indices by state for surface coal producers, underground coal producers, coal consumers, and environmental organizations *(HSURF, HUNDER, HCONSUME,* and *HENVIROS).*[14] Data do not permit similar measures for *SPLITRIGHTS* and *UNRECLAIMED.*[15] Herfindahl indices are negatively related to group size and positively related to the concentration of interests within a group. Accordingly, *HSURF* and *HCONSUME* are expected to have negative effects on *ANTISTRIP*, while *HUNDER* and *HENVIROS* should have positive impacts.

Senator ideology

The final variable to be introduced into the examination of *ANTISTRIP* voting is some (arguably impure) measure of senators' own ideologies. Following the lines of previous research, we rely on the independent (but not disinterested) "pro-environment" rating scale of the League of Conservation Voters (LCV). This rating scale is based on 27 not-surface-mining-related Senate votes taken in the 95th Congress and deemed to be ideologically revealing by the LCV.[16] The LCV notion of environmentalism conforms well with the aforementioned moralistic values of an undeveloped environment.[17] Analogous to *ANTISTRIP*, the frequency of pro-environmental votes is transformed according to (1) and is denoted *PROLCV*. Reflecting the LCV's own stance, *PROLCV* is expected to be positively related to *ANTISTRIP*. The extremes of *PRO-LCV* are occupied by senators with reputations as ideologues--for example, Kennedy (D-MA), Culver (D-IA), Zorinsky (R-NE), and Hatch (R-UT). Of course, this observation begs the question of the purity of ideology.

To the extent, if any, *PROLCV* reflects pure ideology, a move from a lower to a higher *PROLCV* represents a move from a less to a more intense demand for ideological support of an undeveloped environment. The variable *PROLCV* is built up from dichotomous, pro- or anti-environment choices by senators. Holding other things constant, including the opportunity cost of shirking, senators with relatively more intense demands for ideological environmentalism will choose the "pro" position more frequently and, hence, will have higher *PROLCV* values.

To the extent *PROLCV* reflects apparent ideology that is in fact proxying for constituents' interests in SMCRA, *PROLCV* should exhibit significant collinearity with the other factors that explain *ANTISTRIP* voting. Of course, as in any econometric analysis, there may be left-out variables. If these are correlated with the (apparent) ideologies of senators, the hypothesis that pure ideology matters in specific-issue politics may be inappropriately accepted. Consequently, a major part of the effort undertaken in the next major section is aimed at uncovering such a correlation. At this stage, it can only be noted that each of the interests appearing in the record of SMCRA lobbying efforts and suggested by theory has been identified to the extent allowed by the data: all voters at least have "homes" in the selected variables and account is taken of the nature of political organization. To be sure, the groupings of voters according to their interests in coal strip mining most likely do not correspond to the groupings ("constituencies") that originally got a senator elected--as a result of the "bundling" discussed earlier. But, the capture models of regulation do not suggest that the search for left-out variables should begin with these original groupings. Insofar as these models are specific-issue models, the search for left-out variables should be guided by analysis of SMCRA's impacts on consumers' and producers' surplus.

Interstate lobbying and logrolling

Two aspects of the legislative process not included in our empirical model are worth noting here. First, the conception of senators' voting choices embodied in our analysis portrays "captured" senators as casting their ballots based on the likely impact of SMCRA on their own states' constituents--with better organized constituents getting more attention. This obscures the ability of voters to apply pressure across state lines. Data inadequacies do not permit us to formally incorporate this phenomenon. Nevertheless, to the extent that cross-state lobbyers must appeal to within-state impacts in order to be effective, the problem recedes. Moreover, there is no obvious reason why SMCRA-*specific* out-of-state interests should cluster around *PROLCV* or any other measure of ideology based on a bundle of a senator's *non*-SMCRA votes. Still, this possibility becomes a central object of investigation below.

A second aspect of the legislative process not covered explicitly by our model is logrolling. This in part reflects the paucity of help provided by theory and data that would allow measurement of the extent and direction of any logrolling and coalition-forming on the specific issue of SMCRA--of the hundreds of issues to choose from, which issue(s) would a logrolling senator trade his SMCRA vote for? Note, however, there are no apparent a priori reasons why logrolling would make ideology appear any more or any less important relative to constituent interests in explaining SMCRA voting. That is, the willingness of a senator to trade away *either* his constituents' interests *or* his own ideology should be negatively related to the political strength of those interests and the intensity of his ideological preferences, respectively. Furthermore, in the absence of pure ideology, the hypothesis that ideology matters will incorrectly be accepted only if two conditions hold:

1) The non-SMCRA interests that are in fact served when a senator votes against his constituents' SMCRA-specific interests are systematically related to the interests that were served (either indirectly through

logrolling or directly) by the senator's voting on the issues from which *PROLCV* is constructed.

2) At the same time, for the senator buying SMCRA votes by giving up his constituents' interests on other issues, SMCRA-specific constituent interests must be systematically related to the interests that are being served (either indirectly or directly) by his *PROLCV* voting.

With *PROLCV* issues ranging from the regulation of nitrogen oxide emissions from automobiles and the elimination of phosphates in dishwashing detergent to expansion of Redwood National Park and charging congressional staffers for parking privileges, satisfaction of these two requirements seems somewhat implausible. Nevertheless, we address this important question empirically in the next major section--for the cases of both *PROLCV* and measures of ideology that are completely unrelated to the environment.

Finally, for the second condition above to hold without introducing collinearity between *PROLCV* and the included interest variables used to explain *ANTISTRIP*, the SMCRA-specific constituent interests being served by "buying" senators must be unrelated to the interests we have been able to identify. Again, a reading of the history of SMCRA provides little help in identifying such potent left-out variables. Still, this implication suggests a further object for empirical investigation.

Initial results

It is clear that the task of isolating the determinants of legislative voting on an economic issue such as SMCRA is extraordinarily complex. As a first cut, we present the "standard" analysis that has been applied in previous research. Table 1 compares the Capture Model argued for by the economic theory of regulation (i.e., *PROLCV* is excluded) and a Capture-plus-Ideology Model that includes a variable *(PROLCV)* intended to account for senators' ideological preferences. Both models lend support to a multigroup (for example, see Peltzman 1976) capture theory of politics--perhaps amended to include capture by ideologues. Noncoal beneficiaries of the environment, coal consumers, underground coal producers, and surface coal producers all appear to have appreciably influenced senators' voting on SMCRA; and interest groups' organizational capacities appear to have generally pushed senators in expected directions, although without especially strong statistical significance.

Table 1. The Determinants of Anti-Strip-Mining Voting in the U.S. Senate [a]

Explanatory Variable	Capture Model		Capture-plus-Ideology Model		
	Coef.	t-stats.	Coef.	t-stats.	*Beta*
PROLCV			0.466	10.05	0.65
MC	-0.513	-4.78	-0.375	-3.47	-0.22
SURFRES	-16.765	-1.66	-17.198	-1.71	-0.57
UNDERRES	12.512	2.09	14.132	2.37	0.73
SPLITRIGHTS	-26.546	-0.55	68.488	1.40	0.12
ENVIROS	83.375	4.48	0.501	0.02	<u>0.00</u>
UNRECLAIMED	0.019	3.77	0.015	3.03	0.22
CONSUME	-0.350	-1.46	-0.440	-1.83	-0.13
HSURF	-0.294	-1.24	0.017	0.07	<u>0.00</u>
HUNDER	0.305	1.10	0.150	0.54	0.03
HENVIROS	1.935	1.78	-1.286	-1.14	-0.07
HCONSUME	-0.486	-2.42	-0.261	-1.29	-0.08
Constant	-0.154	-0.33	1.414	2.86	
Adj. R^2	0.45		0.74		
Condition-Stat.	25.99		27.47		

[a] Dependent Variable is *ANTISTRIP*. Underlined *Betas* >0.00 before rounding.

The most striking result of Table 1 is the sharp increase in explanatory power that results from the introduction of *PROLCV*. Indeed, it is this type of result that led Kau and Rubin (1979) and Kalt (1981) to conclude that pure ideology was at work in legislative politics. The foregoing discussion, however, argues that such a conclusion is premature. The next section proceeds with a dissection that accounts for the extent to which an extended array of constituent characteristics (including *ENVIROS)* can explain *PROLCV*. At this stage, we can only note that, while the behavior of selected coefficients indicates that *PROLCV* is not completely orthogonal to the set of other explanatory factors, the variable's statistical significance and the condition statistics (Belsley et al.

1980) indicate there is insufficient collinearity to justify the conclusion that *PROLCV* is merely a proxy for the constituent interests identified by the capture theory.

Separating Interests and Ideology

Even if *PROLCV*'s sources--indiscernible constituent interests or the elusive notion of senatorial concerns for the public interest--are unclear, its explanatory power is striking. In the following analysis, we attempt to pry open the black box of ideology from a number of different angles. We first look for a purer measure of senators' own demands for altruistic, publicly interested behavior. Second, after isolating that portion which is most clearly pure, we examine the relative importance of the pure and remaining, arguably interest-proxy, parts of ideology. We then investigate the apparent interest-proxy part of ideology more closely. Finally, to assay whether ideological consumption is economically rational, we subject it to a revealing comparative statics test.

SMCRA voting and social issue ideology

Among the many issues senators vote on are certain moral and ethical matters around which economic-interest lobbying is infrequent. Examples include such issues as child pornography, the neutron bomb, and capital punishment. While Peltzman (1982) rejects ideology as an explanation for voting on economic issues such as SMCRA, he suggests that voting on noneconomic socio-ethical questions is especially likely to be based on individuals' preferences for moral rectitude, that is, pure ideology. Indeed, he finds evidence that voting on such issues reflects senators' own preferences more than does voting on "pocketbook" issues. Following this line of reasoning, we throw *PROLCV* out of the analysis of *ANTISTRIP* and replace it with measures of senators' social issue ideology. These measures are based on senators' voting on, for example, increased penalties for trafficking in child pornography, expanding the applicability of the death penalty, allowing the immigration of avowed communists, and "giving away" the Panama Canal. (Subsequent sections assess whether these measures actually reflect left-out interests and/or capture by ideological constituents.)

Two types of social issue ideology variables are examined. First, *PROLCV* is replaced by (dichotomous) voting on individual issues. Second, two indexes are created (according to (1)) from the sample of individual votes. The sample includes all votes taken in the 95th Congress that could be identified as general socio-ethical questions, uncontaminated by pocketbook concerns.[18] The issues thus identified are the column headings in Table 2. Selection was based on a priori judgment; that is, there was no econometric "fishing."

One of the indexes, the "SI (Social Issue) Index," is based on 34 votes dealing with the 12 non-Panama Canal issues indicated in Table 3. The second index, the "Panama Canal Index," is based on a sample of 25 procedural votes taken during the ratification process for President Carter's Panama Canal Treaty. The ceding of the Panama Canal was selected because a reading of the legislative history indicates that first, it was probably the most striking recent case in which conservatives "stonewalled it" against liberals; and second, no identifiable economic interest groups were coalesced by the issue.

The ideological content of the social issue votes cuts along modern liberal/conservative lines. To provide consistency to expected signs, senators are assigned a value of unity when voting the liberal position (as defined by, for example, the ADA) and a value of zero otherwise. It turns out that politicians consistently package liberalism and environmentalism together--the correlation between the LCV's and the ADA's rating scales is 0.94. Accordingly, if the apparent ideology embodied in *PROLCV* is, in fact, as pure as the ideology expressed in voting on socio-ethical matters, the social issue measures should have strongly positive effects on *ANTISTRIP*. Moreover, overall estimation results should closely resemble those found when using PROLCV.

Table 2 reports representative results when social issue ideology replaces *PROLCV* in the explanation of *ANTISTRIP*. Table 3 shows results of interest when an *individual* vote on one of the socio-ethical issues covered by the SI Index replaces *PROLCV*. The striking finding is how well voting on an issue with as much pocketbook content as SMCRA can be explained by senators' positions on the death penalty, sex education, the neutron bomb, the ceding of the Panama Canal, the immigration of avowed communists, and so on. In every case, the social issue variable has a strongly positive impact on *ANTISTRIP*.[19] Furthermore, the explanatory power of the Capture-plus-Ideology Model is remarkably similar when social issue voting replaces *PROLCV*. As might be expected, this is most evident when indexes are used. The thrust of these first results tilts toward the interpretation of *PROLCV* as reflecting relatively pure ideology.

Table 2. Ideology, Social Policies, and SMCRA Voting:
Representative Results [a]

Explanatory Variable	Communist Immigration		Death Penalty	
	Coef.	t-stats.	Coef.	t-stats.
IDEOLOGY	0.842	5.92	1.013	7.19
MC	-0.503	-4.22	-0.464	-4.23
SURFRES	-21.157	-2.07	-15.152	-1.46
UNDERRES	15.519	3.43	11.025	1.77
SPLITRIGHTS	-1.077	-0.02	-16.656	-0.29
ENVIROS	41.602	2.02	61.048	3.13
UNRECLAIMED	0.014	2.75	0.022	3.86
CONSUME	-0.223	-0.88	-0.301	-1.14
HSURF	-0.048	-0.19	-0.556	-2.19
HUNDER	0.159	0.53	0.435	1.43
HENVIROS	0.164	0.13	1.370	1.18
HCONSUME	-0.466	-2.21	-0.138	-0.64
Constant	0.343	0.69	-0.614	-1.23
Adj. R^2	.54		.66	

[a] Dependent Variable is *ANTISTRIP*.
[b] From Table 1, Capture-plus-Ideology Model.

Table 2. Continued

SI Index		Panama Canal Index		PROLCV [b]	
Coef.	t-stats.	Coef.	t-stats.	Coef.	t-stats.
0.296	9.62	0.193	8.93	0.466	10.05
-0.372	-3.44	-0.434	-4.02	-0.375	-3.47
-16.204	-1.61	-16.845	-1.67	-17.198	-1.71
12.201	2.04	13.079	2.17	14.132	2.37
19.663	0.41	45.120	0.93	68.488	1.40
21.450	1.09	44.194	2.29	0.501	0.02
0.011	2.10	0.013	2.46	0.015	3.03
-0.280	-1.16	-0.293	-1.18	-0.440	-1.83
-0.380	-1.60	-0.428	-1.77	0.017	0.07
0.416	1.50	0.407	1.39	0.150	0.54
0.192	0.17	0.962	0.87	-1.286	-1.14
-0.138	-0.67	-0.197	-0.96	-0.261	-1.29
0.730	1.53	0.111	0.24	1.414	2.86
.71		.67		.74	

Table 3. Ideology, Social Policies, and SMCRA Voting:
Social Issue Votes [a]

Issue	Coefficient	t-stats.	Adj. R^2
Communist Immigration	0.842	5.92	.54
Death Penalty	1.013	7.19	.66
Pardon Draft Resisters	0.902	6.53	.57
Sex Education	1.177	7.70	.64
Neutron Bomb	0.893	5.90	.54
School Desegregation	0.945	6.67	.62
Abortion	0.591	4.73	.53
Child Pornography	0.623	3.52	.44
Pregnancy Disability	1.209	6.07	.56
Pregnancy Discrimination	1.319	7.11	.61
Cuba in Africa	0.882	5.54	.62
Loans to Communists	0.888	6.45	.55
Panama Canal Treaty	1.185	8.64	.65

[a] Capture-plus-ideology specification, Table 2.

Isolating the purest part of senator ideology

In an analysis of voting on the aggregate bundle of issues senators faced in the 96th Congress, Peltzman (1982) demonstrates that, at least on economic issues, measures of senatorial ideology (for example, ADA rating scales and senators' choices of party affiliation) stand in for a detailed list of constituent characteristics that plausibly correspond to their underlying economic interests. In the following analysis, we assume that this finding applies in the particular case of SMCRA. We further allow capture by ideological constituents. We then split measured ideology into that part that can be explained by constituent characteristics and the remaining senator-specific component. Our primary object is to examine whether the latter has any explanatory power.

We first estimate *PROLCV* and the SI Index as functions of the types of factors suggested by Kau and Rubin (1979), and by Peltzman (1982)-- factors such as general constituent characteristics and each senator's *PARTY* (Democrat = 1). Included constituent characteristics consist of demographic variables *and* measures intended to reflect constituents' independent ideological interests. By employing demographic variables, we are accepting the methodology of those who have found that senators' pure ideological goals play no role in legislative politics (Peltzman 1982) and that demographic variables provide suitable proxies for constituents' underlying economic interests.[20]

The variables *ENVIROS* and *HENVIROS* are included to reflect constituents' (environmental) ideological interests. More generally, constituent ideology may be reflected by a measure such as the percentage of the state's vote going to McGovern *(MCGOV)* in the 1972 presidential election. The recognized hopelessness of McGovern's candidacy at election time probably made voting on the basis of investment motives unusually fruitless, and, by Stigler's (1972) argument, votes cast would uncommonly reflect ideological consumption motives.[21] Thus, *MCGOV* is included in the explanation of *PROLCV* and the SI Index. Arguably, it is correlated with left-out constituent characteristics; but the exact source of *MCGOV* is irrelevant to our purpose of isolating that portion of *senators'* voting which is not related to some constituent (economic *or* ideological) interest. The source of *PARTY,* on the other hand, is a matter of concern.

If the list of included constituent characteristics is complete, *PARTY* reflects senator-specific "non-economic factors" (Peltzman 1982) such as a senator's world view (liberal or conservative) at the time of the party affiliation choice. In the absence of a guarantee that our set of constituent characteristics is complete, we perform our analysis from both perspectives: party as ideology and party as proxy for unidentified constituent interests. The latter interpretation is rendered less plausible by the inclusion of *MCGOV.*

The estimated models of *PROLCV* and the SI Index (see our earlier paper) closely resemble the patterns of correlation reported by Kau and Rubin (1979), Kalt (1981), and Peltzman (1982).[22] Their primary role here is to allow the breaking down of ideology. Specifically, *PROLCV* and the SI Index are split into that part predicted by constituent (economic and ideological) interests and a residual component. The fitted component (denoted the constituent part) of *PROLCV* and the SI Index is obtained both with *PARTY* included as a possible left-out interest proxy and with *PARTY* excluded. Correspondingly, the residual, senator-specific component consists of either each model's prediction errors alone or these errors plus the fitted *PARTY* effect. If there is any senator ideology at work in *PROLCV* or SI voting, this senator-specific component is the purest part that might be isolated.

The constituent part and the senator-specific component of *PROLCV* and, alternatively, the SI Index are entered as separate explanatory variables in the model of *ANTISTRIP*. Clearly, given previous results, the constituent part of the ideology measures should have a significant effect on *ANTISTRIP*. Of central interest, however, is the effect of the senator-specific part of the ideology measures. If senators are well policed on strip mining issues or if, when shirking, they do so nonideologically and independent of constituent interests, this variable should not be systematically related to *ANTISTRIP* voting. The alternative hypothesis that the senator-specific variable has a significantly positive impact on *ANTISTRIP* depends on two conditions. First, the variable must be isolating senators' pursuit of their own altruistic, publicly interested goals on general environmental issues *(PROLCV)* or socio-ethical matters (the SI Index). Second, senators must have pursued these goals in their voting on the specific issue of coal strip mining policy.

Table 4 reports estimated *ANTISTRIP* models under the fitting and splitting of *PROLCV*. Table 5 reports the analogous case for SI ideology. As anticipated, the constituent parts of both *PROLCV* and the SI Index have a strongly positive influence on *ANTISTRIP*. Independent of the interpretation of *PARTY* (i.e., ideology or interest proxy), the senator-specific measure also has a highly significant and positive effect on *ANTISTRIP* voting. In fact, in every case, its inclusion appreciably improves the explanatory power of the model.[23] Further, it seems noteworthy that these conclusions are not obviously weaker when looking at the senator-specific part of *social issue* voting.

The results of Tables 4 and 5 may, of course, be due to the exclusion of some as-of-yet-unidentified SMCRA-specific constituent interest--perhaps even an out-of-state interest, or a non-SMCRA interest served indirectly by logrolling. Tables 4 and 5, however, reduce the likelihood that such a variable exists. That is, if such a variable were to exist, it would have to be relatively orthogonal to not only states' identified SMCRA-specific interests, but also to the constituent interest variables used in the explanation of *PROLCV* and the SI Index. Moreover, it would have to be *simultaneously* and causally (in the capture sense) related to voting on coal strip-mining regulation, general environmental issues, sex education, the neutron bomb, child pornography, etc. Pending further search for such a variable, Tables 4 and 5 further suggest that ideology probably should not be excluded from analyses of particular-issue politics.

The role of left-out constituent characteristics

The preceding analysis has assumed that a large part of senators' apparent ideology is correlated with causal constituent (economic or ideological) interests left out of the basic capture-plus-ideology explanation of *ANTISTRIP.* As noted in the first major section, however, such correlations could arise for two very different reasons. On the one hand, it may be happenstance: what looks like senator ideology is the reflection of left-out constituent economic or ideological interests that actually have direct effects on SMCRA voting. On the other hand, *PROLCV* and the SI Index may be entirely pure senator ideology, unrelated to the interests constituents have in the *specific* issue of SMCRA, but related to broad constituent characteristics via Senate elections and voters' interests in putting the "right" ideologies into office--a la Downs.

The problem of inferring causation from correlation is notably difficult. In the case at hand, we approach this problem by focusing on whether there are different implications: 1) when the variables that are correlated with measures of ideology are operating directly on *ANTISTRIP,* as opposed to 2) when policing is imperfect and they operate indirectly through their impact on the types of senators elected (and, hence, the ideologies manifested by shirking senators).

One such difference in implications concerns the way the constituent characteristics (i.e., demographics, ideology, and perhaps *PARTY)* that explain *PROLCV* and the SI Index enter the explanation of *ANTISTRIP.* The same set of characteristics may play a causal role in all three types of voting. The obvious differences in the economic content of SMCRA, general environmental issues, and socio-ethical matters, however, suggest that the roles played by the individual variables in this set will not be identical across the three cases in terms of their size, signs, and significance. Consequently, if the variables that make up the constituent part of ideology play direct causal roles in SMCRA voting, their explanatory power will be higher if they are not constrained to enter the *ANTISTRIP* model in the same linear combinations they have in the explanation of *PROLCV* or the SI Index. On the other hand, the constituent part of ideology may in fact be pure senator ideology in the particular case of SMCRA *and* the route of influence by the set of general constituent characteristics may thus be the indirect Downsian route. If so, constrain-

Table 4. LCV Ideology and Constituent Interests in SMCRA Voting [a]

Explanatory Variable	Excluding Party & Error Part of *PROLCV*			Party & Error Part of *PROLCV*		
	Coef.	t-stat.	*Beta*	Coef.	t-stat.	*Beta*
Senator-Specific Part of *PROLCV*						
Party & Error				0.442	7.73	0.45
Error Only						
Constituent Part of *PROL-CV*	0.615	6.45	0.48	0.527	5.49	0.41
MC	-0.422	-3.91	-0.24	-0.370	-3.42	-0.21
SURFRES	-25.826	-2.54	-0.86	-18.427	-1.80	-0.61
UNDERRES	18.634	3.08	0.96	14.894	2.46	0.77
SPLITRIGHTS	66.982	1.33	0.12	76.481	1.52	0.13
ENVIROS	-8.770	-0.37	-0.03	-7.932	-0.34	-0.03
UNRECLAIMED	0.016	3.15	0.24	0.015	2.97	0.22
CONSUME	-0.493	-2.04	-0.15	-0.455	-1.89	-0.14
HSURF	0.009	0.04	<u>0.00</u>	0.043	0.18	0.01
HUNDER	0.373	1.35	0.08	0.168	0.60	0.04
HENVIROS	-0.630	-0.54	-0.04	-1.474	-1.27	-0.08
HCONSUME	-0.139	-0.67	-0.04	-0.225	-1.08	-0.07
Constant	1.706	3.10		1.590	2.89	
Adj. R^2	.57			.74		

[a] Dependent Variable is *ANTISTRIP*. Underlined *Betas* >0.00 before rounding.

Table 4. Continued

Excluding Error Part of *PROLCV*			Error Part of *PROLCV*			Explanatory Variable
Coef.	t-stat.	*Beta*	Coef.	t-stat.	*Beta*	
						Senator-Specific Part of *PROLCV*
						Party & Error
			0.401	4.89	0.30	Error Only
0.570	8.83	0.56	0.511	7.78	0.50	Constituent Part of *PROLCV*
-0.483	-4.50	-0.28	-0.389	-3.57	-0.22	*MC*
-24.446	-2.42	-0.81	-18.615	-1.83	-0.62	*SURFRES*
17.467	2.91	0.90	14.860	2.47	0.77	*UNDERRES*
80.400	1.62	0.14	75.804	1.53	0.13	*SPLITRIGHTS*
6.150	0.30	0.02	-2.794	-0.14	-0.01	*ENVIROS*
0.017	3.49	0.25	0.015	3.06	0.22	*UNRECLAIMED*
-0.544	-2.26	-0.16	-0.465	-1.92	-0.14	*CONSUME*
-0.115	-0.48	-0.03	0.009	0.04	0.00	*HSURF*
0.571	2.05	0.12	0.223	0.78	0.05	*HUNDER*
-0.883	-0.78	-0.05	-1.379	-1.21	-0.08	*HENVIROS*
-0.032	-0.16	-0.01	-0.205	-0.98	-0.06	*HCONSUME*
1.190	2.42		1.454	2.93		Constant
	.67			.74		Adj. R^2

Table 5. Social Issue Ideology and Constituent Interests in SMCRA Voting [a]

Explanatory Variable	Excluding Party & Error Part of Index			Party & Error Part of Index		
	Coef.	t-stat.	*Beta*	Coef.	t-sta.	*Beta*
Senator-Specific Part of Index						
Party & Error				0.288	7.86	0.44
Error Only						
Constituent Part of Index	0.452	5.55	0.38	0.326	3.94	0.27
MC	-0.432	-4.00	-0.25	-0.369	-3.40	-0.21
SURFRES	-20.969	-2.08	-0.70	-16.575	-1.64	-0.55
UNDERRES	15.148	2.53	0.78	12.433	2.07	0.64
SPLITRIGHTS	16.589	0.34	0.03	22.087	0.45	0.04
ENVIROS	18.950	0.86	0.06	17.641	0.80	0.06
UNRECLAIMED	0.016	3.10	0.24	0.011	2.08	0.16
CONSUME	-0.355	-1.48	-0.11	-0.282	-1.17	-0.09
HSURF	-0.186	-0.78	-0.04	-0.369	-1.54	-0.09
HUNDER	0.457	1.64	0.10	0.426	1.53	0.09
HENVIROS	-0.105	-0.09	-0.01	0.066	0.06	0.01
HCONSUME	-0.178	-0.86	-0.05	-0.121	-0.58	-0.04
Constant	1.227	2.31		0.823	1.55	
Adj. R^2		.54			.71	

[a] Dependent Variable is *ANTISTRIP*.

Table 5. Continued

Excluding Error Part of Index			Error Part of Index			Explanatory Variable
Coef.	t-stat.	*Beta*	Coef.	t-stat.	*Beta*	
						Senator-Specific Part of Index
						Party & Error
			0.233	4.93	0.29	Error Only
0.501	8.44	0.52	0.393	6.20	0.41	Constituent Part of Index
-0.473	-4.41	-0.27	-0.389	-3.58	-0.22	*MC*
-20.761	-2.06	-0.69	-17.593	-1.74	-0.58	*SURFRES*
14.765	2.47	0.76	12.984	2.17	0.67	*UNDERRES*
40.386	0.83	0.07	31.148	0.64	0.05	*SPLITRIGHTS*
19.517	0.97	0.06	14.273	0.71	0.05	*ENVIROS*
0.016	3.23	0.24	0.012	2.27	0.18	*UNRECLAIMED*
-0.413	-1.72	-0.12	-0.315	-1.31	-0.10	*CONSUME*
-0.270	-1.14	-0.06	-0.354	-1.49	-0.08	*HSURF*
0.665	2.38	0.14	0.507	1.80	0.11	*HUNDER*
-0.744	-0.66	-0.04	-0.290	-0.26	-0.02	*HENVIROS*
-0.020	-0.10	-0.01	-0.063	-0.30	-0.02	*HCONSUME*
1.022	2.09		0.916	1.87		Constant
	.65			.72		Adj. R^2

ing these characteristics to enter the *ANTISTRIP* model in the same way they enter the explanation of the ideology measures should not affect their explanatory power.

Results when the general constituent characteristics are constrained to enter the *ANTISTRIP* model as the fitted constituent parts of *PROLCV* and the SI Index are what is reported in Tables 4 and 5. Table 6 compares the explanatory power of the constrained characteristics with that obtained in the unconstrained case (see our earlier paper for full results). Table 6 indicates that, of course, the R^2 is higher when the general constituent characteristics are not constrained. In the SI Index case, the adjusted R^2 also improves when the characteristics are unconstrained--although only slightly. In the *PROLCV* case, however, the adjusted R^2 actually falls when constituent characteristics are unconstrained. In each case, classical tests of the equality of the constrained and unconstrained models provide little confidence that equality can be rejected.

The general constituent characteristics that might have been supposed to be directly affecting SMCRA voting appear to be operating indirectly through the pure ideology of elected and shirking senators. That is, *PROLCV* and the SI Index do not appear to be standing in for otherwise unidentified economic or ideological interests that might have captured senators in their voting on the particular issue of SMCRA. The suggested conclusion is that a senator's overall bundle of votes reflects the constituent preferences that were expressed on election day. The interests of those same constituents, when those interests are subsequently reshuffled by the prospective effects of a particular decision on the Senate floor, however, do not fully control the senator on that decision. The capture theory may work well as a theory of elections, but not so well as a theory of issue-specific politics.

Electoral policing and ideological shirking

If the evident roles of *PROLCV* and the SI Index in SMCRA voting largely reflect senators' own ideological preferences, they do so because of imperfect issue-specific policing. Accordingly, the extent to which shirking senators' notions of the public interest enter their voting behavior should be systematically related to the opportunity costs of shirking. The investigation of this cost is a promising source of comparative statics tests for the presence, importance, and rationality of ideology in representative politics. In general terms, the opportunity cost of shirking should vary directly with constituents' incentives to police (i.e., the producers' and consumers' surplus stakes); and vary inversely with organization-informa-

Table 6.   Ideology and the Path of General Constituent Characteristics in ANTISTRIP Voting

	LCV Ideology: Constituent Characteristics		SI Ideology: Constituent Characteristics	
	Model: Party as Ideology			
	Uncon-strained	Constrained	Uncon-strained	Constrained
R^2	.78	.77 [a]	.79	.75 [b]
Adj. R^2	.73	.74 [a]	.73	.71 [b]
F-Test	84% [c]		14% [c]	
	Model: Party as Interest Proxy			
	Uncon-strained	Constrained	Uncon-strained	Constrained
R^2	.79	.77 [a]	.79	.76 [b]
Adj. R^2	.73	.74 [a]	.74	.72 [b]
F-Test	89% [c]		21% [c]	

[a] From Table 4.
[b] From Table 5.
[c] The level of significance at which equality of the two regressions may be rejected. Lower values signify increased confidence in rejection of equality.

tion costs and institutional impediments to monitoring. The cost of shirking should also be inversely related to the security, somehow measured, with which a senator intending to remain in office holds his or her seat. This security is plausibly related to such factors as the senator's margin of last victory, tenure, committee power (a major source of facilitation services), and personal wealth. These relationships obviously involve substantial simultaneity--tenure, for example, affords senators security, but they get tenure by serving their constituents.

The development of a full simultaneous model of shirking is considerably beyond the scope of this study. Nevertheless, one component of the cost of shirking that is clearly determined exogenously can be examined--the proximity of a senator's next electoral test (Barro 1973). In a world in which voters have positive discount rates and/or memories that decay, a senator can, in a sense, run down his or her security capital in midterm and build it back up again as the next election approaches.

Ideological shirking should, therefore, be directly related to the time remaining in a senator's term.

Table 7 reports one test of this hypothesis. In our sample, 33 senators were up for reelection in 1978. If present, ideological shirking should have been less prevalent *(ceteris paribus)* among these senators than in the sample as a whole during the strip-mining voting of 1977. To examine this, we look for errors in the predictions of the Capture-plus-Ideology Model of *ANTISTRIP.* On any particular vote, the expected outcome, yea or nay, is given by the sign of the senator's predicted *ANTISTRIP* value. The absolute magnitude of this value suggests the confidence to be placed in the expected outcome. An error is inferred when an actual outcome on a vote differs from the expected outcome. An error is interpreted as running against a senator's ideology when its sign is opposite to the sign of the senator's LCV rating.

Table 7. The Effect of Electoral Policing on Ideological Voting

Senator's Electoral Status	Incorrect Predictions in 1977 [a]		of which:	Voted Against LCV Ideology	
	Number	Percent of Total		Number	Percent of Col. 1
Up for Reelection	6	50.0		5	83.3
Not up for Reelection	6	50.0		3	50.0
Total	12			8	

[a] Predictions based on Table 1, Capture-plus-Ideology Model. "Incorrect" signifies sign of predicted *ANTISTRIP* differed from sign of actual *ANTISTRIP* voting in 1977.

Twelve errors are made in predicting SMCRA voting in 1977. Of these, approximately 50 percent were made by the 33 percent of the senators who were up for reelection. Moreover, of the 6 up-for-reelection senators predicted incorrectly, 5 were voting against their ideologies; and the remaining senator voting with his ideology was retiring. Of the 6 not-up-for-reelection errors, only 3 were represented by senators voting against their ideologies. The probability that this pattern was generated by chance is very low.[24] Thus, it appears that the proximity of the next election inhibits ideological shirking: senators shirk less as the policemen approach.

Summary and Conclusions

The evidence thus far suggests the need for some broadening in the economic theory of politics. This theory has effectively precluded from its list of determining factors anything other than the parochial, narrowly self-interested objectives of policymakers' constituents. This reflects the fact that economic, capture models of regulation are largely institution-free. Our analysis has attempted to bring certain aspects of the property rights theory of institutions--policing costs, opportunism, appropriability--to bear on the legislative process. Specifically, we have asked whether slack in control of legislators is empirically important enough to warrant incorporation into positive models of politics. At the level of specific-issue policymaking, the answer appears to be yes. Our results also suggest that the discretionary consumption afforded policymakers by institutional slack is taken, to a substantial degree, in the form of rational altruistic-ideological promotion of self-defined notions of the public interest. At least in the case of federal coal strip-mining policy, this ideological shirking appears to have significantly affected the course of public policy.

If the concept of ideological shirking does prove to be significant, its usefulness will depend on the development of models that can predict the conditions (for example, types of issues, institutional settings, economic contexts) under which ideological shirking is likely to be an important phenomenon. Of course, it still may be that the phenomenon does not even exist. There may yet be constituent interests missing from this and previous analyses that will explain away ideology's importance in specific-issue politics. The search for these interests should continue. For now, it appears that the economic theory of regulation will have to keep the door open to ideological behavior.

Notes

1. These two sources of ideology have often been noted. Downs' (1957) exposition is particularly clear. Jerome Rothenberg (1965), Bruno Frey and Lawrence Lau (1968), and Albert Breton (1974) provide systematic theoretical treatments of pure ideology; and empirical implementation of the concept has been pushed furthest by the literature on the "paradox of voting" (Riker and Ordeshook 1968; Tollison and Willett 1975; and Ashenfelter and Kelley 1975).

2. Of course, in either case, individuals may also receive returns in the form of the esteem of, or even reciprocal favors from, other individuals (Becker 1976).

3. The notion of "public interest" embodied in any particular ideology need

not include the promotion of economic efficiency (Tullock 1982). Indeed, ideologies appear to typically center around the "equity" (i.e., rights and distributional assignments) side of the economists' equity-efficiency dichotomy.

4. Notable exceptions in which ideological shirking appears are the formal models of Rothenberg (1965) and Frey and Lau (1968), although the focus of these models is primarily on policymakers' electoral success. In a model motivated by institutional attributes similar to those considered here and below, Robert Barro (1973) allows slack in the principal-agent relationship and (albeit, nonideological) utility maximization by elected officials.

5. Ideological shirking does not require that separation of ownership and control be *more* prevalent in the legislative setting than in the marketplace. It is sufficient that there be *some* principal-agent slack.

6. Note, also, that shirking in the pecuniary form of taking bribes (at the expense of support maximization) is service to some constituent's interest and would show up accordingly in the empirical analysis of voting below, unless bribery is uncorrelated with measures of constituent influence. In the latter situation, bribery and other forms of nonideological shirking (say, failing to be informed on issues) should show up as white noise.

7. This point is also noted, in the context of a parliamentary system, by Frey and Lau (1968, 358).

8. Votes are taken from Congressional Quarterly, Inc., *Congressional Quarterly Almanac* (1973, 1975, 1977). A descriptive list is available in our 1983 paper.

9. Reserves are from National Coal Association, *Coal Data 1978* (1979). These are highly correlated with the projections of new mine development over 1978-87 reported in McGraw-Hill, Inc., *Keystone Coal Industry Manual* (1977).

10. *CONSUME* is from *Coal Data 1978*. The correlation between *CONSUME* and an alternative measure, total coal Btus consumed per capita, is 0.72. Results reported below are essentially unchanged when the alternative measure is utilized (see our earlier paper).

11. Of the over 50 coal consumers who appeared before congressional hearings on SMCRA, only one was not a utility.

12. The groups are Sierra Club, National Audubon Society, Environmental Defense Fund, Friends of the Earth, National Wildlife Federation, and Wilderness Society (data provided by Resources for the Future, Inc.). The correlation between *ENVIROS* and total hunting and fishing licenses in a state (U.S. Department of Commerce, *Statistical Abstract*,1979) is 0.37. The correlation with state budgets for parks and recreation *(Statistical Abstract*, 1977) is -0.13; and is 0.003 with visits to state and federal forests and parklands (data from Goeldner and Dicke 1981).

13. Data for *SPLITRIGHTS* and *UNRECLAIMED* are from ICF, Inc. and the *Survey of Current Business*.

14. The *Keystone Coal Industry Manual* provides state mine-by-mine data; *HCONSUME* is based on coal-fired electric generating capacity as reported in National Coal Association, *Steam Electric Plant Factors* (1978), *HENVIROS* is

based on the six environmental groups mentioned in note 12 above.

15. The omission does not appear to be consequential; the memberships of *SPLITRIGHTS* and *UNRECLAIMED* are relatively small and easily self-identified. Our earlier paper examined free-rider problems affecting these groups by introducing squared values of *SPLITRIGHTS* and *UNRECLAIMED*. Results are insignificant and do not alter any conclusions of interest.

16. Votes are from LCV, *How Senators Voted on Critical Environmental Issues* (1978) and are listed in our earlier paper.

17. Joseph Sax (1980) provides the archetypical statement of ideological environmentalism:

The preservationist is not an elitist who wants to exclude others, notwithstanding popular opinion to the contrary; he is a moralist who wants to convert them. He is concerned about what other people do in the parks not because he is unaware of the diversity of taste in the society but because he views certain kinds of activity as calculated to undermine the attitudes he believes the parks can, and should encourage. (14)

. . . Engagement with nature provides an opportunity for detachment from the submissiveness, conformity, and mass behavior that dog us in our daily lives; it offers a chance to express distinctiveness and to explore our deeper longings. At the same time, the setting--by exposing us to the awesomeness of the natural world in the context of "ethical" recreation--moderates the urge to prevail without destroying the vitality that gives rise to it: to face what is wild in us and yet not revert to savagery. (42)

18. Votes are from *Congressional Quarterly Almanac* (1977, 1978) and are described in our earlier paper.

19. The *beta* coefficient for the SI Index (0.57) is the second largest in the model.

20. Becker (1983) also argues that demographics provide natural groupings for constituents' interests. However, Arrow's 1963 General Possibility Theorem and the associated literature on coalitions, cycling, and electoral equilibria (see Mueller 1979 for an excellent survey) suggest less confidence in the implicit econometric assumption (embodied in this work and elsewhere) that states' constituent characteristics can be mapped uniquely into their choices of elected representatives. Such concerns over uniqueness and existence, however, do not provide guidance as to why we find below that the explanatory power of constituent interests improves as a senator approaches his next electoral test (if that senator is not retiring!). This is consistent, however, with the interpretation of at least the part of the ideology measures which is *not* related to constituent characteristics as ideological shirking (see subhead "Electoral Policing and Ideological Shirking").

21. George McGovern was president of the ADA in 1976-78.

22. Variables included are *PARTY, MCGOV, ENVIROS,* per capita income, voter educational attainment, the fraction of state personal income generated by manufacturing, voter age, the urban-rural distribution of voters, the rate of growth of the state economy, and a southern dummy. Results of interest here are insensi-

tive to lengthening the list of variables to include, for example, racial characteristics, unionization, and the blue-collar/white-collar split.

23. In every case, the hypothesis that the senator-specific variable has no effect on the model's explanatory power is rejected at above the 99 percent confidence level.

24. Bearing in mind the small sample, a Chi-squared test indicates that the hypothesis that the contingencies in Table 7 were generated by chance can be rejected at above the 99 percent confidence level.

References

Abrams, B. A. and R. F. Settle. 1978. The economic theory of regulation and public financing of presidential elections. *Journal of Political Economy* 86:245-257.

Alchian, A. and R. Kessel. 1962. Competition, monopoly, and the pursuit of pecuniary gain. In *Aspects of labor economics*, ed. H. G. Lewis, 156-183. Princeton, NJ: National Bureau of Economic Research.

Alchian, A. and H. Demsetz. 1972. Production, information costs, and economic organization. *American Economic Review* 62:777-795.

Arrow, K. J. 1972. Gifts and exchanges. *Philosophy and Public Affairs* 1:343-362.

Ashenfelter, O. and S. Kelley, Jr. 1974. Determinants of participation in presidential elections. *Journal of Law and Economics* 18:162-170.

Barro, R. J. 1973. The control of politicians: An economic model. *Public Choice* 14:19-42.

Barzel, Y. and E. Silberberg. 1973. Is the act of voting rational? *Public Choice* 16:51-58.

Becker, G. S. 1957. *The economics of discrimination*. Chicago: University of Chicago Press.

_____. 1974. A theory of social interactions. *Journal of Political Economy* 82:1063-1093.

_____. 1976. Altruism, egoism, and genetic fitness. *Journal of Economic Literature* 14:817-826.

_____. 1983. Competition among pressure groups for political influence. *Quarterly Journal of Economics*. 98:371-398.

Belsley, D. A., E. Kuh, and R. E. Welsch. 1980. *Regression diagnostics: Identifying influential data and sources of collinearity*. New York: Wiley & Sons.

Brennan, G. and J. M. Buchanan. 1982. Voter choice and the evaluation of political alternatives: A critique of public choice. unpublished. Center for the Study of Public Choice, Virginia Polytechnic Institute and State University.

Breton, A. 1974. *The economic theory of representative government.* Chicago: Aldine.

Buchanan, J. M. and G. Tullock. 1965. *The calculus of consent.* Ann Arbor: University of Michigan Press.

De Alessi, L. 1982. On the nature and consequences of private and public enterprises. *Minnesota Law Review* 67:191-209.

Downs, A. 1957. *An economic theory of democracy.* New York: Harper and Row, 1957.

Ferejohn, J. A. 1977. On the decline of competition in congressional elections. *American Political Science Review* 71:166-176.

Fiorina, M. and R. G. Noll. 1978. Voters, legislators, and bureaucracy: Institutional design in the public sector. *American Economic Review Proceedings* 68:256-260.

Frey, B. S. and L. J. Lau. 1968. Towards a mathematical model of government behavior. *Zeitschrift fur Nationalokonomie* 28: 355-380.

Gart, J. J. and J. Zweifel. 1967. On the bias of various estimators of the logit and its variance with application to quantal bioassay. *Biometrika* 54:181-187.

Goeldner, C. R. and K. P. Dicke. 1981. *Travel trends in the United States and Canada.* Boulder: GSBA, University of Colorado.

Hirshleifer, J. 1978. Competition, cooperation and conflict in economics and biology. *American Economic Review Proceedings* 68:238-243.

Jensen, M. C. and W. H. Meckling. 1976. Theory of the firm: Managerial behavior, agency costs and ownership structure. *Journal of Financial Economics* 3:305-360.

Kalt, J. P. 1981. *The economics and politics of oil price regulation.* Cambridge, MA: MIT Press.

_____. 1983. The costs and benefits of federal regulation of coal strip mining. *Natural Resources Journal* 23:893-915.

Kalt, J. P. and M. A. Zupan. 1983. Further evidence on capture and ideology in the economic theory of politics. unpublished. Harvard Institute of Economic Research.

Kau, J. B. and P. H. Rubin. 1979. Self-interest, ideology and logrolling in congressional voting. *Journal of Law and Economics* 22:365-384.

Klein, B., R. G. Crawford, and A. Aleman. 1978. Vertical integration, appropriable rents, and the competitive contracting process. *Journal of Law and Economics* 21:297-326.

Manne, H. G. 1965. Mergers and the market for corporate control. *Journal of Political Economy* 73:110-120.

Mitchell, E. J. 1979. The basis of congressional energy policy. *Texas Law Review* 57:591-613.

Mueller, D. C. 1979. *Public choice.* Cambridge: Cambridge University Press, 1979.

Olson, M. 1971. *The logic of collective action.* New York: Shocken.

Peltzman, S. 1976. Toward a more general theory of regulation. *Journal of Law and Economics.* 19:211-240.

_____. 1982. Constituent interest and congressional voting. unpublished. University of Chicago Economic and Legal Organization Workshop.

Phelps, C. E. 1982. Kalt's *The economics and politics of oil price regulation . . . Bell Journal of Economics* 13:289-295.

Riker, W. H. and P. C. Ordeshook. 1968. A theory of the calculus of voting. *American Political Science Review* 62:25-42.

Rothenberg, J. 1965. A model of economic and political decision making. In *The public economy of urban communities,* ed. J. Margolis. Washington, DC: Resources for the Future, Inc.

Samuelson, P. 1954. The pure theory of public expenditure. *Review of Economics and Statistics* 36:387-389.

Sax, J. L. 1980. *Mountains without handrails, reflections on the national parks.* Ann Arbor: University of Michigan Press.

Schulze, W. D. 1981. *The benefits of preserving visibility in the national parklands of the southwest.* Washington, DC: U.S. Environmental Protection Agency.

Stigler, G. J. 1971. The economic theory of regulation. *Bell Journal of Economics* 2:3-21.

_____. 1972. Economic competition and political competition. *Public Choice* 13:91-106.

Tiebout, C. M. 1956. A pure theory of local expenditures. *Journal of Political Economy* 64:416-424.

Tollison, R. D. and T. D. Willett. 1975. Some simple economics of voting and not voting.. *Public Choice* 24:43-49.

Tullock, G. 1982. A (partial) rehabilitation of the public interest theory. unpublished. Center for the Study of Public Choice, Virginia Polytechnic Institute and State University.

Williamson, O. E. 1975. *Markets and hierarchies: Analysis and antitrust implications.* New York: Free Press.

Zellner, A. and T. H. Lee. 1965. Joint estimation of relationships involving discrete random variables. *Econometrica* 33:382-394.

Congressional Quarterly, Inc. various years. *Congressional Quarterly Almanac.* Washington, DC: Congressional Quarterly, Inc.

ICF, Inc. 1977. *Final report: Energy and economic impacts of H.R. 13950 (Surface Mining Control and Reclamation Act of 1976).* Washington, DC: ICF, Inc.

League of Conservation Voters. 1978. *How senators voted on critical environmental issues.* Washington, DC: League of Conservation Voters.

McGraw-Hill, Inc. various years. *Keystone coal industry manual.* New York: McGraw-Hill, Inc.

National Coal Association. 1979. *Coal data 1978.* Washington, DC: National Coal Association.

_____. 1978. *Steam electric plant factors.* Washington, DC: National Coal Association.

U.S. Department of Commerce. various years. *Statistical abstract of the United States.* Washington, DC: GPO.

_____. various months. *Survey of current business.* Washington, DC: GPO.

Acknowledgments

We thank Harold Demsetz, Allen Jacobs, Paul Joskow, Thomas Romer, Richard Schmalensee, Harry Watson, Mark Watson, and workshop participants at Harvard, MIT, and the University of Chicago for helpful comments and suggestions. Peter Martin, Kevin Mohan, and Margaret Walls provided valuable research assistance. The support of the Sloan Foundation and the Energy and Environmental Policy Center at the Kennedy School of Government has been greatly appreciated.

Chapter 5

Measuring the Ideologies of U.S. Senators: The Song Remains the Same*

Barry C. Burden, Gregory A. Caldeira, and Tim Groseclose

Political scientists generally define ideology as a latent set of values that organizes personal political attitudes. As such, it defies direct observation and makes measuring the ideologies of legislators difficult. Nevertheless, measuring ideology is an important task for legislative scholars. As Krehbiel (1993, 21) reminds us, "empirical research that tests theoretically derived hypotheses must inevitably, if only implicitly, address the question of how legislative preferences should be measured." Fortunately, ideology is believed to affect many *observable* features of legislative behavior, so we can obtain at least indirect measurements of legislators' ideologies. Moreover, since members of legislatures, as elites, are more ideological than the mass public (Converse 1964), the ideological positions of legislators ought, in principle, to be easier to discern, measure, and characterize.

Despite the centrality of ideology, previous attempts to measure legislators' ideologies have produced mixed results. Some researchers

*Reprinted with permission from *Legislative Studies Quarterly* 25, 2 (2000):237-258.

have interviewed or surveyed legislators directly (Bianco 1994; Erikson and Wright 1996; Kingdon 1989; Miller and Stokes 1963; Smith, Herrera, and Herrera 1990; Wright 1978, 1982; Wright and Berkman 1986), though this is difficult to do. More commonly, legislative scholars have turned to roll-call votes to measure the ideology of legislators. Jackson and Kingdon (1992), however, caution against this method. They remind us that forces "including constituencies, members' ideologies, the president's position, party and interest group pressure, and a host of other possibilities"(815) influence the votes of legislators (also Van Doren 1990). Though most of these forces point a legislator in the same direction (Jackson and Kingdon 1992; Kingdon 1989), their simultaneity makes it difficult to glean ideology from voting behavior. Indeed, according to Jackson and Kingdon, "In order to assess the impact of ideology on behaviors such as roll-call votes, measurements of ideology that are constructed independently of the roll-call votes themselves are required" (1992, 815). We agree that "explaining votes with votes" (809) is problematic, but we are not convinced that ideological measures based on roll-call voting records are inappropriate in other settings.

This debate is revived in a recent paper by Hill, Hanna, and Shafqat (1997) in which they offer the most careful and systematic attempt to construct a measure meeting Jackson and Kingdon's challenge. Hill, Hanna, and Shafqat (hereafter HHS) collect newspaper stories about senators during their first campaign for office. In this research note, we are motivated by HHS to compare their measure to eight others that we have gathered. We find no evidence that the HHS scores are able to tap *personal* ideology any better than other measures are. All of the measures do an adequate job of measuring "operative" or "public" ideologies, which are probably of more interest to legislative scholars anyway.

Including the new HHS measure, we compare nine ideological measures from a diverse array of sources including content analysis of newspaper stories, mass surveys, surveys of senators, roll-call voting records, and judgements by Washington insiders. We believe this is the largest collection of ideological measures ever compared in one place. Though no single measure is ideal, they generally lead to similar inferences, which suggests that attempts to improve on existing measures have had limited success. Although the problems with roll-call scores suggested by Jackson and Kingdon surely exist, they are small in practice. We conclude that standard roll-call measures are good proxies of personal ideology and still among the best measures available.

Nine Measures of Ideology

To judge the reliability and validity of the HHS scores, we have assembled eight other measures of ideology for comparison. Five of these measures are based on roll-call voting records, but the other three come from such diverse sources as national citizen surveys and ratings by Washington experts. These measures consist of scores derived by the following organizations and individuals:

1. Americans for Democratic Action (ADA)
2. American Conservative Union (ACU)
3. NOMINATE
4. Heckman and Snyder
5. Levitt
6. Senate Election Studies (SES)
7. *Roll Call*
8. CBS/*New York Times*
9. Hill, Hanna, and Shafqat (HHS)

The first of the roll-call measures is the oft-used Americans for Democratic Action (ADA) scores. These scores run from 0 to 100 and indicate the percentage of the time members voted with the ADA on about 20 key votes each year. Some have criticized the method ADA uses to produce the scores since absences are treated as votes against the group (Box-Steffensmeier and Franklin 1995). Accordingly, we have added American Conservative Union (ACU) scores, which do not penalize members for missing roll calls. Research has shown that interest group ratings also tend to overestimate the degree of extremism in Congress and produce different distributions because of the way votes are selected (Adams and Fastnow 1998; Brunell et al. 1999; Cox and McCubbins 1993; Fowler 1982; Krehbiel 1994; Snyder 1992), though they remain frequent in the literature on Congress.

To move beyond the problems specific to interest group ratings, several alternatives, also based on roll-call votes have been developed. Thus, for our third measure, we turned to NOMINATE, a set of estimates produced by Poole and Rosenthal's multidimensional metric unfolding technique. We use first dimension W-NOMINATE scores, which run from -1 (most liberal) to +1 (most conservative) and account for over 85% of the variance in recent roll-call votes (Poole and Rosenthal 1997). Unlike interest group ratings, NOMINATE relies on *all* of the non-unanimous roll calls and thus avoids the artificial polarization of scores.[1]

The fourth measure comes from Heckman and Snyder (1997) who analyze roll-call data using a statistical method similar to NOMINATE.

Their routine estimates ideal points within a multidimensional policy space to predict legislators' votes. The main differences between Heckman-Snyder and NOMINATE are the parameterizations of the error terms and the utility functions of the legislators. NOMINATE assumes that error terms follow a logistic function, while Heckman and Snyder assume a uniform distribution. NOMINATE uses normally distributed utility functions, while Heckman and Snyder employ quadratic utility functions. These two measures are highly correlated with one another, so Heckman-Snyder scores in their original form do not offer much additional insight. However, Snyder and Groseclose (1997) have re-estimated Heckman and Snyder's scores by constraining the sample to include only lopsided roll calls (i.e., 65% or more in the majority). These scores *are* of interest for our purposes since they should be relatively free of partisan influences. Rational party leaders should save resources for close votes and not waste them pressuring legislators on lopsided votes. Consequently, this measure is less damaged by the Jackson-Kingdon critique and is thus a purer indicator of ideology than standard measures.

The fifth measure is Levitt's (1996) modified ADA scores, which are designed to be purged of non-ideological influences. Levitt models a senator's voting record as a weighted average of four factors: (1) preferences of the caucus, (2) preferences of the constituency, (3) preferences of the "reelection constituency" (Fenno 1978; Goff and Grier 1993), and (4) the senator's personal ideology. Levitt operationalizes these variables as follows: V_{it} is the ADA score of senator i in year t, P_{it} is the mean score of i's caucus, S_{it} is the mean ADA score of the House members from i's state (his or her constituency), C_{it} is the average ADA score of the House members in i's party and state, and Z_i is an estimate of the personal ideology of senator i. Levitt then estimates the constrained regression equation

$$V_{it} = \alpha \, S_{it} + \beta \, S_{it} + \gamma \, E_{it} + (1 - \alpha - \beta - \gamma) \, Z_i$$

where α, β, γ, and $(1 - \alpha - \beta - \gamma)$ are weights on the four variables. We use Z_i, Levitt's estimate of personal ideology.

Moving beyond roll calls, we also have direct assessments of senators drawn from mass surveys. Our sixth measure is the ideological position of senators as assessed by their own constituents surveyed in the pooled Senate Election Studies (SES) conducted in 1988, 1990, and 1992. We use the mean placement for each member, which lies between 1 (extremely liberal) and 7 (extremely conservative), as is standard with the National Election Study scales. Erikson (1990) has demonstrated the reliability and validity of the respondents' estimates when aggregated at the state level as we use them. For our seventh measure, we supplement these indicators with a less traditional source. In 1993, *Roll Call*, a weekly Washington newspaper about Congress, published "The Completely Unofficial Ideological Spectrum of the U.S. Senate." This "spectrum" ranked senators from most conservative to most liberal according to the magazine editors' perceptions.[2] Importantly, this measure should avoid the contamination problems attributed to roll-call votes.

Our eighth comparison measure comes from the self-placements of senators from a CBS/*New York Times* survey of congressional candidates during the 1982 cycle. Senators and their challengers provided their positions on ten different issues, including military spending, abortion, and taxes. The issues and options are the same across senators. From those data, we use a summary ideological scale running from 0 (most liberal) to 10 (most conservative) as in Wright (1989) and Wright and Berkman (1986). Though accurate assessments of personal ideology might be theoretically unattainable, these self reports probably come as close as possible to doing so. This is also the most direct of the nine measures.

Our ninth and final measure of senator ideology comes from a recent article by Hill, Hanna, and Shafqat (1997). HHS are driven by Jackson and Kingdon's concern about roll calls and the practical limitations of interviewing elites to offer an indicator based on newspaper reports written during senators' initial election campaigns. From a content analysis of stories, they construct an ideological measure for members of the 101st Senate, and conduct several tests to demonstrate its reliability and validity. They comb newspaper articles for statements indicative of the *personal* ideology of the candidate during his or her first campaign for the Senate. For each statement, a trained coder decides whether it has ideological importance and, if so, whether it is "liberal" or "conservative." Each senator then receives a score based on the number of liberal relative to conservative judgments.

The raw values for senators on all of these measures are presented in Appendix A for researchers who may wish to use them elsewhere. Scatterplots among all nine measures are presented in Appendix B.

Hindrances to the Measurement of Legislative Ideology

Because ideology is unobservable and thus unknown, the best a measure can do is to estimate it with high levels of reliability and validity. If a measure is plagued with systematic errors that taint the measure in a consistent manner, then the measure is said to have a bias and be invalid.

If a measure is operationalizing ideology well but with a lot of random fluctuation that makes it inefficient, it has error and is unreliable. The ideal measure minimizes both error and bias to produce the most accurate ideological estimates. Clearly all measures are subject to some error and bias, the absolute levels of which are impossible to determine. Our goal is to roughly assess the relative amounts of these problems in the diverse group of measures that we have assembled. Without detailing every imperfection in these measures, we have identified three important categories of problems that could jeopardize their accuracy. We now briefly describe these three types, focusing on how they affect the new HHS measure in particular and traditional roll-call measures to a lesser extent, since their limitations are already known in the literature.

Contamination by forces other than personal ideology

Perhaps the most common criticism of ideology measures is that they are contaminated by factors other than ideology. Non-ideological factors may add both error and bias to measures. Though it undoubtedly exists, the extent of the contamination depends on which measure is being used and how ideology is conceptualized. Rohde (1991) makes a useful distinction between the *personal* and *operative* preferences of legislators. Personal preferences reflect a legislator's unique, internal ideology, free of other influences; operative preferences include one's personal views as well as other influences and reflect choices made in context. Though Jackson and Kingdon define ideology as a member's personal preferences, many legislative scholars define ideology in terms of operative preferences. If we adopt the latter definition, roll-call votes are suitable if not ideal measures (Mayhew 1974). And if forces such as constituency preferences and partisanship influence the past roll-call votes of a legislator, then constituency and party are likely to do so on votes in the future. Consequently, to predict votes in the future, one would *want* a measure influenced by variables such as party, constituency, and lobbying.

Even if one conceptualizes ideology as *personal*, traditional roll-call measures are probably a good proxy for ideology. We are not convinced that non-roll-call measures such as the HHS indicator are better than roll-call measures at avoiding contamination. Recall that HHS assessed the positions of senators recorded by newspaper reporters during their initial campaigns for office. Surely candidates for the Senate craft positions and statements at least partly in response to the preferences of constituents, thus making them operative preferences instead of pristine reflections of personal values. Of course, pressure from party leaders is less likely to influence these statements than it is to influence roll-call votes, but constituency pressure may have a *larger* impact on these statements than it does on roll-call votes (see Krehbiel 1993). Similar concerns apply to the preferences of financial contributors who are often ideologically extreme party activists. Preferences of campaign contributors are likely to figure in the statements of Senate candidates, even and perhaps especially during initial campaigns.

Noncomparable scales

Some ideology scores are not comparable across members, chambers, or time because the underlying scales differ across members. Simply because measures of two phenomena share the same numerical range does not mean that they can be directly compared. And comparing senators located on different scales could introduce serious bias. For instance, suppose a student scores a 90 on an algebra test while another earns a 75 on a calculus test. Obviously, we cannot conclude that the former student has the better mathematical skills, even if these scores have no error associated with them. The underlying scales produced by the tests are not the same, even though the possible range of scores for both is 0 to 100.

This problem sometimes plagues roll-call measures. When confined to the same chamber and year, roll-call measures rely on a common set of votes to evaluate legislators and are comparable. The problem arises when scores from different years or chambers are compared directly (Groseclose, Levitt, and Snyder 1999; Poole and Rosenthal 1997). For example, ADA scores are based on a different subset of votes each year and in each chamber, so the raw values are not strictly comparable. When the roll calls used in the analysis are constant or an appropriate correction is made to simulate constancy, scores for different senators are mapped to the same scale. The *Roll Call* rating system we use does not suffer from this problem, though the candidate (CBS/*NYT*) and constituent (Senate Election Study) measures might, if respondents--whether elites or citizens--interpret the questions differently or use different reference points when answering.

Though the HHS technique does not rely on different sets of votes as roll-call measures do, it is at least as affected as them by the use of nonconstant scales. Because the set of issues used to judge any two senators will be different, the scales used to evaluate the two senators will also differ. The mix of issues covered by reporters is highly sensitive to the character of a senator's opponent in her or his first race. Reporters tend to cover hot campaign issues, just as newspapers are more likely to report airplane crashes than safe landings even though the latter are more representative (Patterson 1994). Though an issue might not be important to a candidate nor beneficial for him to raise, his opponent can bring attention to it and thus force him to address an issue he would otherwise de-emphasize. So a Republican challenger could cause an incumbent Democrat who is really a moderate to appear liberal by raising the salience of particular issues if it benefits his party's agenda, particularly in terms of "issue ownership" (Petrocik 1996). In short, newspaper stories might say more about the issue-space in a campaign than they do about the senator's true position on the political spectrum. HHS compound this problem by coding only "issue(s) distinctive to the immediate campaign," purposefully avoiding past and future decisions, statements, or behaviors of Senate candidates that might provide a broader view of where they stand.

The small *n* problem

Recall that because ideology is unobservable, the best one can do is estimate the true value for each legislator. Small sample sizes increase the error of such estimates. Statistically speaking, estimates become more precise (i.e., efficient) as the sample size, n, increases. Just as readers should be wary of a correlation or other point estimate based on a small n, ideology estimates with similar sample sizes should also be treated with skepticism. Interest group ratings (ADA and ACU here) are based on just 20 or so votes per year. Setting aside the question of the representativeness of these votes, the small number is troublesome. At a minimum it makes scores "clump"; members can have only one of 20 ideologies. Severe clumping effectively makes ideological measures discrete rather than continuous and thus limits their usefulness. The CBS/*NYT* survey also faces this problem since it is based on just 10 questions posed to senators and their challengers. For these scores and the interest group ratings, the sample size is small but constant across members. The Senate Election Study is a bit better with state samples of 40 to 50 respondents.

HHS sample sizes, which are measured in newspaper stories rather than votes or issues, vary dramatically across members. Though some senators' estimates are based on many stories, it is difficult to find enough newspaper stories to compute reliable ideological scores for most senators. Following Segal and Cover (1989), HHS content analyzed stories from *The Chicago Tribune, The Los Angeles Times, Washington Post,* and *The New York Times* published during the calendar years in which senators initially ran for office. Although these newspapers cover political events around the nation, many candidates received coverage in only a handful of stories, even in home state papers (Franklin 1995). Despite enormous effort, the HHS procedure only yielded scores for 69 senators. Supplemental sources were then used, but five senators could still not be evaluated. Many of those who did generate "enough" codable stories had scores based on what we believe are insufficient numbers of sources.[3] Half of the senators generated 10 or fewer stories to code. The paucity of material in many races, in our view, makes these estimates of ideological positions unreliable and inefficient. Minimally, it causes scores to clump at common values such as 50, where eight of the 95 senators were placed.

Comparing Ideological Measures

We now turn to some simple comparisons among the nine measures. Note that not all measures produced values for every senator. Some of these are due to insufficient data (such as the five missed by HHS) but most are due to imperfect temporal overlap of the nine datasets. Our reference point is the 101st Senate (1989-90), which HHS used as their source of cases. Other measures were collected before or after that point. For example, the CBS/*NYT* survey was conducted in 1982, so it does not include senators who were elected afterwards. The *Roll Call* ranking was not done until 1993, after some of those serving in the 101st Senate had departed. Each measure exists for at least half of the 100 senators, and all but three of the measures account for more than 90 senators. Listwise, however, only 34 senators have values on every measure.

Theoretically, the CBS/*New York Times* survey of candidates should measure personal ideology best. Unlike roll-call measures, which may be influenced by lobbying, partisanship, and legislative agendas, these data from candidates provide the most direct, personal indicators available. The presence of this measure among potentially tainted indicators provides an ideal setting in which to examine the validity of the HHS measure. If the investigators are correct that their measure more accurately taps personal ideology than do existing measures, then the HHS and CBS/*New York Times*' measures ought to be more highly correlated with one another than with any other measures.

Simple correlations, shown in Table 1, simply do not support this hypothesis. Both listwise and pairwise correlations are reported, but we shall focus on the listwise estimates in the lower triangle of the table. With the exception of constituents' estimates in the SES, the HHS scores correlate with the CBS/*New York Times* measure at a lower not higher level than do other measures. This result alone suggests that the new con-

Table 1. Correlations Among Nine Ideological Measures

	HHS	1989 ADA	1989 ACU	NOMI-NATE	*Roll Call*
HHS		.86	.87	.87	.90
1989 ADA	.86 (95)		.94	.93	.94
1989 ACU	.83 (95)	.91 (100)		.95	.92
NOMINATE	.84 (95)	.95 (100)	.93 (100)		.96
Roll Call	.87 (73)	.95 (73)	.90 (73)	.96 (73)	
Levitt	.87 (50)	.93 (51)	.94 (51)	.92 (51)	.93 (41)
SES	.75 (95)	.82 (99)	.78 (99)	.86 (99)	.85 (73)
CBS/*NYT*	.83 (67)	.87 (70)	.83 (70)	.87 (70)	.87 (50)
Heckman-Snyder	.84 (95)	.93 (100)	.93 (100)	.99 (100)	.94 (73)

Note: Entries in lower triangle are absolute values of pairwise correlations. The number of cases is in parentheses below the corresponding correlation. Entries in the upper triangle are absolute values of listwise correlations ($n = 34$ for all).

Table 1. Continued

	Levitt	SES	CBS/ *NYT*	Heckman-Snyder
HHS	.90	.72	.81	.86
1989 ADA	.93	.78	.82	.91
1989 ACU	.90	.79	.83	.95
NOMINATE	.90	.88	.84	.98
RollCall	.92	.86	.84	.93
Levitt		.78	.88	.90
SES	.77 (52)		.75	.84
CBS/*NYT*	.87 (50)	.74 (71)		.83
Heckman-Snyder	.92 (51)	.84 (99)	.87 (68)	

Table 2. OLS Estimates for Ideology Equations

	HHS	NOMI-NATE	1989 ADA	1989 ACU	*Roll Call*
Democrat	71.8*	83.6*	72.2*	5.4	26.7*
	(5.9)	(4.6)	(6.9)	(5.6)	(7.0)
Republican	43.8*	39.9*	17.8*	61.4*	70.1*
	(6.3)	(4.9)	(7.4)	(7.0)	(7.3)
State mass ideology	-13.5	-22.1	-15.3	49.0*	45.7
	(26.1)	(19.8)	(29.8)	(28.1)	(34.0)
Democratic elite ideology	-0.32	-1.6*	-3.3*	0.60	3.2*
	(1.0)	(.79)	(1.2)	(1.1)	(1.3)
Republican elite ideology	-2.1*	-3.2*	-3.1*	3.0*	2.3
	(1.2)	(0.9)	(1.4)	(1.3)	(1.5)
South	-12.2*	3.2	-2.9	5.5	2.8
	(4.6)	(3.6)	(5.4)	(5.1)	(5.3)
n	90	94	94	94	69
Adjusted R^2	.94	.97	.93	.94	.95
MSE	12.8	10.0	15.0	14.1	12.80

Note: All dependent variables have been rescaled to range from 0 (most conservative) to 100 (most liberal). Coefficient standard errors are in parentheses.
* $p < .05$, two-tailed test.

Table 2. Continued

	SES	Levitt	CBS/ NYT	Heckman- Snyder
Democrat	51.1*	78.1*	96.2*	92.4*
	(2.4)	(12.2)	(9.5)	(5.6)
Republican	36.7*	39.7*	55.1*	46.8*
	(2.6)	(13.9)	(10.5)	(5.9)
State mass ideology	-25.8*	-54.0	-56.9	-28.3
	(10.4)	(68.8)	(42.6)	(23.8)
Democratic elite ideology	-.73	-1.9	-0.18	-.1.1[sic]
	(0.41)	(2.0)	(1.6)	(.95)
Republican elite ideology	0.10	-5.4*	-6.1*	-4.4*
	(0.47)	(2.4)	(1.9)	(1.1)
South	-1.15	6.1	-1.4	3.5
	(1.86)	(10.5)	(7.7)	(4.3)
n	94	52	67	94
Adjusted R^2	.99	.90	.91	.97
MSE	5.2	17.3	17.7	11.9

tent analytic measure does no better than existing roll-call measures at tapping personal ideology.   Such varied measures as NOMINATE, Heckman-Snyder scores, and *Roll Call* rankings average an *r* of .95 with one another while HHS correlates at about .86.[4] The SES estimate by constituents is the only measure correlating at a comparably low level, but we can discount this outlier because of the small sample sizes (sometimes just 20 or 25 respondents) in each state. If we set aside the results for the SES, the lowest correlations in the matrix involve the HHS measure.

The determinants of the measures provide another check on validity. We have accordingly regressed each of the eight measures of ideology on six independent variables that ought to affect ideology. In view of the partisan sources of much ideological division in American politics, we include the senators' partisanship on the right-hand side as two dummy variables, one for each party (Poole and Rosenthal 1997).[5] We also include measures of the ideology of Democratic and Republican elites in the senators' states (Erikson, Wright, and McIver 1993) to account for the responsiveness of senators to partisan activists (Fiorina 1974; Goff and Grier 1993; Shapiro et al. 1990).   And the long-standing uniqueness of southern politicians requires us to specify a regional dummy. We have also included a measure of state ideology (from Erikson, Wright, and McIver 1993) to control for any state-specific effects. To insure comparability of coefficients across equations, we have rescaled all of the ideological measures by linear transformations to range from 0 (most liberal) to 100 (most conservative).

The results of linear regressions in Table 2 indicate the uniqueness of the HHS measure, even though the other measures come from such disparate sources as roll-call analyses, subjective placements by Washington insiders, self-reports by senators, and surveys of citizens. For our purposes, perhaps the important difference is the southern dummy, which turns up statistically significant in the HHS equation but not in any of the other eight. The HHS equation generates predicted values for southern senators about 12 points lower than other senators, even after controlling for other state- and party-related variables. How can we account for this difference?

There is bias in the HHS scores that stems from the tendency for reporters to write articles about the unusual and to avoid coverage of the mundane, as we noted above. Reporters are trained to cover interesting and different news, leading them to overreport cases of Democrats taking conservative positions and Republicans taking liberal positions. Sam Nunn often votes with his fellow Democrats, but this is not unusual news. It is more striking news when he breaks ranks and sides with the Republicans. This distortion is most likely when evaluating southern Democrats, who were more conservative than their northern colleagues even in the 1980s (Rohde 1991). More evidence for this assertion appears in Figure 1, where we present a scatterplot of HHS against NOMINATE scores. (We find a similar pattern when we compare to the other measures.) If the two measures were synonymous, all points would cluster around the 45-degree line drawn. Some, of course, do; but southern Democrats constitute a systematic set of deviations. All but two of the scores for southern Democrats are *below* the line, indicating that the HHS measure portrays them as more conservative than does NOMINATE.[6] Consistent with our argument, reporters who focus on what makes these legislators unusual exaggerate the conservative tendencies of southern Democrats.

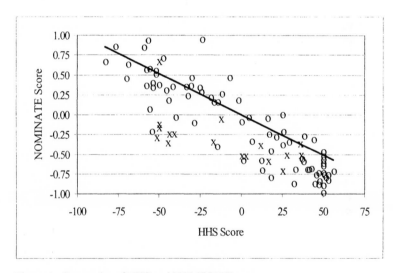

Figure 1. Scatterplot of HHS and NOMINATE
Note: x = Southern Democratic senators; o = all other senators

Traditional roll-call measures, such as ADA scores and NOMINATE, do not produce this bias for southern Democrats, and these measures show a high degree of validity. They are correlated at levels greater than .90 with Levitt's measure, suggesting that, although the confounding effects of party and constituency exist, they are small. This is supported further by rankings from *Roll Call* magazine since ADA scores and NOMINATE correlate even more strongly with this measure. NOMI-

NATE is correlated at extremely high levels (.95) with Heckman and Snyder's scores, even though the two measures derive from different samples of roll-call votes. Although ADA's correlation with Heckman and Snyder (.87) is not as great, this is still high.

Discussion

These results lead us to conclude that roll-call based measures operationalize legislator ideology at least as well as alternative measures do. Our simple analysis of members of the 101st Senate suggests that they may actually be better at tapping the operative preferences of members. As the folk wisdom suggests, all of the measures do an adequate and similar job of measuring ideology. In short, the song remains the same. Our primary critique of the new HHS measure is theoretical. Though it satisfies the Jackson and Kingdon critique, it is plagued by all three of the problems we identified, while some other measures are only affected by one or two of them.

We acknowledge that roll-call measures tend to pick up confounding forces such as constituency and party, but find that the effects of these factors are overwhelmed by ideology. Measures that attempt to remove extraneous forces are still correlated very highly with traditional roll-call measures such as ADA scores or NOMINATE. Further, this is consistent with a multitude of studies showing the high reliability of roll-call measures (e.g., Adams and Fastnow 1998; Box-Steffensmeier and Franklin 1995; Clausen 1973; Poole and Rosenthal 1997). Hill, Hanna, and Shafqat, in creating a newspaper-based measure of senatorial ideology, have managed to avoid the Jackson-Kingdon critique, but fall prey to other problems. Despite renewed criticism, roll-call measures serve as good proxies of the personal ideologies of legislators and, more importantly, are still the most comprehensive and road-tested measures available. No measure is ideal and so researchers should select the appropriate ideology measure based on the application and the relative importance of minimizing error and bias.

Appendix A

Senator	HHS	NOMI-NATE	1989 ADA	1989 ACU	*Roll Call*	SES	Levitt	CBS/ *NYT*	Heckman -Snyder
Adams	32.0	-0.850	95	4		3.74			0.120
Armstrong	-59.5	0.869	0	100		4.70	-12	10	-0.170
Baucus	6.5	-0.314	80	19	34	3.92		4	0.027
Bentsen	-45.0	-0.335	45	36		4.11	29	6	0.038
Biden	50.0	-0.597	90	14	10	4.04		0	0.101
Bingaman	37.0	-0.537	65	15	27	3.94		3	0.096
Bond	-30.5	0.485	5	85	64	4.75			-0.132
Boren	-50.0	-0.143	30	63	43	4.46	19	6	-0.004
Boschwitz	-25.5	0.361	15	81		4.92	12	7	-0.087
Bradley	50.5	-0.740	85	15	22	4.00	80	0	0.108
Breaux	-44.0	-0.224	40	30		4.28			0.023
Bryan	-15.0	-0.382	55	30	35	4.28			0.053
Bumpers	16.5	-0.577	90	21	17	4.11	79	3	0.086
Burdick	50.0	-0.716	85	11		4.37		3	0.113
Burns		0.506	0	85		4.74			-0.136
Byrd	11.5	-0.373	60	14	38	4.22	42	3	0.057
Chafee	25.0	0.026	35	39	40	4.51		3	-0.005
Coats		0.498	10	86					-0.132
Cochran	-58.0	0.378	0	78	68	4.70	3	9	-0.100
Cohen	-29.0	-0.074	45	50	41	4.83		5	0.020
Conrad	50.0	-0.445	70	29	32	4.05			0.055
Cranston	44.5	-0.856	85	4		3.24	91	0	0.127
D'Amato	-56.0	0.086	35	48	57	4.78	9	10	-0.010
Danforth	-14.5	0.181	15	71	54	4.72	26	6	-0.041
Daschle	50.0	-0.631	80	7	19	3.78			0.064
Deconcini	29.0	-0.330	60	32		3.90	38	6	0.063
Dixon	17.0	-0.226	55	32		4.22	44	3	0.022
Dodd	40.0	-0.669	65	22	11	3.57	69	0	0.106
Dole		0.449	5	86		5.19	0	7	-0.137
Domenici	-2.0	0.205	10	88	53	4.88		9	-0.056
Durenberger	4.5	-0.015	40	41	48	4.54	50	4	0.016
Exon	-54.5	-0.195	35	36	47	4.39		6	0.006
Ford	44.0	-0.288	45	25		4.09	53	6	0.026

Appendix A. Continued

Senator	HHS	NOMI-NATE	1989 ADA	1989 ACU	Roll Call	SES	Levitt	CBS/ NYT	Heckman -Snyder
Fowler	18.0	-0.442	60	15		3.80			0.072
Garn	-50.0	0.689	5	96		5.03		10	-0.155
Glenn	27.5	-0.490	65	26	25	3.97	64	3	0.072
Gore	1.0	-0.567	55	19	24	4.35	59		0.067
Gorton	-24.5	0.302	15	75	59	4.95	14	4	-0.091
Graham	36.0	-0.352	50	36	33	4.40			0.052
Gramm	-56.0	0.599	0	96	71	5.22	-13		-0.171
Grassley	-70.0	0.469	25	86	60	4.47	-1	9	-0.123
Harkin	41.0	-0.676	95	14	1	3.71	99		0.123
Hatch	-54.0	0.415	5	93	65	5.26		9	-0.106
Hatfield	38.5	-0.242	80	21	26	5.07	82	3	0.053
Heflin	-12.5	-0.029	25	75	51	4.74	16	8	-0.017
Heinz	16.0	-0.020	35	54		4.72	53	4	0.009
Helms	-77.0	0.873	5	100	75	5.89	-13	9	-0.188
Hollings	-41.0	-0.230	45	50	44	4.18	36	2	0.018
Humphrey	-83.0	0.682	10	96		5.14		9	-0.143
Inouye	50.0	-0.510	70	11	21	4.17		1	0.064
Jeffords	25.5	-0.187	40	44	28	4.41			0.048
Johnston	21.5	-0.253	30	32	42	4.44	25	5	0.048
Kassebaum	-17.0	0.179	20	57	46	4.98	42	5	-0.084
Kasten	-46.0	0.329	10	89		4.33	-7	9	-0.096
Kennedy	50.0	-0.880	85	7	2	3.67	82	2	0.131
Kerrey	50.0	-0.550	80	11	18	4.14			0.064
Kerry	45.5	-0.737	95	11	5	3.38	80		0.092
Kohl	42.5	-0.661	95	11	8	4.23			0.101
Lautenberg	47.0	-0.724	80	7	4	3.56	86	0	0.113
Leahy	47.5	-0.822	100	0	7	3.76		0	0.143
Levin	38.0	-0.578	80	14	20	3.63	87	1	0.096
Lieberman	12.0	-0.566	75	32	29	3.97			0.096
Lott	-52.0	0.577	5	96	72	5.08			-0.147
Lugar	-34.0	0.375	10	75	66	5.64	-5	7	-0.097
Mack	-58.0	0.584	5	96	72	5.00			-0.152
Matsunaga	33.0	-0.669	75	0		4.14		1	0.089
McCain	-54.0	0.355	5	93	61	4.76			-0.113

Appendix A. Continued

Senator	HHS	NOMI-NATE	1989 ADA	1989 ACU	*Roll Call*	SES	Levitt	CBS/ *NYT*	Heckman -Snyder
McClure	-48.0	0.729	0	93		5.06		10	-0.169
McConnell	-7.0	0.488	10	89	69	4.46	-8		-0.125
Metzenbaum	50.0	-0.966	95	7	3	3.52	103	1	0.148
Mikulski	47.0	-0.860	90	8	6	3.52			0.128
Mitchell		-0.646	80	11		4.28		1	0.093
Moynihan	18.0	-0.774	75	4	14	3.35	75	1	0.112
Murkowski	-31.0	0.387	5	5	63	5.12		8	-0.103
Nickles	-69.0	0.651	0	96	70	5.08	-12	10	-0.185
Nunn	-51.5	-0.274	35	37	45	4.74	22	5	0.045
Packwood	0.0	-0.073	30	61	49	4.49	52	4	0.020
Pell	53.0	-0.746	85	4	15	4.31		0	0.116
Pressler	-12.0	0.276	35	75	58	4.59		8	-0.101
Pryor	2.5	-0.508	80	27	31	4.20	64	2	0.083
Reid	25.0	-0.355	65	21	37	4.45			0.052
Riegle	56.0	-0.692	85	12	12	4.12	90	2	0.087
Robb	-17.5	-0.330	45	36	36	4.25			0.037
Rockefeller	0.0	-0.508	80	14	13	4.41	67		0.073
Roth	-50.0	0.390	0	81	56	4.79		6	-0.085
Rudman	-19.0	0.238	25	70		5.19		5	-0.076
Sanford	36.5	-0.493	65	19		3.50			0.083
Sarbanes	53.0	-0.812	85	7	16	3.72	98	3	0.116
Sasser	25.0	-0.695	85	8	23	4.28	66	5	0.098
Shelby	-50.0	-0.102	25	57	50	4.77			-0.025
Simon	51.5	-0.778	100	14	9	3.43	71		0.109
Simpson	-42.0	0.368	10	70	62	4.49		8	-0.110
Specter	-40.0	-0.014	40	57	52	4.56	68	3	0.010
Stevens		0.116	20	20		4.88		8	-0.031
Symms	-57.0	0.958	0	96		5.62		10	-0.207
Thurmond	-52.0	0.529	5	96	67	5.02	-9	9	-0.149
Wallop	-24.0	0.965	0	100	74	5.09		8	-0.198
Warner	-44.5	0.205	5	89	55	4.71	2	10	-0.053
Wilson	-33.0	0.262	10	93		5.32		7	-0.080
Wirth	12.5	-0.682	95	7		3.72			0.101

Appendix B

Scatterplots Among All Nine Ideology Measures

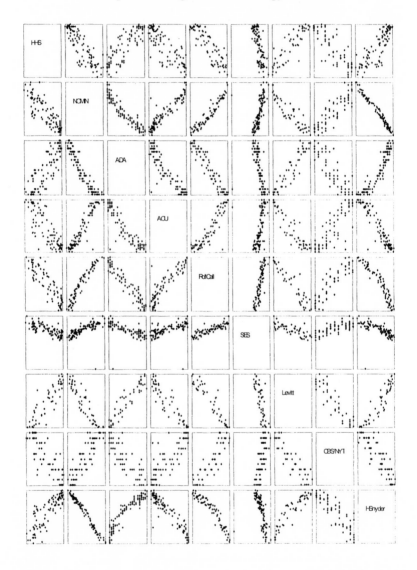

Notes

1. NOMINATE scores also have the benefit of approximate standard errors, which indicate the confidence associated with the point estimates. Other measures contain an *unknown* amount of uncertainty; and, as a result, the point estimates are usually treated as the "truth."

2. The editors compiled the spectrum after consulting "voting scores from liberal and conservative groups, prior statements of political philosophy, and overall reputations. And then we relied on our intuition. For the newly elected senators, we perused campaign positions and statements, considered reputations, and gleaned information from the trade publication *PAC Manager,* published by the National Association of Manufacturers. For the two appointees, we applied past positions and statements, vague impressions, and a healthy dollop of guesswork" (1993, 95).

3. The mean number of stories for the 95 senators was 18.6. Though the mean is low, even it is inflated because of the large number of stories found on senators from states in which the papers are located. When we remove senators from these three states (California, Illinois, and New York, but not DC), the mean number of stories drops to 12.7. Assuming that the typical senator had about 15 stories, the standard error of such estimates would be around 13 and so the 95% confidence intervals around them are more than 25 points wide!

4. HHS correlate their scores with ACU and other measures but do not report the crucial correlations among the other measures. Our results are the same if one uses rankings instead of raw scores or Spearman's rho instead of Pearson's r.

5. Two exhaustive and mutually exclusive dummy variables may be included since a constant is not estimated.

6. Regression analyses point to the same conclusion. After we convert the measures to a common [0,100] interval and regress HHS on the other six measures and a dummy for southern Democrats, both of the independent variables are statistically significant. In most cases the southern Democrat coefficient is around -15, suggesting that HHS underpredicts them by 15 points. The dummy for southern Democrats is rarely significant when other measures are used as dependent variables.

References

Adams, G. D. and C. Fastnow. 1998. On the differences between legislative ideology measures. Presented at the annual meeting of the Midwest Political Science Association, Chicago.

Bianco, W. T. 1994. *Trust: Representatives and constituents.* Ann Arbor: University of Michigan Press.

Box-Steffensmeier, J. M. and C. H. Franklin. 1995. The long campaign: Senate elections in 1992. In *Democracy's feast: Elections in Amer-*

ica, ed. H. F. Weisberg. Chatham, NJ: Chatham House.

Brunell, T. L., W. Koetzle, J. DiNardo, B. Grofman, and S. L. Feld. 1999. The R^2=.93: Where then do they differ? Comparing liberal and conservative interest group ratings. *Legislative Studies Quarterly* 24:87-102.

Clausen, A. R. 1973. *How congressmen decide: A policy focus.* New York: St. Martin's Press.

The completely unofficial Senate ideological spectrum. 1993. *Roll Call.* January 18.

Converse, P. E. 1964. The nature of belief systems in mass publics. In *Ideology and discontent*, ed. D. Apter. New York: Free Press.

Cox, G. W. and M. D. McCubbins. 1993. *Legislative leviathan: Party government in the House.* Berkeley: University of California Press.

Erikson, R. S. 1990. Roll calls, reputations, and representation in the U.S. Senate. *Legislative Studies Quarterly* 15:623-640.

Erikson, R. S. and G. C. Wright. 1996. Voters, candidates, and issues in congressional elections. In *Congress reconsidered*, ed. L. C. Dodd and B. I. Oppenheimer. Washington, DC: Congressional Quarterly Press.

Erikson, R. S., G. C. Wright, and J. P. McIver. 1993. *Statehouse democracy: Public opinion and policy in the American states.* New York: Cambridge University Press.

Fenno, R. F., Jr. 1978. *Home style: House members in their districts.* Boston: Little, Brown.

Fiorina, M. P. 1974. *Representatives, roll calls, and constituencies.* Lexington, MA: D.C. Heath.

Fowler, L. L. 1982. How interest groups select issues for rating voting records of members of the U.S. Congress. *Legislative Studies Quarterly* 7:401-413.

Franklin, C. H. 1995. Words and deeds: Not-so-cheap talk in U.S. Senate campaigns, 1988-1992. Presented at the annual meeting of the Midwest Political Science Association, Chicago.

Goff, B. and K. Grier. 1993. On the (mis)measurement of legislator ideology and shirking. *Public Choice* 76:5-20.

Groseclose, T., S. D. Levitt, and J. M. Snyder, Jr. 1999. Comparing interest group scores across time and chambers: Adjusted ADA scores for the U.S. Congress. *American Political Science Review* 93:33-50.

Heckman, J. J. and J. M. Snyder, Jr. 1997. Linear probability models of the demand for attributes with an empirical application to estimating preferences of legislators. *RAND Journal of Economics* 28:S142-

S189.

Hill, K. Q., S. Hanna, and S. Shafqat. 1997. The liberal-conservative ideology of U.S. Senators: A new measure. *American Journal of Political Science* 41:1395-1413.

Jackson, J. and J. W. Kingdon. 1992. Ideology, interest group scores, and legislative votes. *American Journal of Political Science* 36:805-823.

Kingdon, J. W. 1989. *Congressmen's voting decisions*. 3rd ed. Ann Arbor: University of Michigan Press.

Krehbiel, K. 1993. Constituency characteristics and legislative preferences. *Public Choice* 76:21-37.

_____. 1994. Deference, extremism, and interest group ratings. *Legislative Studies Quarterly* 19:61-77.

Levitt, S. D. 1996. How do senators vote? Disentangling the role of voter preferences, party affiliation, and senator ideology. *American Economic Review* 86:425-441.

Miller, W. E. and D. E. Stokes. 1963. Constituency influence in Congress. *American Political Science Review* 57:45-56.

Patterson, T. E. 1993. *Out of order*. New York: Alfred Knopf.

Petrocik, J. R. 1996. Issue ownership in presidential elections, with a 1980 case study. *American Journal of Political Science* 40:825-850.

Poole, K. T. and H. Rosenthal. 1997. *Congress: A political-economic history of roll-call voting*. New York: Oxford University Press.

Rohde, D. W. 1991. *Parties and leaders in the postreform House*. Chicago: University of Chicago Press.

Segal, J. A. and A. D. Cover. 1989. Ideological values and the votes of U.S. Supreme Court justices. *American Political Science Review* 83:557-565.

Shapiro, C. R., D. W. Brady, R. A. Brody, and J. A. Ferejohn. 1990. Linking constituency opinion and Senate voting scores: A hybrid explanation. *Legislative Studies Quarterly* 15:599-621.

Smith, E. R. A. N., R. Herrera, and C. L. Herrera. 1990. The measurement characteristics of congressional roll-call indexes. *Legislative Studies Quarterly* 15:283-295.

Snyder, J. M., Jr. 1992. Artificial extremism in interest group ratings. *Legislative Studies Quarterly* 17:319-343.

Snyder, J. M., Jr. and T. Groseclose. 1997. Party pressure in congressional roll-call voting. Manuscript. Massachusetts Institute of Technology.

Van Doren, P. M. 1990. Can we learn the causes of committee decisions from roll-call data? *Legislative Studies Quarterly* 15:311-340.

Wright, G. C. 1978. Candidates' policy positions and voting in U.S.

congressional elections. *Legislative Studies Quarterly* 3:445-464.

———. 1989. Level-of-analysis effects on explanations of voting: The case of the 1982 US Senate elections. *British Journal of Political Science* 19:381-398.

Wright, G. C. and M. Berkman. 1986. Candidates and policy in United States Senate elections. *American Political Science Review* 80:567-588.

Acknowledgments

We thank Kim Hill, Keith Poole, Jim Snyder, and Jerry Wright for providing data. Laura Arnold, Melissa Collie, Kim Hill, and Herb Weisberg provided helpful comments at different stages of the project.

Chapter 6

Senate Voting on Abortion Legislation Over Two Decades: Testing a Reconstructed Partisanship Variable*

Mark J. Wattier and Raymond Tatalovich

The longstanding tradition of roll call analysis has given rise to an academic debate over whether political party affiliation is simply an artifact of an underlying ideological dimension in congressional voting behavior. This debate over whether party or ideology is the driving force in congressional voting has been joined on theoretical and conceptual grounds, but even more troublesome are the methodological problems of trying to evaluate the efficacy of these two specific variables. A high degree of multicollinearity between party and ideology precludes including both variables in the same multivariate analysis. Equally problematic are the problems in comparing a dichotomous (party) variable against the usual kinds of interval scales for ideology, because standardized statistical techniques inevitably will show that, *ceteris paribus,* a continuous variable will outperform a dichotomous variable. This paper offers a solution to this methodological dilemma by reconstructing a "partisanship" variable which embeds an ideological dimension within party affiliation. As

*Reprinted with permission from the *American Review of Politics* 16 (1995):167-183.

a test of its predictive powers, this new variable is compared to traditional party and ideological variables in an analysis of abortion voting in the Senate over two decades.

Is It Party or Ideology?

The early studies of congressional voting highlighted party and constituency as the salient predictors of legislative behavior (Turner 1951; MacRae 1958; Truman 1959). Members of Congress would follow their party identification, it was observed, unless they experienced conflicting pressures from the districts or states. For the "typical" Republican or Democrat elected from generally safe districts, party and constituency were mutually supportive and led to a high degree of cohesion among Republicans and Democrats. Indeed it was observed that party loyalty among legislators was a function of ideological voting insofar as districts with certain demographic attributes tended to elect conservative Republicans and other types of districts generally elected liberal Democrats (Froman 1963). The outliers--conservative Democrats and liberal Republicans--deviated because their districts contained more than the average numbers of voters who identified with the opposing party.

But many recent studies report that legislative voting on a range of policies is characterized by a liberal-conservative dimension (Overby 1991; Mueller 1986; McCormick 1985; McCormick and Black 1983; Smith 1981; Schneider 1979; Bernstein and Anthony 1974; Moyer 1973; Russett 1970). This body of research questions the impact of constituency opinion as well as party affiliation. On the former, rather than search for positive cues from constituency on legislative voting, it operates on the assumption that, as with roll calls on strategic weapons systems, members of Congress follow their ideology "as long as the cost of doing so is not prohibitive" (Lindsay 1990, 957). Thus Representatives and Senators will avoid votes that would alienate their constituents but, in the absence of that uncertainty, they prefer to follow their own ideological predispositions rather than try to uncover the true feelings of their districts or states.

Party affiliation is conceptualized as an artifact because "political parties per se are not the primary variable; rather, the fundamental dimensions of belief that give rise to the parties are the primary variables" (Poole 1988, 129). Thus what causes most Democrats to vote together is the clustering of liberal attitudes among Democrats, and a similar clustering of conservative attitudes produces an even more unified vote among Republicans. Consequently, if congressional parties lack the cohesion of parliamentary parties, it is mainly because

> the Democratic party is much less homogeneous than the Republican
> party. The Republicans are concentrated at center right to far right. The
> bulk of the Democratic party is concentrated at center left to far left,
> but substantial numbers of Democrats are located at center right and far
> right. (Poole and Daniels 1985, 381)

On operational grounds, what Poole and Daniels (1985) mean is that party, when subjected to a multivariate analysis, is always entered as a dichotomous ("dummy") variable, usually with Democrats coded 1 and Republicans as 0. That operationalization bunches liberal Northern Democrats and conservative Southern Democrats into one category and, among Republicans, the small number of Northeastern liberals with the majority of conservatives. This kind of party affiliation variable cannot capture the range of ideological positions among Republicans or Democrats that would influence the gradations of liberal to conservative voting.

Research on Abortion Voting

There is a substantial literature on abortion voting and, for our purposes, many researchers have argued that ideology is far more important than party in explaining those roll calls. Indeed the most extensive analyses have argued that party was marginal or without importance, a finding which seems almost counterintuitive given other research that points to abortion as a cleavage issue dividing the two parties' presidential candidates and their platforms (Daynes and Tatalovich 1992). More recent studies indicate that abortion is beginning to operate as a party realigning issue within the electorate (Abramowitz 1995; Wattier, Daynes and Tatalovich 1996) and within Congress (Adams 1992).

Three roll calls in 1976 on the original Hyde Amendment, banning Medicaid funding of abortions unless the mother's life was endangered, were examined by Vinovskis (1980) using multiple classification analysis. He found that the Americans for Democratic Action (ADA) rating of liberal voting by Representatives was the most important predictor, and second ranked was religion. At first party affiliation appeared to be an important predictor as well but

> after we controlled for the effects of the other variables, the differences
> between Republicans and Democrats not only disappeared, but on two
> of the three roll-call votes Democrats were now slightly more likely to
> favor the Hyde Amendment than Republicans.(242-243)

Peltzman's (1984) analysis confirmed that ideology was the most important predictor of congressional voting on abortion, but the most extensive study of House abortion voting (Tatalovich and Schier 1993) found that the ADA Score was the strongest predictor in eight Congresses. The ADA scores signified that Representatives who generally voted liberal on legislation tended to vote pro-choice on abortion bills. As to party, Tatalovich and Schier (1993, 131-132) concluded that

> [t]he effect of party on abortion voting in the 93rd, 94th, 96th, and 97th Congresses is not statistically significant. And where party does exhibit a statistical association with voting on abortion, the relationship is negative in three instances. Only after taking account of the substantial effect of ideology on voting pro-choice is there a slight tendency for Republicans to be more supportive of abortion than Democrats.

Both studies, by Vinovskis and by Tatalovich and Schier, used the "raw" ADA score to measure ideology and they included a dichotomous variable for party affiliation. While Vinovskis as well as Tatalovich and Schier faithfully reported that "ideology" was markedly stronger than party, their findings may be a statistical artifact--interval variables (i.e., ideology) usually produce larger correlations than a nominal party variable (Poole and Daniels 1985).

Research on Senate abortion voting used either party or a proxy for ideology, but not both, as was done in the analyses of House roll calls. Also the previous Senate studies focused on a single roll call: the June 28, 1983 roll call by which the Senate defeated (49-50) the pro-life Hatch-Eagleton Amendment (HEA) to the Constitution. Granberg (1985,127) found that the odds of a pro-HEA vote increased if the Senator was a Republican, but the measure he used for ideological voting (Americans for Constitutional Action Score) was not significant in his 11-variable regression model. The HEA also was subjected to a logistic regression analysis by Strickland and Whicker (1986), comparing it to a vote on a pro-life bill sponsored by Senator Jesse Helms (R-NC), but no measure of ideology was included in their analysis. However both ideology (ADA Scores) and party were used in the latest analysis of the HEA by Chressanthis, Gilbert, and Grimes (1991). They found that party was insignificant and that "ideological measures may be more important than constituent interests in voting outcomes on abortion legislation"(596).

Methodology

In this analysis the Senate votes on abortion were subjected to regression analysis using the same model to assess whether the predictors of pro-choice voting have changed over two decades. Our dependent variable is an additive scale that indicates the percentage of times each Senator voted pro-abortion in each two-year period.[1] Each roll call was scored 1 for a pro-abortion position and 0 for an anti-abortion position. An abstained or absent vote was coded as missing. The dependent variable, in other words, reflects the percentage of votes in which each Senator supported the pro-choice position. The separate votes were then summed and divided by the number of votes cast to create a dependent variable that varies between 0.00 (pro-life) and 1.00 (pro-choice). This procedure allows us to make comparisons across the eight Senates from 1973 through 1988. The intercorrelation matrix for each group of Senate votes shows them to be highly intercorrelated, suggesting that the votes represent a single policy dimension.[2]

The religious affiliation of Congresspersons was highly influential according to the research by Vinovskis (1980) and Tatalovich and Schier (1993) and has been associated with "free voting" on abortion by Members of Parliament in Great Britain (Hibbing and Marsh 1987). Cook, Jelen and Wilcox (1992, 94) agree that the Roman Catholic Church "has been the most visible opponent of legal abortion. Indeed, for many, abortion *is* a Catholic issue." While the views of abortion by lay Catholics are not monolithic, attitudes generally and especially among Catholics who are more religious tend to be conservative with respect to abortions (Cook, Jelen and Wilcox 1992, 101-108; also see Chandler, Cook, Jelen and Wilcox 1994, 136-137). *It is hypothesized that Catholic Senators will cast more anti-abortion votes than non-Catholic Senators. Therefore non-Catholics are coded 1 (pro-choice) and Catholics are coded 0 (pro-life).*

Our choice of variables to measure constituency effects were dictated by two considerations. First we needed state-wide demographics which are associated with party competition and ideological divergence so that one common set of constituency variables can be used to reconstruct both the ADA Score and our new "partisanship" variable. Second, we needed demographics that serve as proxies for mass opinion toward abortion policy so credible alternatives can be tested alongside party and ideology. Choosing demographic attributes with no relationship to abortion attitudes would bias the findings and elevate the importance of party or ideology as predictors of senatorial voting behavior. Included therefore are median family income, percent urban, and percent non-white. These demographics were drawn from the 1970 Census to analyze the 93rd through 96th Congresses and from the 1980 Census to analyze the 97th through 100th Congresses.

Peter Skerry (1978, 70) was one of the early observers to note that a reverse class cleavage affects the abortion issue, which he attributed to "a larger cultural conflict between certain strata of the upper-middle class--the highly educated professionals, scientists, and intellectuals--and the mass of Americans who comprise the working and lower-middle classes." Researchers have confirmed that socio-economic status predicts support for legal abortion. Especially people with higher educations but additionally "[t]hose citizens in high-prestige jobs and who have high family incomes are also more supportive of legal abortion" (Cook, Jelen and Wilcox 1992, 50). To tap this class linkage, Vinovskis (1980) included the percentage of families below $3,000 income while Tatalovich and Schier (1993) included median family income. *Therefore we hypothesize that Senators from states with lower median family incomes will tend to vote pro-life on abortion bills.*

There is a pronounced urban bias to the distribution of abortions and abortion clinics in the United States (Henshaw and Van Vort 1994, 101-103). Also Tatalovich and Daynes (1989) determined that hospitals in large cities were more likely to offer abortion services along with maternal services than hospitals located in small towns and rural places. Opinion polls do not emphasize residence as a primary determinant of abortion attitudes. A study in the late 1960s found some relationship between city size and approval of abortion, particularly in very large cities (Mileti and Barnett 1972), and more recent analysis confirms that people raised in cities are less likely to oppose abortion than those from rural areas (Cook, Jelen, and Wilcox 1992, 52). The general expectation is that states with more urban areas are likely to have more tolerant attitudes toward abortion. *Therefore we hypothesize that Senators from states with smaller proportions of urban dwellers will tend to vote pro-life on abortion bills.*

Since 1965 "a consistent finding in public opinion surveys of abortion attitudes has been that black respondents are less in favor of legal abortion than white respondents," observed Hall and Ferree (1986, 193), whose research determined that the racial "gap in prochoice attitude is as great in the 1982-84 period as it was 10 years before, and the pattern of lesser black support for legal abortion is consistent on an item-by-item basis over the decade" (204). Thus they disagree with the conclusion by Combs and Welch (1982, 518) that "[w]hile the overall gap between the two racial groups has narrowed since 1972, blacks were still less likely to support abortion than whites." Moreover the racial differential is more pronounced in the South (Secret 1989). So even though black women have abortions at much higher rates than white women, and the fact that the Congressional Black Caucus has been committed to pro-choice notwithstanding, even today blacks are found to have less liberal views on abortion than whites (Cook, Jelen and Wilcox 1992, 44-48). *Therefore we hypothesize that Senators from states with larger populations of non-whites will vote more pro-life on abortion bills.*

Several analysts have used the raw ADA Score to examine voting on abortion legislation (Tatalovich and Schier 1993; Chressanthis, Gilbert, and Grimes 1991; Vinovskis 1980). Many interest groups rate how legislators vote on key bills of importance to their membership, but the scores calculated by the Americans for Democratic Action (ADA), a liberal advocacy group, are regularly used by legislative scholars as a proxy for ideological voting, if not ideology. A classic essay by Philip E. Converse (1964, 207) conceptualizes ideology as a "belief system" or "a configuration of ideas and attitudes in which the elements are bound together by some form of constraint or functional interdependence." Key to this conceptualization of ideology is the notion of "constraint" which has special relevance to how political elites assess issues.

As Poole (1988, 118) explains:

> From an observer's point of view, the constraint means that certain issue positions are bundled together, and the knowledge of one or two issue positions makes the remaining positions very predictable. To know that a member of Congress favors an increase in the minimum wage makes it highly likely that the member favors increased spending to aid the homeless. These relationships are typically summarized by the words "liberal" and "conservative," and informed observers of the U.S. political landscape can easily tick off the issue positions normally associated with these words.

Interest group ratings have been validated as accurately reflecting a left-right dimension (Poole and Daniels 1985) and thus are good surrogates for ideology. It may not be obvious, however, that a "new" issue on the political agenda can be automatically bundled as "liberal" or "conservative" until the implications become apparent with the passage of time. Abortion was not politicized until the 1973 Supreme Court decision that constitutionalized a right to abortion during the first trimester of a pregnancy. Also issues evolve over time with the result that political coalitions once associated with a given issue may change. *Therefore we hypothesize that Senators with lower ADA scores will tend to vote more pro-life on abortion, and vice versa.* But what intrigues us is whether the 1970s votes on abortion legislation were related to a liberal-conservative ideological dimension and if that linkage has been strengthened during the

1980s.

However, because we are predicting behavior (abortion votes) from behavior (key ADA votes), this relationship may inflate the ADA score as a predictor and thus diminish "party effects" and constituency impacts. This methodological problem lies at the heart of a serious critique of this approach by Jackson and Kingdon (1992, 809) who argue that ADA values are flawed because

> [u]se of these scales to represent representatives' ideology in a model of their voting behavior turns out to be simply a tautology. It is explaining votes with votes. The problem is that the interest groups score, the explanatory variable, and the votes being modeled, the dependent variable, are almost certain to be tapping the same or related dimensions.[3]

Our methodology attempts to address this concern in three ways.

First, if abortion votes could themselves be scaled on a left-right dimension, then the ADA score or any left-right scale would be an inflated predictor. We attempt to compensate for this potential bias by (1) removing abortion votes from the ADA scale and re-calculating the scores and (2) averaging the scores for two years to create a congressional session score.

Second, three different multiple regression models are presented and each has different combinations of variables. By comparing the results across models, particularly changes in the explainable variance and changes in the beta weights, we can assess the impact of ideology with or without party and constituency effects and with or without ideology. It already has been noted that party affiliation and ADA scores are not included in the same model for reasons of multicollinearity.

Third, and most important, the "raw" ADA scores which Jackson and Kingdon criticize are not used in this analysis. Since ADA scores may "represent" constituency forces and not simply their personal worldview, we sought to eliminate this source of bias. Following the methodological technique of Segal, Cameron, and Cover (1992), the ADA scores for all Senators were reconstructed by controlling for constituency influences on ADA voting in order to isolate "residual" effects as reflecting their "personal" ideology. We regressed the ADA scores (minus all abortion votes) against our three demographic variables (urban, non-white, median family income) and also three state attitudinal variables (ideology, partisanship, political culture[4]) in order to derive residual (unpredicted) values of the ADA scores for use in the regression models. In sum, the "residual" values--not the original ADA score--are utilized as the "personal ideol-

ogy" measure in this analysis and, though the raw ADA scores are correlated with the "residual" values, there is no one-to-one relationship
between the residuals and how the ADA rated individual Senators.[5]
The use of a dichotomous variable for party affiliation causes other
methodological problems, as already noted. Our methodological innovation is to derive a "partisanship" variable based on **both** party affiliation
and ideology. We used probit analysis to predict the party of each Senator
(Republican = 0; Democrat = 1) using state ideology, state partisanship,
state political culture, region, and those "residual" values for "personal"
ideology for each year. (The only variable that differs from model to
model is personal ideology; see Appendix.) By substituting an interval
variable for partisanship, which accounts for the gradations of ideological
positions within each congressional party, we have addressed the concerns by Poole and Daniels (1985) that a dichotomous party variable loses
predictive power when matched against an interval variable for ideology.

Findings

To evaluate the importance of party versus ideology and demographic variables as predictors of abortion voting in the Senate, three
alternative multiple regression models were derived for the eight Senates
(Table 1). Each model includes urban, non-white, median family income,
and the religious affiliation of the Senators. The alterations involve the
use of party, ideology, or partisanship. The first includes the reconstructed ADA value but no party or "partisanship" variable. The second
includes the dichotomous party affiliation variable but no "partisanship"
variable or reconstructed ADA value. The third includes the reconstructed "partisanship" variable without the ADA values. Ideally one
would include the ADA values and party affiliation or the reconstructed
"partisanship" variable in the same equation, but that option was disal-
lowed because of obvious multicollinearity problems.[6]

The results generally do **not** comport well with the findings on
abortion voting in the House of Representatives. Recall that Vinovskis
(1980) and Tatalovich and Schier (1993) found that party had no impact,
with ideology the strongest predictor. By comparing the Beta Weights
between the first and third models, ADA is a stronger predictor than party
affiliation in every instance. However the predictive power of party
affiliation rose markedly during the 1985-86 and 1987-88 Senates, which
is consistent with the argument by Adams (1992) that abortion is becoming a realigning issue for both parties. In every case the model with ADA
also accounts for more explainable variance than the model for party affil-

Table 1. Regression Models Comparing Reconstructed ADA Scores, Party, and
Partisanship as Predictors of Senate Abortion Voting, 1973-1988 [a]

Reconstructed ADA Variable (IDE)			Dichotomous Party Variable (PTY)			Reconstructed Partisanship Variable (PSN)		
				1973-1974				
MFI [b]	.341*	.058	MFI	.386*	.053	MFI	.327*	.057
	.1258			.1358			.1209	
IDE	.300*	.052	PTY	.045	.105	PSN	.329*	.204
	.1545			.0444			.6632	
REL	.128	.148	REL	.093	.154	REL	.114	.146
	.1812			.1344			.1621	
BLK	-.069	.006	BLK	-.072	.006	BLK	-.123	.006
	-.0035			-.0038			-.0064	
URB	-.063	.005	URB	-.074	.005	URB	-.060	.005
	-.0022			-.0025			-.0021	
Const.	-.7096		Const.	-.7574		Const.	-1.0192	
Adj R^2	.140		Adj R^2	.088		Adj R^2	.158	
				1975-1976				
MFI	.495*	.038	MFI	.444*	.033	MFI	.567*	.038
	.1398			.1175			.1602	
IDE	.384*	.036	PTY	.205*	.074	PSN	.396*	.188
	.159			.1622			.7969	
REL	.203*	.097	REL	.220*	.103	REL	.192*	.097
	.2200			.2431			.2074	
BLK	-.041	.004	BLK	-.071	.004	BLK	-.127	.004
	-.0017			-.3030			-.0053	
URB	-.212	.004	URB	-.079	.003	URB	-.222	.004
	-.0059			-.0022			-.0061	
Const.	-.5051		Const.	-.6543		Const.	-1.1116	
Adj R^2	.289		Adj R^2	.191		Adj R^2	.281	

Table 1. Continued

Reconstructed ADA Variable (IDE)			Dichotomous Party Variable (PTY)			Reconstructed Partisanship Variable (PSN)		
			1977-1978					
MFI	.299*	.042	MFI	.294*	.034	MFI	.250*	.043
	.0858			.0796			.0932	
IDE	.383*	.038	PTY	.276*	.076	PSN	.324*	.177
	.1524			.2186			.5294	
REL	.226*	.114	REL	.243*	.113	REL	.205*	.118
	.2658			.2864			.2412	
BLK	-.053	.004	BLK	-.084	.004	BLK	-.171	.005
	-.0022			-.0035			-.0070	
URB	-.074	.004	URB	-.000	.003	URB	-.088	.004
	-.0020			-.0000			-.0024	
Const.	-.2606		Const.	-.4818		Const.	-.5531	
Adj R^2	.195		Adj R^2	.155		Adj R^2	.133	
			1979-1980					
MFI	.396*	.039	MFI	.366*	.034	MFI	.330*	.040
	.1164			.1010			.0969	
IDE	.447*	.036	PTY	.318*	.075	PSN	.481*	.127
	.1853			.2599			.6470	
REL	.217*	.110	REL	.215*	.113	REL	.283*	.110
	.2685			.2638			.2939	
BLK	.080	.004	BLK	.003	.004	BLK	-.103	.005
	.0035			.0001			-.0045	
URB	-.091	.004	URB	-.056	.003	URB	-.068	.004
	-.0025			-.0016			-.0019	
Const.	-.6296		Const.	-.6579		Const.	-.8233	
Adj R^2	.307		Adj R^2	.202		Adj R^2	.307	

Table 1. Continued

Reconstructed ADA Variable (IDE)			Dichotomous Party Variable (PTY)			Reconstructed Partisanship Variable (PSN)		
			1981-1982					
MFI	.371*	.041	MFI	.244	.038	MFI	.332*	.041
	.1187			.0724			.1062	
IDE	.416*	.041	PTY	.270*	.085	PSN	.457*	.119
	.1925			.2428			.5910	
REL	.242*	.107	REL	.278*	.113	REL	.267*	.106
	.2854			.3302			.3150	
BLK	.006	.004	BLK	-.078	.005	BLK	-.119	.005
	.0001			-.0038			-.0056	
URB	-.098	.004	URB	.031	.004	URB	-.094	.004
	-.0030			.0009			-.0029	
Const.	-.8237		Const.	-.6967		Const.	-.9464	
Adj R^2	.258		Adj R^2	.142		Adj R^2	.279	
			1983-1984					
MFI	.296*	.036	MFI	.262*	.040	MFI	.273*	.037
	.0936			.0831			.0860	
IDE	.528*	.037	PTY	.334*	.081	PSN	.537*	.117
	.2403			.2940			.7299	
REL	.257*	.095	REL	.266*	.108	REL	.291*	.097
	.2961			.3122			.3357	
BLK	-.046	.004	BLK	-.138	.005	BLK	-.202*	.004
	-.0022			-.0067			-.0096	
URB	.007	.003	URB	.035	.004	URB	-.026	.003
	.0002			.0011			-.0008	
Const.	-.7568		Const.	-.8008		Const.	-.9141	
Adj R^2	.387		Adj R^2	.214		Adj R^2	.372	

Table 1. Continued

Reconstructed ADA Variable (IDE)			Dichotomous Party Variable (PTY)			Reconstructed Partisanship Variable (PSN)		
			1985-1986					
MFI	.278*	.038	MFI	.197	.035	MFI	.189	.038
	.0899			.0587			.0610	
IDE	.589*	.039	PTY	.539*	.078	PSN	.612*	.110
	.2768			.4822			.7995	
REL	.151	.098	REL	.196*	.102	REL	.148	.098
	.1766			.2278			.1732	
BLK	.079	.004	BLK	-.052	.004	BLK	-.051	.004
	.0038			-.0025			-.0025	
URB	-.101	.004	URB	-.034	.003	URB	-.074	.004
	-.0032			-.0010			-.0023	
Const.	-.3685		Const.	-.3894		Const.	-.4474	
Adj R^2	.362		Adj R^2	.281		Adj R^2	.373	
			1987-1988					
MFI	.287*	.035	MFI	.183	.033	MFI	.302*	.036
	.0824			.0490			.0874	
IDE	.582*	.036	PTY	.499*	.077	PSN	.607*	.100
	.2434			.4039			.6520	
REL	.106	.092	REL	.137	.099	REL	.149	.094
	.1113			.1432			.1557	
BLK	.042	.004	BLK	-.120	.004	BLK	-.147	.004
	.0018			-.0052			-.0063	
URB	-.157	.003	URB	-.063	.003	URB	-.204	.003
	-.0044			-.0018			-.0057	
Const.	-.1327		Const.	-.1229		Const.	-.4192	
Adj R^2	.329		Adj R^2	.204		Adj R^2	.315	

[a] Values are standardized (top left: Beta Weight) and unstandardized [bottom: (b)] regression coefficients and Standard Error (right); asterisk indicates statistical significance at least at the .05 level.

[b] The variables are: IDE = reconstructed ADA Score, REL = Religion, PTY = Party (dichotomous variable), PSN = Partisanship (interval variable), URB = Urban, BLK = Black, MFI = Median Family Income.

iation. However, unlike the situation in the House, the dichotomous party affiliation variable was statistically significant in every model beginning with 1975-76, which suggests that party affiliation is overall a stronger cue for Senate voting than for House voting on abortion.

Studies of House voting also determined that religion was quite strong, but religion seems to be **less** salient for Senate voting. As was the case in the House, however, every coefficient was positive to signify that non-Catholic Senators were more pro-choice than Catholic Senators. Looking at the third regression model, religion was not statistically significant in 1973-74 or 1987-88 and was third ranked behind median family income and party affiliation in 1977-78 and 1979-80. It ranked behind median family income in 1975-76 and behind party affiliation in 1983-84 and 1985-86. Only in 1981-82 was religion the strongest predictor in the model. Religion fares even worse in the first model when the reconstructed ADA value is entered: insignificant in three models and third ranked (behind median family income and ADA or vice versa) in five other Senates.

On constituency effects, Tatalovich and Schier (1993, 131-132) found no impact from urbanism or income and very modest non-white influences. Our findings show a fairly strong class influence on Senate voting. The positive coefficients with median family income--that Senators from more affluent states tend to vote pro-choice--not only agree with the literature on abortion attitudes but are consistent across four models. Income was a significant predictor in 25 of the 32 regression models and was first or second ranked in 23 instances. Thus, the "reverse" class dynamic causes Senators to vote liberal on abortion legislation even though an upper income profile generally relates to conservative voting on economic and social-welfare measures.

Most of the previous research on the House and the Senate strongly indicated that party is relatively unimportant but that "ideology" was very important. This analysis casts serious doubt on that interpretation, based on the compelling effects of our reconstructed partisanship variable. A comparison of the first model, with reconstructed ADA, against the third model, with the reconstructed partisanship variable, shows that for all Senates but one (1977-78) **partisanship** is markedly **stronger** than the ADA values as a predictor of voting on abortion. On the whole, as would be expected, more "partisan" Democrats vote more pro-choice and more "partisan" Republicans vote more pro-life. In sum, partisanship outperforms the reconstructed ADA values because our estimates for partisanship were based on both ideological diversity and constituency forces among Republicans and Democrats.

The beta weights in the second model, with a dichotomous party affiliation variable, when contrasted against those in the third model, with the newly reconstructed partisanship variable, show how much superior this interval variable is. The improvement in the Beta Weights ranged from .048 (1977-78) to .284 (1973-74).

Conclusion

Is it party or ideology? No doubt scholars will continue to raise this question, and they may even raise it in a softer version: under what conditions is it party or ideology? Either question, we think, will misdirect research on political elites. Instead we pose an alternative research question: what are the effects of "strong" or "weak" partisanship on decision-making by political elites?

Recent research on political parties has focused on what could be characterized as the "demise-and-rise" debate. Parties are either defunct or rejuvenated, or somewhere in-between on the way to one of these two extremes. Each key aspect of party--party in the electorate, party as an organization, and party in government--has been witness to this debate. This paper suggests that the partisanship of legislators (i.e., party in government) has influenced voting on abortion bills. Heretofore much literature suggested that abortion voting was dominated by ideology only, but that conclusion hinged on a conceptualization of party as being devoid of an ideological component. To the contrary, party and ideology are not two distinct and separate decision criteria but rather they are aspects *of* one construct--partisanship. The evidence for this new conceptualization is that our model with reconstructed partisanship outperforms models with party or with ideology. Party is not simply one or another group, scored as 1 or 0; party is a coalition of members who have varying degrees of commitment to the core beliefs of their group.

Studies of the mass electorate since the 1950s (Campbell, Converse, Miller and Stokes 1960; Nie, Verba and Petrocik 1979) have examined both the direction and intensity of partisanship by differentiating between "weak" and "strong" Republicans or Democrats whereas, in contrast, for some time aggregate studies of elites have focused only on direction. The results of this analysis strongly argue against using party affiliation as conventionally operationalized. A dichotomous variable for party is not an effective measure to capture the diversity of opinion among Senators-- or Representatives--of either political party.

These findings begin to redress the methodological inequities in comparing party affiliation against interval measures of "ideology" based on group ratings. The reconstructed partisanship variable, unlike the dummy variable for party affiliation, more accurately reflects the ideological diversity among Republicans and especially Democrats. Recall that this measure was derived from personal ideology and constituency influences (state political culture, state partisanship, state ideology) as well as region. An ideological component is therefore **embedded** in the estimated values for partisanship.

Thus we have demonstrated a way to measure intensity as well as direction for political elites, which seems to produce stronger results than previously found on a research topic where party has been shown to not matter. The empirical contribution of this analysis for congressional voting research is that, henceforth, scholars ought to build upon our work and substitute an estimated value for partisanship instead of using a dummy variable for party affiliation.

Appendix

We used probit analysis to predict the party of each Senator (Republican=0; Democrat=1) using as predictors the measures of state ideology and state partisanship devised by Wright, Erikson and McIver (1985), the state political culture variable devised by Sharkansky (1969), region (south=1 and non-south=0), and the "residual" values for "personal" ideology for each year. The probit model was used to generate a probability estimate of a Senator being 1 (or a Democrat), and the resulting estimates ranged from 0 to 1 with all intermediate values, meaning that this generated variable is an interval measure. The probit models correctly predicted from 67% to 86% of the Senators' party affiliations and the variables for party affiliation and partisanship were intercorrelated in the .44 to .79 range. From 1973-74 through 1987-88, the correlation coefficients between the partisanship and party affiliation variables and the percentage of actual party affiliations corrected predicted are: .54 and 74.2%; .44 and 67.3%; .51 and 71.3%; .59 and 73.9%; .69 and 83.2%; .69 and 83.3%; .68 and 78.9%; .79 and 86.4%. Final validation that we derived a reasonably "reliable" variable for partisanship is that our reconstructed measure outperforms the dichotomous party variable as a predictor of legislative voting.

Notes

1. Any roll call where less than 25% of the Senators voted in opposition was omitted from the analysis. Scale scores were created for Senators who voted on a majority of the roll calls selected for analysis. The number of roll calls included for each Senate follow 1973-74, 1 vote; 1975-76, 7 votes; 1977-78, 16 votes; 1979-80, 15 votes; 1981-82, 6 votes; 1983-84, 9 votes; 1985-86, 7 votes; 1987-88, 9 votes.

2. The reliability of each abortion scale was checked with Cronbach's Alpha. The average Alpha for the seven scales (1975-76 through 1987-88) was .95, varying from .97 and .92.

3. Our firm belief is that, if the Jackson and Kingdon (1982) critique is allowed to stand unchallenged, then the ability of most scholars to pursue roll call analysis will be severely limited, because it is impractical to survey all members of Congress at regular intervals (assuming they would be forthcoming in their responses) in order to obtain the kind of exogenous variable for ideology that Jackson and Kingdon require. Indeed it is noteworthy that the third edition of Kingdon's (1989) classic on voting behavior in Congress simply replicates the data from the same subset of 60 Representatives who were interviewed in 1969, twenty years earlier. All attempts to update those findings were speculative in nature or based on secondary sources. Because voting analysts usually desire to know what motivates *all* House members on an issue, particularly a new issue like abortion, the use of any subset of legislators could yield biased results. Thus for most studies every legislator would need to be interviewed in order to pursue roll call analysis using the Kingdon strategy.

An externally validated measure of ideology (using surveys or interviews) might not, in fact, yield a perfect measure of ideology because attitudes are one step removed from behavior. Which is a more accurate predictor of legislative behavior--a measure based on what legislators say (interviews) about issues or their worldview or a measure based on what legislators actually do (roll call votes)? However valid on theoretical grounds the Jackson and Kingdon critique might be, we have no evidence that attitudes are a more effective predictor of future policy choice when compared to a surrogate based on past voting behavior. Jackson and Kingdon pointed to research on mass electoral behavior as properly utilizing attitude measures, but a devastating review of forty years of research in this tradition by Wicker (1969,75) concluded: "Most socially significant questions involve overt behavior, rather than people's feelings, and the assumption that people's feelings are directly translated into action has not been demonstrated."

Finally, there must be some theoretical grounds for finding an observed relationship even if the estimate of that relationship is relatively crude. Our assumption (and one shared by many legislative analysts) is that abortion as an issue *does* tap into the legislators' ideology, expressly one based on whether the government should interfere in the private lives of citizens. Thus the Jackson and Kingdon critique poses a CATCH-22, because the theoretical rationale for expecting a relationship between ideology and abortion voting are the same reasons why the ADA Scores are inflated at the expense of party and constituency.

4. These state attitudinal variables were derived by Sharkansky (1969) and Wright, Erikson, and McIver (1985).

5. Beginning with 1973-74 and ending with 1987-88 the coefficients between the ADA score (excluding abortion votes) and the "residual" values for personal ideology follow: .788; .772; .795; .823; .817; .864; .876; and .818.

6. Beginning with 1973-74 through 1987-88, the correlations between dichotomous party and personal ideology (.637; .562; .563; .642; .724; .682; .731; .720) but especially between the reconstructed partisanship variable and personal ideology (.717; .565; .634; .761; 781; .747; .826; .781) show the potential for a multicollinearity problem.

References

Abramowitz, A. I. 1995. It's abortion, stupid: Policy voting in the 1992 presidential election. *Journal of Politics* 57:176-186.

Adams, G. 1992. Abortion: Evidence of an issue evolution. Paper presented to the annual meeting, Midwest Political Science Association, Chicago.

Bernstein, R. A. and W. W. Anthony. 1974. The ABM issue in the Senate, 1968-1970: The importance of ideology. *American Political Science Review* 68:1198-1206.

Campbell, A., P. E. Converse, W. E. Miller, and D. E. Stokes. 1960. *The American voter.* New York: John Wiley.

Chandler, M. A., E. A. Cook, T. G. Jelen and C. Wilcox. 1994. Abortion in the United States and Canada: A comparative study of public opinion. In *Abortion politics in the United States and Canada: Studies in public opinion,* ed. T. G. Jelen and M. A. Chandler. Westport, CT: Praeger.

Chressanathis, G. A., K. S. Gilbert, and P. W. Grimes. 1991. Ideology, constituent interests, and senatorial voting: The case of abortion. *Social Science Quarterly* 72:588-600.

Combs, M. W. and S. Welch. 1982. Blacks, whites, and attitudes toward abortion. *Public Opinion Quarterly* 46:510-520.

Converse, P. E. 1964. The nature of belief systems in mass publics. In *Ideology and discontent,* ed. D. E. Apter. New York: Free Press.

Cook, E. A., T. G. Jelen, and C. Wilcox. 1992. *Between two absolutes: Public opinion and the politics of abortion.* Boulder, CO: Westview.

Daynes, B. W. and R. Tatalovich. 1992. Presidential politics and abortion, 1972-1988. *Presidential Studies Quarterly* 22:545-561.

Froman, L. A., Jr. 1963. *Congressmen and their constituencies.* Chicago: Rand McNally.

Granberg, D. 1985. The United States Senate votes to uphold *Roe v. Wade. Population Research and Policy Review* 4:115-131.

Hall, E. J. and M. M. Ferree. 1986. Race differences in abortion attitudes. *Public Opinion Quarterly* 50:193-207.

Henshaw, S. K. and J. Van Vort. 1994. Abortion services in the United States, 1991 and 1992. *Family Planning Perspectives* 26:100-106,

112.

Hibbing, J. R. and D. Marsh. 1987. Accounting for the voting patterns of British MPs on free votes. *Legislative Studies Quarterly* 12:275-297.

Jackson, J. E. and J. W. Kingdon. 1992. Ideology, interest group scores, and legislative votes. *American Journal of Political Science* 36:805-823.

Kingdon, J. W. 1989. *Congressmen's voting decisions.* Ann Arbor: University of Michigan Press.

Lindsay, J. M. 1990. Parochialism, policy, and constituency constraints: Congressional voting on strategic weapons systems. *American Journal of Political Science* 34:936-960.

MacRae, D., Jr. 1958. *Dimensions of congressional voting: A statistical study of the House of Representatives in the Eighty-first Congress.* Berkeley and Los Angeles: University of California Press.

McCormick, J. M. 1985. Congressional voting on the nuclear freeze resolutions. *American Politics Quarterly* 13:122-136.

McCormick, J. M. and M. Black. 1983. Ideology and voting on the Panama Canal treaties. *Legislative Studies Quarterly* 8:45-63.

Mileti, D. S. and L. D. Barnett. 1972. Nine demographic factors and their relationship to attitudes toward abortion legalization. *Social Biology* 19:43-50.

Moyer, W. 1973. House voting on defense: An ideological explanation explanation. In *Military force and American society*, ed. B. Russett and A. Stephan. New York: Harper & Row.

Mueller, K. J. 1986. An analysis of congressional health policy voting in the 1970s. *Journal of Health Politics, Policy and Law* 11:117-135.

Nie, N., S. Verba, and J. R. Petrocik. 1979. *The changing American voter.* enlarged ed. Cambridge: Harvard University Press.

Overby, L. M. 1991. Assessing constituency influence: Congressional voting on the nuclear freeze, 1982-83. *Legislative Studies Quarterly* 16:297-312.

Peltzman, S. 1984. Constituent interest and congressional voting. *Journal of Law and Economics* 27:181-210.

Poole, K. T. 1988. Recent developments in analytical models of voting in the U.S. Congress. *Legislative Studies Quarterly* 13:117-133.

Poole, K. T. and R. S. Daniels. 1985. Ideology, party, and voting in the U.S. Congress, 1959-1980. *American Political Science Review* 79:373-398.

Russett, B. 1970. *What price vigilance: The burden of national defense.* New Haven, CT: Yale University Press.

Schneider, J. E. 1979. *Ideological coalitions in Congress.* Westport, CT:

Greenwood Press.

Secret, P. 1989. The impact of region on racial differences in attitudes toward legal abortion. *Journal of Black Studies* 17:347-369.

Segal, J. A., C. M. Cameron, and A. D. Cover. 1992. A spatial model of roll call voting: Senators, constituents, presidents, and interest groups in Supreme Court confirmations. *American Journal of Political Science* 36:96-121.

Sharkansky, I. 1969. The utility of Elazar's political culture. *Polity* 2:66-83.

Skerry, P. 1978. The class conflict over abortion. *Public Interest* (Summer):69-84.

Smith, S. T. 1981. The consistency and ideological structure of U.S. Senate voting alignments, 1957-1976. *American Journal of Political Science* 25:780-795.

Strickland, R. A. and M. L. Whicker. 1986. Banning abortion: An analysis of Senate votes on a bimodal issue. *Women & Politics* 6:41-56.

Tatalovich, R. and B. W. Daynes. 1989. The geographical distribution of U.S. hospitals with abortion facilities. *Family Planning Perspectives* 21:81-84.

Tatalovich, R. and D. Schier. 1993. The persistence of ideological voting on abortion legislation in the House of Representatives, 1973-1988. *American Politics Quarterly* 21:125-139.

Truman, D. B. 1959. The congressional party: A case study. New York: Wiley.

Turner, J. 1951. *Party and constituency: Pressures on Congress.* Baltimore: Johns Hopkins University Press.

Vinovskis, M. A. 1980. The politics of abortion in the House of Representatives in 1976. In *The Law and Politics of Abortion*, ed. C. E. Schneider and M. A. Vinovskis. Lexington, MA: Lexington Books.

Wattier, M. J., B. W. Daynes and R. Tatalovich. 1996. (forthcoming) Abortion attitudes, gender, and candidate choice in presidential elections: 1972 to 1992. *Women & Politics.*

Wicker, A. W. 1969. Attitudes versus actions: The relationship of verbal and overt behavioral responses to attitude objects. *Journal of Social Issues* 4:41-78.

Wright, G. C., R. S. Erikson, and J. P. McIver. 1985. Measuring state partisanship and ideology with survey data. *Journal of Politics* 47:469-489.

Section 3:

Problem Definition and Redefinition, Agenda Setting, and Public Policy

Chapter 7

Problem Definition, Agenda Access, and Policy Choice*

David A. Rochefort and Roger W. Cobb

The process of public policymaking has commonly been depicted in terms of a natural logical sequence. Through the accumulation of information, a troubling social condition comes to light and is documented. Next it is the job of public officials to assess that problem and its causes and to respond as efficiently as possible through such means as new legislative enactments. Attention continues until the distressing concern is alleviated. This "rationality perspective" has been utilized by many writers on the governmental process, appearing in such varied disciplinary literatures as economics, political science, management, administrative science, and budgeting (Dye 1984, 31).

Yet empirical evidence repeatedly refutes this portrayal. For example, mismatches often exist between measures of the seriousness of a problem and the level of attention devoted to it. Lineberry (1981, 301-304) demonstrated the discrepancy over time between the official poverty rate and the public's perception of poverty as an important problem facing this country. He concluded that other factors, in addition to "objective condi-

*Reprinted with permission from *Policy Studies Journal* 21, 1 (1993):56-71.

tions," could be responsible for an issue's standing. Some of those factors, present in this and other areas of public policy, include the intensity of issue advocacy, leaders' openness to the issue, and the salience of competing problems.

Not only is there a degree of arbitrariness about what is taken to be a serious problem, but controversy often surrounds how a given issue will be understood. As Dery (1984, xi) has written, "problems do not exist 'out there'; they are not objective entities in their own right." From pollution, to child abuse, to AIDS, to illiteracy, there are divergent perceptions of any problem's origin, impact, and significance within the societal context. Use of language is critical in determining which aspect of a problem will be examined (Stone 1988; Baumgartner 1989). Rhetoric can help lodge a particular understanding of a problem in the minds of the public and protagonists. Even if one conception manages to attain dominance at a given moment, however, this interpretation can later be dislodged, effectively altering the substance of the problem being worked on. Viewed over a sufficient span of time, this evolutionary pattern of issue transformation is perhaps more the rule than the exception within our dynamic political environment.

Although rational decisionmaking, strictly considered, hardly ever occurs in government, the model of rationality "remains important for analytic purposes because it helps to identify barriers to rationality. It assists in posing the question: Why is policy making not a more rational process?" (Dye 1984, 32). And it is largely in response to this question that alternative decisionmaking models--centering on political pressures, time- and knowledge-limitations, bureaucratic operations, etc.--have been fashioned (Lindblom 1959; Allison 1971; Lowi 1979). Useful as these alternative perspectives may be, none addresses directly what is arguably the most fundamental source of "nonrational" political phenomena, namely, the intersubjective nature of social experience and its impact both on issue initiation and policy formulation. Only recently has a body of research begun to accumulate on this topic under the academic rubric of studies in "problem definition." Hogwood and Gunn (1984, 109) define this term as encompassing .

> the processes by which an issue (problem, opportunity, or trend), having been recognized as such and placed on the public policy agenda, is perceived by various interested parties; further explored, articulated, and possibly quantified; and in some but not all cases, given an authoritative or at least provisionally acceptable definition in terms of its likely causes, components, and consequences.

The purpose of this paper is to organize, clarify, and elaborate upon this emerging problem-definition perspective. Specific objectives are as follows: a) to examine the malleable nature of public issues on which the entire process of problem definition depends, b) to consider certain common types of problem definition as forms of description with powerful consequences for agenda access *and* for policy design, c) in a field of work dominated by narrow case studies, to supply myriad illustrations, from across the contemporary political scene, of the pervasive daily significance of problem definition, and d) to set out a plan of continuing research on the elements and ramifications of problem definition. To provide a necessary foundation, we begin by reviewing what others have contributed to the growing literature in this area.

Themes in Previous Work

The concept of problem definition has evolved chiefly out of two separate strains of work. The first comes from those who study social conflict. One of the key mechanisms for gaining advantage in a social conflict is the deft interpretation of an issue to best exploit the advocate's interest. As Schattschneider (1960, 66) wrote some 30 years ago: "The definition of the alternatives is the supreme instrument of power." Since there is no one fixed definition of an issue, it is subject to the interpretative maneuvers of the protagonists. In this light, social conflict becomes a process of successive, competitive problem definitions by opposing sides angling for advantage and issue expansion.

A second tradition comes from those who argue that there is no objective social reality, that all versions are in fact socially created. As Cobb and Elder (1983, 172) write, "Policy problems are not simply givens, nor are they matters of the facts of a situation, they are matters of interpretation and social definition." In a complicated world, people are looking for categories or ways of making sense out of complex phenomena. Problem definition is one way of organizing information and assigning personal meaning to it, although as Combs (1981, 55) states, "reality is always more complex, inchoate, contradictory, and inexplicable than our images and metaphors of it." Blumer (1971, 301) makes plain the connection between this process and policymaking in noting that:

> Social problems lie in and are produced by a process of collective definition. The process of collective definition is responsible for the emergence of social problems, for the way in which they are seen, for the way in which they are approached and considered, for the kind of remedial plan that is laid out, and for the transformation of the remedial

plan in its application.

More recent work on problem definition has centered on four major themes, with some research fitting under more than one heading. The first slant stresses causality. What produced the problem? Where did it come from? Here analysts have examined how responsibility comes to be assigned to an individual, group, technology, etc., with a distinct negative bias. In this connection, Stone (1989, 293) notes that competing players fight over explanations of culpability, with the process "resembling a great tug of war between political actors asserting competing causal theories." Edelman (1988, 17) similarly comments that "to evoke a problem's origin is to assign blame or praise." Applying these notions to the study of plant closings, Portz (1990) discovered three alternative explanations of the problem by affected communities: management failures, high labor costs, and changing market conditions. The way in which local actors responded to such economic dislocations significantly depended on the interpretation adopted.

Causal argument leads to a second, more encompassing theme of the contemporary literature. Here the focus is a problem's overall "image." Nimmo (1974, 9) identified an image "as a subjective representation of something previously perceived." He noted four components: perceptual (direct observation), cognitive (interpreting the referent), affective (feeling), and conative (the action potential). Rochefort (1986, 133-136) applied this approach to the study of social welfare policy by showing that every policy problem has several distinguishing elements: causation, nature, the problem's extensiveness, and the characteristics of the group affected. Others have examined the encapsulation of entire problems in simple phrases that evoke instant recognition and response. In this way, problems can be compressed into symbolic terms used by each side fighting for an effective edge through affective imagery. Jones and Baumgartner (1989) found that the battle over nuclear power was completely turned around when the original symbols of efficiency and progress were replaced by ones of danger and cost. Kingdon (1984) explained how transportation and health disputes in Washington hinged, in part, on the symbols attached to the policy alternatives, which in a sense became those alternatives.

A third theme in the literature emphasizes how problem definition depends not on the problem itself so much as what is to be done about it. Thus, some believe that solutions determine how problems will be defined. Wildavsky (1979, 42) has argued that public officials will not take a problem seriously unless there is a proposed course of action attached to it. In a sense, the solution begets the problem. As he states, "A problem is linked to a solution; a problem is a problem only if something can be done about it." Further, Wildavsky predicts that if any proposed solution is implemented, it creates a whole new set of issues, thereby ensuring that no public problem ever really dies. Elder and Cobb (1984, 24) observe, as well, that "the availability of solutions makes problems possible." These terms "solve" and "solution" are of necessity relative because most analysts adopting this viewpoint do not believe that problems are, in any final sense, solvable.

A fourth approach to problem definition directs attention to those who are defining the problem, in particular, a person, group, or interest who manages to claim the situation as their just province and to keep competing definitions out of bounds. Gusfield (1981, 10-11) developed the notion of "problem ownership," drawing an analogy with such characteristics of property as control, exclusiveness, transferability, and potential loss. Who, then, are the "problem owners" in the population? Generally, they are people with special status and educational attainment (often professionals) who are highly respected. The key politically is who is seen to have the legitimacy to deal with an issue needing public intervention.

This past work still leaves major gaps in the study of problem definition. For instance, not enough attention has been paid to the varied dimensions of problem description, including not only problem responsibility but also other attributions. Nor has the relationship of problem definition to policy outcomes been adequately studied. Questions remain, too, about the connection between problem definition and the process of agendasetting by which issues rise and fall in political prominence. Examining the evolving nature of governmental paperwork as a public issue--from the bureaucracy's need to collect standardized data from many sources, to governmental intrusiveness--Weiss (1989, 118) correctly observed that problem definition is related to but not synonymous with agenda access. All of these concerns, however, are but different reflections of the inherent fluidity of policy issues, a subject that deserves further attention.

Why Are Public Issues So Malleable?

The first thing to note about the malleability of public issues--their openness to competing interpretations as well as factual distortion--is that they are not unique in this way. We live in a complex, ultimately mysterious, world in which more stimuli constantly bombard us than can be consciously processed, and in-depth understanding is typically achieved only for specialized areas of long-term study or experience. To state that "our lives take shape under the impact of associations and meanings which are not necessarily of our making and choosing" (Sederberg, 1984, 5) is to put it mildly. Further, as Simon (1985) has explained, people have only a limited capacity for processing large amounts of information and new pieces of data are constantly entering into the picture. The natural tendency is to focus short term and on those particular items that manage to gain our attention.

Cognitive psychologists distinguish between "general" and "phenomenal" realities. The former refers to the actual bases of existence. The latter refers to "the constellation of thoughts, perceptions, and feelings" which make up each person's "constructed reality" (Wegner and Vallacher, 1977, 4). The physical environment, other people's behavior, even one's own qualities as an individual all enter into this construction and are taken as true. Applying this insight politically, Hogwood and Gunn (1984, 109) state, "we each create our own reality, and this is nowhere more true than in the way we identify problems or issues, and interpret and relate them to our mental map of some larger situation."

Processes of perception as well as argumentation (Majone, 1989) underlie the phenomenal aspect of public issues. Multiple influences that operate simultaneously, within sequential chains, and as part of hierarchical structures convey the intricacy of social problem solving. In a picture of many possible influences, selecting certain factors to the exclusion of others is an act of explanation that aggressively promotes a particular version of reality. Brewer and deLeon (1983, 89) assert that "with increased complexity come increases in the number and diversity of system interpretations, in part because of the biased and distorted views affected individuals bring with them to the problem context." In the following passage, economist Ellwood (1989, 8) sets out some alternative factors that could be cited to explain lack of resources in the case of a two-parent family:

> Suppose we find that a two-parent family with three children is poor even though the father is working full time. What is the cause of the family's poverty? One could say that the father's wages are too low, that the mother is not willing to work, that the family cannot find affordable day care, that the couple was irresponsible to have children when they could not support them, or that the father did not get enough education or has not worked hard enough to get a "good" job. Even if we talked to the family, it is possible that we would not be able to agree on just one "true" reason.

Needless to say, for each of these different viewpoints there are strong adherents in society, who consequently favor different policy solutions. Often, selecting which independent variables to emphasize in a complicated "explanation-rich" situation hinges on the observer's level of analysis. Where, on the continuum from micro-individual behavior to macro-social forces, does the problem-definer focus attention? As a case in point, recent media reports (Black, 1990) have revealed that black men in America have a much greater involvement with the criminal justice system than other population subgroups: approximately one-quarter in their 20s are either in prison or on probation or parole. Seeking to explain these data, one observer could highlight the irresponsible and immoral behavior of the individuals involved, while another would stress the special economic disadvantages facing the black community, whose overall poverty rate is three times as high as in the general population.

Measurement is a process that always involves discretion and inconsistency. No two analysts will approach the task of gauging a social problem's magnitude, rate of change, or distribution in exactly the same way. Whether a problem exists, how bad it is, who or what is responsible, and what future trends will occur are all perceptions that can depend on the measuring approach used.

Illustrations abound. How about the issue of nonwhite illegitimate births, sometimes labeled a contemporary social calamity in the U.S.? Do the numbers justify this concern? It depends on what you choose to look at. Whereas illegitimate births as a proportion of all births in this population are climbing sharply, this is chiefly because births to married nonwhite women have fallen. Little actual growth has taken place in the rate of births to unmarried nonwhite women over the past decade (Ellwood 1989, 68-69). The poverty rate, a prime socioeconomic indicator, is also disputed on measurement grounds (DeParle 1990a). Among varied criticisms are that it fails to take proper account of yearly inflation in nonfood costs such as housing, and that it neglects to factor in the cash value of in-kind benefits. Depending upon the calculating method applied, the national poverty rate ranges from 9% to 18% (the official rate stands at 13%). Evaluating the success of antidrug programs is similarly complicated by the relevance of a bevy of alternative measures including seizures, treatment rates, arrests, drug-related homicides, and use estimates (Ayres 1990), not to mention the different targeting strategies of antidrug policy (Sharp 1990). Conclusions differ markedly depending on the numbers employed.

Deciding what an issue "is really about" is somewhat an exercise in ranking priorities. Some issues require choice between the interests of two or more affected groups. Those voting in Aspen, Colorado's recent referendum on the banning of fur coat sales affirmed that the coat-wearers' use of the fur took precedence over the rights of the fur-bearing creatures (Johnson 1990). Not all issues involve life and death questions for one of the affected parties, but many do come down to weighing the respective claims of identified competitors. Or, the priority choices may concern abstract values, such as the abortion debate's freedom of choice vs. a right to life. Another kind of value choice concerns the toleration of alternative adverse consequences. The acid rain debate, for one, offers no painless solution. To allow manufacturers to continue to produce harmful emissions for the sake of economic productivity damages the environment. But tough regulation of these manufacturers runs the risk of unemployment and general economic stagnation. Such difficult tradeoffs appear in many areas of public policy, requiring ethical as well as economic valuations that directly shape problem definition.

Problem Definition as Problem Description

How did a distressing social condition come into being? What key features distinguish this problem from other social issues, providing guidance for the design of specialized remedies? What are the characteristics of the group identified with, or affected by, the problem? What is the nature of the appropriate solution, and is it feasible? In interpreting social reality, problem definition is a political expression that advances answers to all of these essential policy questions, yet we have only just begun to delineate the main categories of problem description and their common options (e.g., Peters 1986, 45-56; Hogwood and Gunn 1984, 108-127). Summarizing existing work in this area and adding to it, Table 1 presents a road map for this analysis. Current illustrations are discussed in greater detail.

Problem causation

Invariably the way a problem is defined includes some statement about its origins. As previously noted, the question of culpability is the most studied aspect of problem definition. An important distinction is whether a problem is attributed to individual versus impersonal causes. Much of the traditional debate between liberalism and conservatism can in fact be explained by the relative stress given to these two competing perspectives. Consider, for example, what has come to be known as the "underclass" problem. Those on the left highlight failures of the eco-

Table 1. An Anatomy of Problem Description

Dimension of Problem	Options
Problem Causation	personal - impersonal intended - accidental blame allocated - blame avoided simple - complex
Nature of the Problem	
Severity	degrees of severity
Incidence	growing, stable or declining social patterns: by class, population, cohort, age, etc.
Novelty	unprecedented - familiar
Proximity	personally relevant - a general social concern
Crisis	crisis - noncrisis emergency - nonemergency
Characteristics of the Problem Population	worthy - unworthy deserving - undeserving familiar - strange sympathetic - threatening
End - Means Orientation of Problem Definer	instrumental - expressive
Nature of the Solution	available - nonexistent acceptable - objectionable affordable - unaffordable

nomic and cultural systems, while those on the right commonly cite the lack of individual effort (DeParle 1990a). In the realm of technology, much play has been given to the role of human versus equipment error in accounting for complex system failures such as in nuclear power plants. The latter attribution is more likely to result in stronger standards and regulation because responsibility is not linked to idiosyncratic human performance and capability.

The recent courtroom trial of Captain Joseph Hazelwood of the Exxon Valdez oiltanker was a very visible exercise in choosing where to allocate blame for a social catastrophe (After Trial 1990). Government prosecutors made the case that the 11-million-gallon spill of crude oil into Alaska's Prince William Sound resulted from Hazelwood's intoxication and recklessness while guiding his ship through the channel. Contrary to much of the negative publicity surrounding the captain's trial, however, Hazelwood was eventually acquitted of these felony charges and convicted only of a misdemeanor of negligence. Subsequently, this judgment has added momentum to the cause of those arguing that society must concentrate not on individual "scapegoating" but improving mechanisms for oil spill prevention and cleanup, including, among other measures, better oil tanker design and quicker spill response systems.

Thinking in causal terms seems to be an ingrained human propensity. When an event happens, an immediate response is to identify the underlying reasons why it occurred. Stone (1988) refers to the distinction between intended and accidental causes. Intended causes are described as some purposive human action designed to bring about a particular result. In the case of public policymaking, if the action is perceived to be successful, it is labeled as "rational;" if unsuccessful, a search for the source of failure ensues, often associated with such notions as "victims" and "conspiracies." Accidental causes have to do with natural intervention, "the result of accident and fate." Whatever the perceived agent, "the different sides in an issue act as if they are trying to find the 'true' cause, but they are always struggling to influence which idea is selected to guide policy" (Stone 1988, 149-154). Once the public has identified a guilty party, it is disappointed if appropriate punishment is not dealt out. Thus, recent poll data show that a majority of citizens believe that the owners and managers are most responsible for the savings and loan debacle, and there is widespread dissatisfaction with an administration clean-up that has sent few "culprits" to jail (Nash 1990).

Certain problems are defined very simply, specifying single causal agents. Others take note of a variety of influences. Problem definitions of these two types may predispose the political system to different outcomes. Generally, narrowing the focus to just one or two causal factors is a signal that the problem definer is ready for immediate action. More complex formulations (Stone 1988, 152-154), on the other hand, may represent a strategy to head off prompt response. Overwhelmed with the poorly understood interaction of many causes, policymakers may simply throw up their hands and claim the foolishness of intervention at the present time. They may recommend deeper study instead. Yet there are important exceptions to this common pattern. Multicausal explanations and the multipronged solutions they engender can be among the most sophisticated policy endeavors and also those that have the greatest chance of building support (Light 1985).

Nature of the problem

A social problem may be represented along many dimensions beyond that of causality. These ascribed characteristics increase or decrease the chances of public action, just as they may prefigure key aspects of policy design.

Severity

One crucial descriptive dimension is severity, i.e., how serious a problem and its consequences are taken to be. Is this an issue meriting space on a crowded public agenda? In acquiring a high priority standing politically, it helps if an issue affects large numbers of people. Alternatively, devastating impacts on a few can also make a problem noteworthy. How strongly the severity label gets applied is a matter for contentious debate, since this element of problem definition is pivotal to capturing the attention of public officials and the media.

Recent events have seen just such debate concerning a collection of environmental issues, with disputants vehemently disagreeing over so-called objective facts. Global warming is a good illustration (Shabecoff 1990a). While admitting the existence of the problem, the Bush Administration officially tended to characterize it as far from catastrophic and not deserving of corrective measures so strong that they would damage the economy. However, some opponents, both within and outside the administration, warn that the situation is already grave, a looming disaster. Accordingly, they criticize the administration for its go-slow posture. Nuclear winter, a companion environmental issue, has stimulated a parallel debate over severity (Lessons 1990). Under the most terrifying scenarios, a nuclear exchange could produce an environmental disaster leading to the extinction of human life on earth. Gainsayers view this as alarmist, arguing that more research has to be done to delineate likely impacts of the use of these weapons.

Incidence

A social problem's incidence is an important descriptive dimension that represents the overall scope of people affected as well as those groups disproportionately at risk. And like other aspects of problem definition, incidence too can be a debatable question that intermixes politics and available information. Sometimes the issue is one of change over time, i.e., is a problem declining, stable, or growing, and if it is growing, at what rate? Linear or even exponential projections are the most ominous, and when accepted as valid, tend to create the most pressure for quick public intervention. Release of new projections of this kind by researchers captures much of the space in today's newspapers. Some varied recent examples include startling forecasts of the rate of global deforestation (Shabecoff 1990b), surging traffic problems in New York City resulting from high increases in the number of motor vehicle registrations (Levine 1990), and concerns about a trend toward declining airline safety (Lavin 1990). Yet much depends on the way information is aggregated and presented for such situations, as shown by the latter issue in which one sees a growing absolute number of airline accidents but a falling rate per overall number of flights.

Incidence patterns across society can also be depicted in varying fashions. Sometimes an issue's social-class dimension is brought to light. Nelson (1984, 15) showed that the association of child abuse with class-based concerns "had long lasting effects on the shape of child abuse policy." During the Bush Administration, a capital gains tax cut has also been approached as a class issue (Wehr, 1989). Opponents label it an unwarranted "handout to the rich," as supporters seek to challenge this interpretation by predicting an economic stimulation that would benefit all in society through more jobs and higher tax receipts. Alternatively, a social issue may be identified with a particular population cohort. The current focus (Preston 1984) on growing poverty among children at the same time that poverty rates among the elderly have fallen dramatically is an emerging issue that stresses the use of age as a defining measure of incidence.

Novelty

When an issue is described as novel, unprecedented, or trailblazing, it can have a number of effects. One, of course, is to win attention. Then as time passes and the novelty wanes, the public and media become bored with an issue and are distracted from it (Downs 1973; Bosso 1989). But issues that have not been seen before are difficult to conceptualize and they lack familiar solutions. Thus, a tension arises, as the issue is publicized and onlookers expect resolution, yet no consensus exists within the political system on how to tackle the problem. For example, when a new drug appears with promise for treating a serious public health problem like AIDS, the public and elected officials alike are understandably excited. However, new drugs carry potential risks as well as benefits which must be carefully assessed through a process that many critics find too time-consuming (Groopman 1989). Similar difficulties occur with other types of medical breakthroughs such as in genetics research. Each new discovery brings with it a host of ethical and practical concerns requiring analysis and discussion.

Proximity

To characterize an issue as having proximity is to argue that it hits close to home or directly impinges on a person's interest. If the case can be made successfully, members of the audience will become concerned and may express this politically. For this reason, issue proponents constantly seek to expand their base by claims of personal relevancy. Viewed in this light, it was no surprise to hear the National Commission on Children, on the occasion of release of its new report on child poverty in America, describe this problem not only in terms of "personal tragedies" but also as "a staggering national tragedy." To quote panel chairman John D. Rockefeller IV, "The health and vitality of our economy and our democracy are increasingly in danger." Added Harvard Professor T. Berry Brazelton, "We know these kids are going to cost us billions in the future. They're going to be the terrorists of the future" (U.S. panel 1990, A22).

Crisis

"Crisis" may be one of the most used terms in the American political lexicon. It is applied to denote a situation where corrective action is long overdue and dire circumstances exist. The dividing line between a mere problem and an actual crisis is indeed a hazy one which issue advocates are prone to cross rhetorically when they see momentum for their cause waning. The national deficit is an example of an issue that has frequently been associated with the term crisis, although not all politicians or economists agree the label is appropriate (Ortner 1990). In 1986, the death of two prominent athletes from a drug overdose coupled with the appearance of a new form of cocaine helped convert the drug problem into a concern of "crisis proportions." Yet, ironically, some evidence indicates that at the time drug usage was actually declining (Baumgartner 1989, 201-210).

"Emergency" is a term often used synonymously with crisis. Discussing the homelessness problem, Lipsky and Smith (1989) explained how defining the situation as an emergency has enabled quick responses but also tended to produce temporary band-aid solutions such as shelters instead of more comprehensive, long-term reforms related to housing, unemployment, and mental health care.

Characteristics of the problem population

Not only are problems given descriptive definition, so too are the afflicted groups and individuals. This especially occurs in social welfare policymaking, whose purpose is to transfer resources or deliver services to specified target populations. Political willingness to make these commitments is generally conditioned by societal perceptions of the people who are going to benefit. Further, the balance between assistance and coercion in policy design--an important dimension of government's use of its "policy tools" (Schneider and Ingram 1990)--is struck by how positive or negative these perceptions are.

Several attitudinal axes help to structure aggregate impressions. Is the group worthy or unworthy (deserving or undeserving) of assistance? Underlying this question is the recurrent notion of culpability. Are members of the group seen as familiar or strange? Social deviants and other out-group members do not receive equivalent consideration to persons with whom the public readily identifies. Related to these issues is the distinction between sympathetic and threatening populations. Rochefort (1986) utilized these attributes to account for varying forms of public intervention concerning groups like the elderly, working and welfare poor, and the mentally ill. Examining public opinion data, Cook (1979) also demonstrated a link between the favorability of attitudes toward different claimant groups and popular support for providing aid to those groups. She concludes that "all things being equal people we like and find attractive and pleasant seem to get more help" (1979, 41).

Current disagreement over appropriate public policy toward sex offenders substantiates these general observations. Those who view abusers as unfortunate victims of a psychiatric syndrome argue for corresponding therapeutic treatment. Others who perceive the offender as a responsible moral actor advocate traditional criminal punishment. Notes one psychologist in the former camp,

> States must now pay for more social services for the elderly and for AIDS victims . . . and do so in a climate of no new taxes. It is not popular to say we're going to spend scarce dollars to treat sex offenders, a silent, disliked group. (Diesenhouse 1990, 6)

Ends-means orientation of the problem definer

An interesting twist on the theme of problem definition concerns the ends-means orientation of those defining the problem. In some situations issue advocates premise their stance on an instrumental basis which sets out a deliberate course of action carefully calculated to achieve a desired end. At other times, however, the means and not the ends of public action will be uppermost for issue definers. In effect, this amounts to viewing public policy in expressive terms and the very process of implementation as the embodiment or corruption of certain cherished values. Curious debates can ensue when issue opponents differ in their focus on ends and means, for the two sides lack a shared conceptual orientation essential even to meaningful argument.

A revealing instance of this phenomenon in contemporary domestic politics has been the controversy over distribution of sterile needles to IV drug users for preventing the spread of AIDS (Rochefort and Pezza 1991). Proponents in several cities throughout the country have advanced the plan as a rational, purposive public health initiative, given that common use of dirty needles among the addict population ranks as one of the primary means of transmitting the AIDS virus. To bolster their case, some cite evidence of positive impacts in selected European cities that have already undertaken the measure (Purdom 1990). Yet for many opponents, the important issue is not whether distributing sterile needles to drug addicts is an effective anti-AIDS device, but whether it is an acceptable form of government activity to support the illegality of drug use. The resulting conflict has been especially intense, with little basis for compromise between such dissimilar perspectives.

Nature of the solution

The definitional struggle in public policymaking extends from aspects of the problem and those affected by and interested in it to include descriptive qualities of the solution. Until and unless general political agreement also crystallizes on this matter, government remains without the wherewithal to act. Brewer and deLeon (1983, 18) term this the "estimation" stage of policy analysis, which "emphasizes empirical, scientific, and projective issues to help determine the likelihoods and consequences of candidate options . . .[and] assessments of the desirability of such outcomes."

The most basic concern at this stage of the process is solution availability: Do key actors believe that means exist to accomplish what needs to be done? Or does it seem folly and a waste of resources to invest in a given course of action? For better or worse, the political realm is a magnet for nostrums that have neither been applied nor evaluated on a macro-social scale. Therefore, it often becomes a guessing game for decisionmakers--an exercise in faith or skepticism--to choose between aggressive intervention or restraint. Nuclear power plants to produce cheap and reliable electricity, health education programs to promote better living habits in the population at large, employment and training initiatives to counter chronic welfare dependency, recycling to resolve a growing trash disposal problem--each of these constructions matches a widely recognized social goal with a touted solution whose practical effectiveness is the subject of unabating controversy.

A solution's acceptability does not refer to effectiveness of action but to whether that action conforms to standard codes of behavior. In many ways, this attribute offers another vantage point on the ends-means distinction already introduced. The heart of the matter is ethical: Are there established social principles that forbid a certain remedial approach even as the problem at hand worsens and could feasiblely be contained? War in the Middle East has once again raised the issue of chemical warfare. Experience shows these weapons to be a lethal component of a country's military arsenal, capable of inspiring great terror among the enemy. But does a civilized nation unleash this kind of destructive power, no matter what the circumstances? The question of acceptability also frequently attends the development of new technologies. A recent example is the implantation of fetal tissue into the brains of sufferers of Parkinson's Disease (Kolata 1990). Although the technique apparently holds great promise for combating this nervous condition, widespread opposition has arisen based on fear the surgery will encourage abortions.

Supposing a proposed policy intervention is agreed upon, available, and acceptable, one more potential barrier still remains, that of affordability. The issue is straightforward. Do political actors perceive that adequate resources exist to pay for what needs to be done? Especially in these days of government deficits, decisionmakers are cautious in making financial commitments. Meanwhile, demands are ongoing for expanding existing programs and for adding new ones. Considerable information now suggests the positive educational and social impacts of America's Head Start program for preschool age disadvantaged children (Chira 1990). Yet, even despite this apparent success and broad-based support for the program, legislative and executive policymakers are at odds over how much money should be added to Head Start and whether all eligible children can possibly be served. Comparable fiscal qualms beleaguer the nation's effort to improve its high infant mortality rate. Much is understood about the complex of prenatal services that could help the situation and has been summarized in several high-level government reports (Tolchin 1990). It remains controversial, however, just how these services will be provided and especially through what sources of funding. Affordability debates invoke various kinds of standards depending on the rhetorical objectives of participants. Dollar comparisons with other operating or proposed programs, references to overall budgetary constraints, and estimates of the cost of action measured against the probable economic (and social) costs of failing to act are all common.

Future Research on Problem Definition

Problem definition is fast becoming one of the most widely invoked concepts in the policy analysis literature, yet casually so and often with little evident awareness on the part of users about kindred scholars or the full potential of the approach. Thus the perspective is yet in an immature theoretical state, with further progress dependent on establishment of a common vocabulary, delineation of key concepts, and the comparison and categorization of preliminary research efforts. Contributing to this sense of coherency in the study of problem definition has been a central aim of this article.

The next step in the theory-building process must be to continue to formulate and test hypotheses about the impacts of alternative definitional arguments. As discussed above, already a number of important "if, then" propositions can be stated which relate policy design to such varying problem constructions as whether causation is perceived to be personal or impersonal, human or mechanical, intended or accidental, and plural or singular. Attributions like severity, incidence, novelty, proximity, and crisis-nature are hypothesized to determine a public issue's salience; while availability, acceptability, and affordability predict whether the policymaking process will result in the enactment of a solution. These generalizations need to be added to--by research relating problem definition to some ordered set of policy design choices (e.g., Schneider and Ingram 1990)--and evaluated in a variety of political contexts that investigate the mediating role of cultural and institutional factors. Other questions concern the way professional and other interests come to exercise authority over the definition process, and how long-established problem definitions in specific policy areas may undergo sudden transformation (Polisar and Wildavsky 1989; Taylor 1988; Rochefort 1986). Attention must also be given to the impact of problem definition on the process of policy implementation, including the unravelling of previously accepted definitions at this stage (Weiss 1989).

We end on a normative note. Given the tendency of the political system repeatedly to define its issues along certain conceptual lines, are there aspects of reality which for some reason are systematically screened out that could, if deliberately incorporated, improve regime performance? The usual resistance to addressing issues in terms of race and class in an inegalitarian capitalist society is plain. Sederberg (1984, 117) touches on this point in writing,

> The dominant distribution of values and resources, after all, also reflects an explanation or related set of explanations, and as such confronts the problem of adequacy. If the established order is necessarily imperfect, the need for change must be recognized.

And growing reliance on specialized experts, even on questions whose broad value implications outweigh their technical nature, unnecessarily restricts participation in the identification of problems and their solutions. In circumstances like these, the process of problem definition has import for democratic theory far beyond what its semantic trappings might suggest.

References

After trial, Valdez captain says he is more cynical. 1990, March 25. *New York Times*, Part I, 26.

Allison, G. 1971. *Essence of decision*. Boston: Little, Brown.

Ayres, B. D. 1990, February 12. Drug statistics bring hope to capital. *New York Times*, B9.

Baumgartner, F. R. 1989. *Conflict and rhetoric in French policymaking.* Pittsburgh, PA: University of Pittsburgh Press.

Black, C. 1990, March 4. America's lost generation. *Boston Globe*, 69-70.

Blumer, H. 1971. Social problems as collective behavior. *Social Problems* 18:298-306.

Bosso, C. 1989. Setting the agenda: Mass media and the discovery of famine in Ethiopia. In *Manipulating public opinion*, ed. M. Margolis and G. Mauser, 153-174. Pacific Grove, CA: Brooks-Cole.

Brewer, G. D. and P. deLeon. 1983. *The foundations of policy analysis*. Homewood, IL: Dorsey Press.

Chira, S. 1990, February 14. Preschool aid for the poor: How big a Head

Start? *New York Times*, A1.

Cobb, R. W. and C. D. Elder. 1983. *Participation in American politics: The dynamics of agenda-building.* Baltimore: Johns Hopkins University Press.

Combs, J. E. 1981. A process approach. In *Handbook of political communication,* ed. D. D. Nimmo and K. R. Sanders, 39-62. Beverly Hills, CA: Sage.

Cook, F. 1979. *Who should be helped? Public support for social services.* Beverly Hills, CA: Sage.

DeParle, J. 1990a, August 26. What to call the poorest poor? *New York Times*, Part IV, 4.

_____. 1990b, September 3. In rising debate on poverty, the question: Who is poor? *New York Times,* 1.

Dery, D. 1984. *Problem definition in policy analysis.* Lawrence: University of Kansas Press.

Diesenhouse, S. 1990, April 22. Do sex offenders belong in treatment or in jail? *New York Times*, Part IV, 6.

Downs, A. 1973. Up and down with ecology--the issue-attention cycle. *Public Interest* 32:38-50.

Dye, T. 1984. *Understanding public policy.* Englewood Cliffs, NJ: Prentice-Hall.

Edelman, M. 1988. *Constructing the political spectacle.* Urbana: University of Illinois Press.

Elder, C. D. and R. W. Cobb. 1984. Agenda-building and the politics of aging. *Policy Studies Journal* 13:115-130.

Ellwood, D. 1989. *Poor support.* New York: Basic Books.

Gusfield, J. 1981. *The culture of public problems.* Chicago: University of Chicago Press.

Hogwood, B. W. and L. A. Gunn. 1984. *Policy analysis for the real world.* London: Oxford University Press.

Johnson, D. 1990, February 12. An unlikely battle in snow country: Aspen to vote on banning fur sales. *New York Times*, A18.

Jones, B. and F. Baumgartner. 1989. Shifting images and venues of a public issue. Presented at the annual meeting of the American Political Science Association, Atlanta.

Kingdon, J. 1984. *Agendas, alternatives and public policies.* Boston: Little, Brown.

Kolata, G. 1990, February 3. Fetal tissue seems to aid Parkinson patient. *New York Times*, A1.

Lavin, C. 1990, February 9. Why airline safety looks worse as it gets better. *New York Times*, A1.

Lessons of nuclear winter. 1990, February 5. *New York Times*, A18.

Levine, R. 1990, April 10. Rise in cars chokes New York area's roads. *New York Times*, A1.

Light, P. 1985. *Artful work: The politics of Social Security reform.* New York: Random House.

Lindblom, C. E. 1959. The science of "muddling through". *Public Administration Review* 19:79-88.

Lineberry, R. 1981. *Government in America.* Boston: Little, Brown.

Lipsky, M. and S. R. Smith. 1989. When social problems are treated as emergencies. *Social Service Review* 63:5-25.

Lowi, T. 1979. *The end of liberalism.* New York: Norton.

Majone, G. 1989. *Evidence, argument, and persuasion in the policy process.* New Haven, CT: Yale University Press.

Nash, N. C. 1990, August 26. Public dismay over S & L crisis grows, poll finds. *New York Times*, Part I, 30.

Nelson, B. 1984. *Making an issue of child abuse.* Chicago: University of Chicago Press.

Nimmo, D. 1974. *Popular images of politics.* Englewood Cliffs, NJ: Prentice-Hall.

Ortner, R. 1990. *Voodoo deficits.* New York: Dow Jones-Irwin.

Peters, B.G. 1986. *American public policy: Promise and performance.* 2nd ed. Chatham, NJ: Chatham House Publishers.

Polisar, D. and A. Wildavsky. 1989. From individual to system blame: A cultural analysis of historical change in the law of torts. *Journal of Policy History* 1:129-155.

Portz, J. 1990. *The politics of plant closings.* Lawrence: University of Kansas Press.

Preston, S. 1984, December. Children and elderly in the U.S. *Scientific American* 251:44-49.

Purdom, T. 1990, February 14. Dinkins to end needle plan for drug users. *New York Times*, B1.

Rochefort, D. A. 1986. *American social welfare policy.* Boulder, CO: Westview.

Rochefort, D. A. and P. Pezza. 1991. Public opinion and health policy. In *Health politics and policy*, ed. T. Litman and L. Robins, 247-269. Albany, NY: Delmar.

Schattschneider, E. E. 1960. *The semi-sovereign people.* New York: Holt.

Schneider, A. and H. Ingram. 1990. Behavioral assumptions of policy tools. *Journal of Politics* 52:510-529.

Sederberg, P. C. 1984. *The politics of meaning.* Tucson: University of Arizona Press.

Shabecoff, P. 1990a, February 6. Bush asks cautious response to threat of global warming. *New York Times*, A1.

_____. 1990b, June 8. Loss of tropical forests is found much worse than was thought. *New York Times*, A1.

Sharp, E. B. 1990. Agenda-setting and policy results: Lessons from three drug policy episodes. Presented at the annual meeting of the American Political Science Association. San Francisco, CA.

Simon, H. 1985. Human nature in politics: The dialogue of psychology with political science. *American Political Science Review* 79:293-304.

Stone, D. A. 1988. *Policy paradox and political reason*. Glenview, IL: Scott, Foresman.

_____. 1989. Causal stories and the formation of policy agendas. *Political Science Quarterly*, 104, 281-300.

Taylor, S. 1988, April 21. Alcoholics lose lawsuit on some V.A. benefits. *New York Times*, Part I, 27.

Tolchin, M. 1990, June 17. Two-thirds of states have programs to cut costs of teen pregnancies. *New York Times*, Part I, 22.

U.S. panel warns on child poverty. 1990, April 27. *New York Times*, A22.

Wegner, D. and R. Vallacher. 1977. *Implicit psychology*. New York: Oxford University Press.

Wehr, E. 1989. Bush's capital gains plan revives old debate. *Congressional Quarterly Weekly Report* 47:369-372.

Weiss, J. 1989. The powers of problem definition: The case of government paperwork. *Policy Sciences* 22:97-121.

Wildavsky, A. 1979. *Speaking truth to power*. Boston: Little-Brown.

Chapter 8

The Behavioral Study of Political Ideology and Public Policy Formulation*

Carl Grafton and Anne Permaloff

Our objective is to suggest a methodology for gauging ideological change and its relationship to change in public policy. The methodology is applied to a theory outlined in an earlier article that examined the impact of ideology on policy for economics and business (Grafton and Permaloff 2001--Chapter 10 in this volume). We then expand the methodology to another area of policy to test its applicability. Because liberals and conservatives dominate federal and state governments in the United States, we concentrate on these ideologies.

We define a political ideology as an action oriented model of people and society (Parsons 1951, 349; Johnston 1996, 13; van Dijk 1998, 8). An ideology contains prescriptions for public policy. We define ideological change as a revision of a prescription or a new prescription. Although most definitions of ideology contain references to public policy prescriptions, histories of ideologies pay surprisingly little attention to public policy except for discussions of the New and Fair Deals (e.g., Hoover 1987; Young 1996; Dorrien 1993). Even when public policy is a central topic, it is typically presented only as part of a historical narrative (Brink-

*Reprinted with permission from *The Social Science Journal* (forthcoming).

ley 1998; Thompson 1981), and references to public policy in textbooks on ideology appear only as examples (Van Dyke 1995). Ideological theorists are even less likely to discuss public policy (e.g., Rawls 1971; Devigne 1994). And, we have found no histories, textbooks, or theoretical treatises regarding ideology that contain testable theories of ideological change.

Not only are theoretical and historical treatments of ideology disconnected from public policy, since the 1960s both liberals and conservatives have been engaged in complex internal debates that render each writer's description of his or her own side of questionable value (Young 1996; Farganis 1993; Garry 1992; Devigne 1994; Dorrien 1993).

Many political psychology studies include the part played by ideology in thinking processes and the functions ideology fulfills in the human personality (Iyengar and McGuire 1993). Ideology helps people understand the relationships among events, facilitates the making of consistent judgments over time, and aids in the efficient processing of information (Apter 1964, 20; Young 1977). Researchers in this area do not make systematic connections between ideology and public policy nor do they pay significant attention to ideological change.

Much effort has been devoted to statistical analyses of the impact of ideology on policy formulation especially in Congress where roll call votes and the characteristics of legislators and their districts are quantifiable (Richardson and Munger 1990; Kalt and Zupan 1984). Also, research on public opinion shows shifts along the liberal-conservative ideological continuum and changing perceptions of the distance between the voters and such institutions as Congress and the presidency (Flanigan and Zingale 2002). Other work concentrates on the relationship between social class and ideology (Ornstein and Stevenson 1999). Gleiber and Shull (1992, 441-467) are unusual in their focus on the importance of ideological position and intensity of preference in presidential policy-making. In addition, they make the point that ideology on a liberal-conservative scale encompasses a range of interests and like Kingdon (1984) that ideology serves as a handy shorthand for the study of public policy preferences. These and many similar studies offer no general theory relating ideology to public policy, and they make no attempt to explain ideological change.

The extensive literatures on government problem definition, agenda setting, and policy formulation pay little attention to ideology even though the policy areas with which these literatures deal are often highly animated ideologically (Dearing and Rogers 1996; Rochefort and Cobb 1994). The leading authors in these literatures use such examples as affirmative action and energy policy. They discuss these policies in terms of ideological labels (liberals versus conservatives), not underlying ideological values or ideological change. Paul Sabatier's (1991) advocacy coalition approach includes "belief systems" that might be mistaken for ideology, but his belief systems are much closer to David Truman's (1960) concept of interests.

Marxian theory asserted the inevitability of conflict between capitalists, workers, and the bourgeoisie. Ralf Dahrendorf (1959, 290-293) offers a version of conflict theory more sophisticated than Marx's that centers on conflict between dominant and subjugated groups. Conflict theory views conflict as normal. We make no such assumption. Dahrendorf, Marx, and other conflict theorists also assume that political conflict is structured around polarized dominant and subjugated groups. It is easy to imagine that this pattern sometimes obtains, but, again, we see no reason to assume its presence.

Discourse theory and frame theory also fail to address the issues of concern in this research. According to Nossiff (1998), discourse and frame theory seek to explain how triggering events can lead to the definition of issues in particular ways and the use of discourse by interest groups to frame issues and specify desirable policies and get their issues and solutions onto the societal and governmental agenda. (See also Snow, Rochford, Worden, and Benford 1986). Despite Nossiff's assertion that discourse and frame theory attempt to explain the relationship between triggering events and agenda setting, we have found no discourse and frame theory work that does so beyond the bounds of specific case studies nor does there appear to be a location in these theories for the relationship between triggering events and agenda setting. Furthermore, we see little attempt to identify patterns of triggering events or types of triggering events that lead to particular types of discourse or frames.

Discourse and frame studies appear to focus on particular cases rather than the broad, long lived frames of liberalism and conservatism. Many of these case studies present imaginative and perceptive accounts of conflict or consensus between liberals and conservatives, but the quality of these studies owes more to the intelligence of the authors than the power of the analytical tools they wield. Frame and discourse theories tend to present framing and discourse as tools for or elements of ideological or interest group struggle, but that broader ideological conflict tends to go unexamined (e.g., Jacoby 2000; Bergeron 2001; Alba 2000; Coles 2002).

A Device for Theory Development

Fred S.Roberts (1976) and Robert Axelrod (1976) offer a way to develop theories of ideological change and connect them to our ideological indicator, newspaper and journal of opinion editorials. Roberts uses cognitive maps called signed digraphs that model dynamic systems. For example, he depicts a partial digraph model of energy demand: Number of factories ---(+)---> Energy use ---(-)---> Quality of the environment (Roberts 1976, 146). The digraph is read: as number of factories increases (the positive sign), energy use increases, and as energy use increases, quality of the environment decreases (the negative sign). The digraph can be adapted to depict decision-making.

Axelrod (1976, 6) uses cognitive maps to depict beliefs that went into decision-making cases. His standards for the derivation of a cognitive map are: the methods should be unobtrusive; the map should be driven entirely from data, not a priori research assumptions; and the map should be complete, detailed and valid. In reading source materials such as accounts of decision-making, the cognitive map maker should focus on statements of cause and effect (Wrightson 1976, 292). The approach described below meets these standards.

Gauging Ideological Positions

Many empirical studies of the public policy impact of ideology use as measures of ideology ratings of members of Congress provided by interest groups most notably Americans for Democratic Action (ADA). The ADA index is sometimes appropriate for roll call analysis, but the reduction inherent in summarizing one year's votes as a single number misses important strands of ideology and ideological change, and these indexes represent only matters brought to a vote (Jackson and Kingdon 1992; Burden, Caldeira, and Groseclose 2000).

We suggest newspaper and journal of opinion editorials as a way to measure ideology. They include all policy areas on or near the public agenda and a wide range of issues. The eccentricities of individual authors are constrained by the institutional nature of publishing. Temporary foibles can be restricted further by using more than one publication to gauge a particular ideology (Lasswell, Lerner and Pool 1952, 17). We conceive of liberals as the national political community whose thinking can be gauged by the editorials of the *New York Times* and *Washington Post*. For conservatives we reference the editorials of *National Review* magazine and the *Wall Street Journal*. We assume that the editors of these publications usually will not reside on the leading edge of ideological development. Those on the leading edge will tend to be ideological theorists (who pay relatively little attention to public policy) and policy specialists (who are sometimes difficult to pinpoint ideologically). We randomly sampled 1,377 days of the newspapers and 326 issues for the biweekly *National Review* for the years 1961-1998 for a total of 13,827 editorials. Among the ways we tested the ideological bona fides of these four publications was by comparing one element of their editorial policy (support for the president's policies) to Mark A. Zupan's (1992) translation of the ADA ratings of members of Congress into synthetic ADA support ratings for the presidents from Harry Truman through George Bush and using Zupan's methodology extending his synthetic ADA ratings through 1999. (For a detailed description see Grafton and Permaloff, forthcoming.) The variation explained between the synthetic ADA scores and the publications' presidential support scores are: *New York Times* .56; *Washington Post* .42; the *Wall Street Journal* .77; and *National Review* .63 (the last two are negative relationships). All are statistically significant beyond .001. Time series plots produce similar results.

Editorials prior to 1961 were not included in the sample due to continuity problems with the conservative publications. *National Review* was founded in 1955, and prior to the 1960s *Wall Street Journal* coverage focused mostly on economic news. When coverage of a policy area must predate 1961 because of its long history, we use a combination of secondary sources, editorials, and news stories. Our coverage rarely extends farther back than the New Deal because that period marks the beginning of contemporary politics.

Our coding scheme for editorials categorizes them into such major policy areas as: economics; civil rights; the environment, energy, and transportation; and labor relations (Grafton and Permaloff 2001). Some of these major areas, such as economics and civil rights, were subdivided into more specialized areas and others were not. While the labels are ours, the publications concentrated on these topics or their sub topics as isolated wholes. Editorials were also coded with reference to ideological values which are discussed later.

The Case of Incomes Policies

In another study we developed hypotheses regarding ideological change with regard to public policy for business and economics during the period 1961-1998 (Grafton and Permaloff 2001). Ideological change or lack thereof was largely explained using a modified theory of market failure that distinguished among policy areas that exhibited efficient and responsive operation of the market, temporary market dislocations, partial market breakdown, or complete market breakdown. In essence we found that for both liberals and conservatives most core values did not change over time, but other values changed in specific ways.

One element of public policy for business and economics from 1961-1998 concerned so-called incomes policies in the Kennedy, Johnson, and Nixon administrations. Incomes policies are tools used by government to control inflation including persuasion, voluntary guidelines, jawboning, and mandatory wage and price controls. The formulation of public policy in this area is represented in digraph form in Figure 1. One element of our thesis in our earlier publication was that temporary market dislocations such as inflation in the 1960s and 70s produced liberal proposals for increased federal influence and control over the economy that were opposed by conservatives. Another part of our thesis was that liberal policies developed under temporary market dislocations tend to fail (as did income policies in the Kennedy, Johnson, and Nixon administrations) and were abandoned by liberals. This and the other parts of our market failure thesis can be characterized using the digraph framework.

The digraph begins with the social system in equilibrium (see Parsons 1951, 491; Merton 1968; Truman 1960). It assumes stability until social, economic or technical (SET) change occurs (Grafton 1975, 1991). The SET change depicted is inflation of unknown origins in the Kennedy administration and later inflation that probably resulted from Johnson administration attempts to fund the Vietnam War and new domestic programs plus expansionist monetary policies (Saulnier 1968). SET change causes the mobilization of activist interest groups (AIGs) which most often, we hypothesize, are of the left. Economists were the first AIG to measure the inflation and identify it as a threat, and they played a large part in formulating incomes policies. Herbert Stein (1988, 143) characterizes incomes policies as "part of the standard doctrine of liberal intellectuals during the Kennedy-Johnson years . . . ." In this case the most influential AIG members were advisors to Presidents Kennedy and Johnson who advocated the full range of incomes policies short of mandatory controls (Cochrane 1975).

Berger and Luckmann (1966, 79) are consistent with how we regard the role of AIGs, seeing "role specialization to the point where role specific knowledge [AIGs] becomes altogether esoteric as against the common stock of knowledge", e.g., generalist-opinion leaders or editorial writers. Similarly, Rochon (1998, 8) finds that: "The creation of new

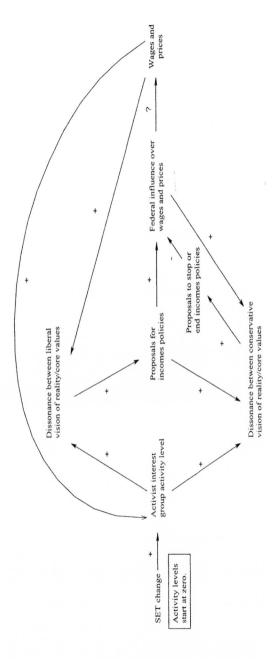

Figure 1. Incomes Policies Signed Digraph

The period from Kennedy to Nixon represents several cycles through the diagram. Another cycle repeated after the Arab oil boycott. Wage and price increases generated liberal proposals for incomes policies enacted over conservative opposition. No rigorous economic theory supported these policies. Wages and prices did not respond to incomes policies (except perhaps that Nixon wage and price controls delayed increases) turning liberals against incomes policies. Conservative proposals to end controls were essentially unopposed.

values begins with the generation of new ideas or perspectives among small groups of critical thinkers. . . ."

In Figure 1 "Activist interest group activity level"--in this case economists--results in dissonance between the liberal vision of reality and liberal core values. Many psychologists and sociologists conceive of ideology as a core of rarely changing values and one or more outer layers of more flexible attitudes, opinions, and policies (Young 1977, 7; Rokeach 1960, 39-51.) Talcott Parsons (1951, 349, 351) addresses another dimension of value structure by distinguishing between an ideology's evaluative and cognitive aspects. In Western ideologies there is a strain toward internal consistency between them (see also van Dijk 1998, 315). The core values in our model rarely change and they are almost purely evaluative. The vision of reality is changeable, depends heavily on new information and is almost purely cognitive.

The most vivid example of incomes policy in the Kennedy administration was the president's sharply worded criticism in 1962 of a price increase by U.S. Steel Corporation. The Kennedy action was strongly supported by the *Times* (Storm 1962). In Figure 1 proposals for increased federal influence over wages and prices produce increased dissonance between the conservative vision of reality and core values. This produces conservative counterattacks (Guideposts 1964; Up, Steel! 1963).

Figure 1 connects federal influence over wages and prices to wages and prices with an arrow marked by a question mark signifying a doubtful relationship between the two. Johnson administration attempts to influence wages and prices with voluntary guidelines and negotiation (another run around the digraph) resulted in criticism, not praise, from the *Times* (Storm 1962; Whose Job 1966) because, according to the newspaper, the Johnson administration was implementing them badly. Even worse, the *Times* (Demise 1966; Whose Job 1966) argued that few economists believed that voluntary wage and price controls and negotiation could work in the face of an inflationary fiscal policy. The *Times* (Tax Debate 1966) soon advocated a tax increase to control inflation and once again, conservatives were opposed (Too Much 1967).

President Nixon was against incomes policies including mandatory wage and price controls (De Marchi 1975, 295, 299). Initially, his appointees shared this view. By mid 1969 the *Post* (Banker 1969), beginning yet another run around the digraph, suggested the possibility that unspecified "government controls" might be necessary to curb the continuing inflation.

Figure 1 summarizes much of what occurred in the Kennedy and Johnson years, but it captures only part of the 1969-1971 period. Liberal advocacy of mandatory wage and price controls was unenthusiastic (Incomes 1971; Applying 1969; Yes 1970). However, Nixon administration economist Arthur Burns, a moderate, became convinced that the market had partially broken down; he became probably the most influential advocate of wage and price controls in the United States (De Marchi 1975, 310-311). The authors' modified theory of market failure sees the perception of partial market breakdown as a common reason for liberal advocacy of increased government involvement in the market. Ultimately, liberals became the strongest (but always unenthusiastic) advocates of mandatory wage and price controls (fitting our original theory and the digraph image). It is rare for an ideological moderate to spearhead such an effort. By 1971 liberals were pushing for mandatory wage and price controls (Incomes 1971). The continued unenthusiastic tone of most liberal advocacy of this policy is symbolized by the title of one *Post* editorial: "Yes, the Freeze is Unfair"(1971).

Another aspect of the 1969-1971 period not captured in the digraph is what is almost universally described as political opportunism by the Democrats in Congress and President Nixon. In August 1970 Congress passed the Economic Stabilization Act giving the president authority to control wages and prices. This move is often explained as the Democrats' way to avoid responsibility for inflation. They had given the president the tools with which to stop inflation. If he chose not to use the authority, he could be blamed. If he used it and failed to stop inflation, he could be blamed. And, if he used it and certain workers or businesses were hurt, he could be blamed. In August 1971 Nixon announced a comprehensive wage and price freeze. His turnabout is explained by most observers as arising from his fear of reelection defeat, not from ideological considerations.

As the digraph suggests, conservatives opposed liberal proposals for controls and highlighted flaws in their operation (Cheers 1969; Success 1972; Remembering 1971) while always weak liberal support for controls waned (Ceiling 1973; Small Business 1972; On Prices 1972). It became clear to nearly everyone that federal wage and price controls were not in fact reducing the rate of wage and price increases or at best that controls were suppressing inflationary forces that would be explosively released upon the end of controls (Rockoff 1984, 210-214; Jones 1975, 7-9; Kosters 1975; Weber 1975, 380; Pohlman 1975, 16-20). Conservative pressure to end controls was essentially unopposed.

Our modified theory of market failure distinguishes among successful market operation, market misbehavior, and partial or complete market breakdown. Complete market breakdown means that the market cannot function theoretically and in fact does not function. No convincing evidence exists that inflation in the waning months of the Johnson administration into the Nixon administration resulted from market breakdown. Indeed, the market response to the inflationary public policy of the Johnson administration was inflation. Market misbehavior is defined as economic movements that produce widespread unhappiness (e.g., inflation and stock market downturns). Part of our theory holds that liberals tend to retract policies proposed or enacted as a response to market misbehavior. Our modified theory of market failure helps explain the movement through phases of the digraph's operation.

One problem with characterizing this series of events with an image on a printed page is that the strength of the relationships symbolized by the arrows varied markedly over time. For example, initial liberal advocacy of wage and price controls weakened and left the field clear for effective conservative opposition. Nevertheless, our modified market failure hypotheses combined with the digraph characterize this 15 years of public policy fully but parsimoniously. The digraph also helps in the development of hypotheses. This topic will be discussed later.

Policy Other than Business and Economics

The use of the digraph allows us to examine the dynamics of change, but by itself it cannot explain what core values were being violated by the policies examined. While our modified theory of market failure provides a fairly complete explanation of the relationship between ideology and public policy regarding business and economics, this theory says nothing about other areas of domestic public policy.

Janda, Berry, and Goldman (JBG) (1992, 175) have developed a succinct model that encompasses much of how historians and theorists (e.g., Young 1996; Van Dyke 1995; Rossiter 1995; Gray 1995; Gold 1992; Heywood 1992; Reichley 1981; Manning 1976; Levin-Waldman 1996; Berlin 1969; Hayek 1960; Green 1986; Hobhouse 1911) have characterized liberal and conservative differences. According to JBG, a liberal tends to favor equality over freedom and freedom over order. A conservative tends to favor freedom over equality and order over freedom. JBG omit the critical element of the economic system, and they ignore divisions in both liberal and conservative camps. Nevertheless, their work may serve as the beginning of a model if we consider attitudes toward freedom, equality, and order as core values or building blocks for ideological prescriptions for domestic public policy not involving business and economics.

To reaffirm the JBG model's utility we conducted a paragraph by paragraph content analysis of characterizations of liberalism and conservatism in the last ten years of refereed social science journals in the online collection EBSCO Host (Academic Search Elite). Our focus was on how the articles characterized liberalism and conservatism in terms of equality, freedom, and order (Permaloff and Grafton forthcoming). Simplifying our findings substantially, the JBG model was largely confirmed.

Although it may be too simplified, the JBG model can explain the operation of digraphs that focus on domestic public policy not involving business or economics. To illustrate this point we derived a digraph of liberal and conservative public policy on abortion (Figure 2). This digraph begins in the 1930s when abortion had been illegal in most states for a half century and some doctors observed that dangerous back alley abortions were occurring and that the women suffering these procedures were poor. Due to Depression era unemployment and poverty, women increasingly asked doctors for help with unwanted pregnancies.

In 1933 two politically radical physicians published books that essentially called for the legalization of abortion. A more moderate advocacy of abortion legalization by the physician Frederick J. Taussig was published in 1936. Taussig proposed a law that would permit abortions for the retarded, victims of rape, underage girls, and the poor (Reagan 1997). World War II interrupted the abortion legalization activities of AIGs. In 1955 Planned Parenthood sponsored a national conference which issued a statement calling for a liberalization of abortion laws (Reagan 1997, 219-220). A proposal by the American Law Institute (ALI) for a model law followed the outlines of the Planned Parenthood statement. These actions predated by years positions taken by the *Times*.

The work of AIGs preceded (and probably led to) changes in the editorial direction of the *Times*. *Times* news coverage in the period 1950-1960 treated abortion the same as any crime such as robbery. In 1959 the *Times* printed its first stories (not editorials) that appeared to be inclined positively toward abortion (e.g., Legal Abortions 1959). The first post WWII editorials regarding abortion were published in 1965; they favored the ALI model (e.g., Dilemma 1965). By 1969 the *Times* advocated that state abortion laws be struck down by federal courts. This amounted to a position favoring outright legalization (Changing 1969), a position depicted in Figure 2 as "Federal power over states."

An important question is whether American liberalism's core beliefs changed from (say) the end of World War II to the year of the first *Times* pro abortion editorial nearly two decades later. Overall, liberalism's core values did not appear to change appreciably in this time period (Hamby

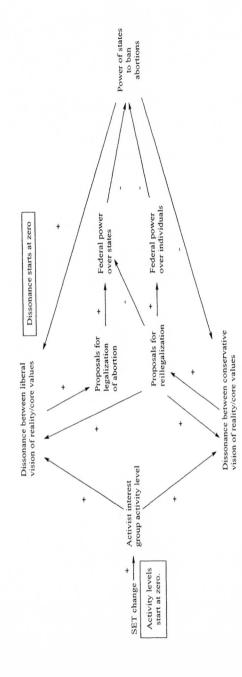

Figure 2. Abortion Signed Digraph

Proposals for legalization or reillegalization might be represented by an index measuring distance from the status quo. Thus, increased liberal dissonance will produce an increase in the proposals for legalization index and increased conservative dissonance will produce an increase in the proposals for reillegalization index. A positive sign means that an increase in a variable causes an increase in the connected variable. A negative sign means that an increase in a variable causes a decrease in the connected variable. For example, an increase in the power of states to ban abortions causes an increase in liberal dissonance and a reduction in conservative dissonance.

1973; Van Dyke 1995). *Times* and *Post* editorials concerning New Deal and Fair Deal issues suggested no significant value change during this time. Yet, the *Times* went from ignoring abortion editorially and presenting it in news accounts as the equivalent of robbery to endorsing abortion legalization. The liberal position had done a full turnaround. AIGs were demonstrating that so-called back alley abortions were killing thousands of women a year (a violation of liberal core values concerning order) and that disproportionate numbers of those women were poor (a violation of liberal core values concerning equality). What changed were not the liberal core values engaged by the issue of abortion, but how the *Times* editors viewed the world. That new view clashed with their unchanged core values. This dissonance energized the *Times*' call for legislative and constitutional changes.

For some conservatives the relatively sudden legalization of abortions produced a new vision of reality and a dissonance between that vision and the conservative value of order. There was a split between *National Review* and the *Journal* immediately after *Roe v. Wade*. While *National Review* was opposed to legalized abortion and remains so, the *Journal* was supportive (Abortion 1973). This conflict between two elements of conservatism may partly explain the relatively ineffective conservative opposition to abortion during the period under study. Just as the dissonance between the liberal vision of reality and liberal core values generated proposals for reform, the comparable dissonance for *National Review* conservatives produced a counterattack. Their conservative activism was not the result of a change in conservative core values.

Our abortion digraph depicts a state of tension between liberals and some conservatives that cannot be stabilized without the reduction in dissonance in one or both sides. Either core value changes must occur or one or both sides must change their visions of reality.

A General Model

The two cases suggest a general model. Social, economic, or technological (SET) change is transformed by activist interest groups (AIGs) into a new vision of reality that is incompatible with ideological core values. Why do newspaper editors (our central ideological indicator) listen to AIGs? The answer may be that ideologues require some level of consistency between core values and what they view as reality, and sometimes AIGs are able to make a compelling case. Also, editors may find it in their career interests to promote change.

Once liberal dissonance starts movement (assuming that liberals initiate change) in the form of proposals for policy change that are picked up by the president or members of Congress, these proposals can directly affect the conservative vision of reality. Liberal proposals may be considered threatening to conservative core values although not all liberal proposals are viewed negatively by conservatives. The resulting dissonance between conservative core values and their new vision of reality will trigger opposition to liberal proposals. At the same time, AIGs that are concerned with other interests more than ideology will enter the debate and join in support or opposition to the liberal proposals. Whenever change is initiated by conservatives, the digraph movement is a mirror image of the above description.

There are many instances when the dissonance process stops before a policy is enacted. AIGs may not necessarily make a compelling case that generates dissonance between an ideological vision and core values. Just as dissonance may produce protest or outrage that falls short of a proposal for a policy, a proposal may not be enacted into law or an executive branch policy. In the case of incomes policies, failure to control inflation and lack of liberal enthusiasm for such policies combined with ideological opposition from conservatives to end incomes policies. In the case of abortion, anti-abortion forces largely failed due to ideological opposition from liberals and disunity among conservatives.

Operationalizing Our Approach: Some Hypotheses

Digraph construction facilitates the formulation and testing of hypotheses regarding ideological change and the impact of ideology on public policy. The following hypotheses (partially collected from earlier portions of this discussion) seem worthy of investigation:

> When a new policy proposal appears in an editorial (representing main stream liberalism or conservatism), the policy will have been initiated by an AIG located to the left of liberals or to the right of conservatives.
> Liberal dissatisfaction (dissonance) with a given situation will be based on its violation of liberal core values, not core value change; this will result in proposals for policy change.
> Liberal proposals to change the unsatisfactory situation will take the form of policies designed to change state or federal power over individuals, business and/or the states.
> Liberal reform proposals will change the conservative vision of reality, producing dissonance between that conserva-

tive vision and conservative core values.
Conservative dissonance will generate proposals to resist liberal proposals.

Liberal or conservative policy proposals/reforms and resulting liberal-conservative debate will precede federal government policy changes such as legislation.

Liberal or conservative policy proposals are sometimes not enacted for such reasons as ideological opposition or technical infeasibility.

Enacted policy changes that address liberal dissonance will intensify conservative dissonance and result in conservative proposals to reverse the changes in policy.

Once the process of ideological change begins, the system will cycle in an unstable manner (usually for years) until changes occur in one or both visions of reality.

Disunity among either liberals or conservatives will produce a relatively stable policy favoring the more unified side.

The combination of signed digraphs, editorials in newspapers and journals of opinion, and secondary sources related to the topics discussed in the editorials provides a foundation for the behavioral study of ideology and public policy formulation. This analytical framework and these data can generate testable hypotheses. These in turn can be used together with theories of agenda setting and policy formulation to explain the role of ideology and ideological change in policy development and problem redefinition.

References

Abortion and privacy. 1973, January 26. *Wall Street Journal*, editorial page.

Alba, A. 2000. The tax policy regime in American politics, 1939-1945. *Congress and the Presidency* 27:59-80.

Applying corporate brakes. 1969, July 12. *Washington Post*, editorial page.

Apter, D. ed. 1964. *Ideology and discontent*. New York: Free Press.

Axelrod, R. 1976. *Structure of decision*. Princeton, NJ: Princeton University Press.

Banker in the briar patch. 1969, July 6. *Washington Post*, editorial page.

Berger, P. L. and T. Luckmann. 1966. *The social construction of reality*. New York: Doubleday.

Bergeron, S. 2001. Political economy discourses of globalization and society. *Journal of Women in Culture and Society* 26:983-1006.

Berlin, I. 1969. *Four essays on liberty*. Oxford: Oxford University Press.

Brinkley, A. 1998. *Liberalism and its discontents*. Cambridge, MA: Harvard University Press.

Burden, B. C., G. A. Caldeira, and T. Groseclose. 2000. Measuring the ideologies of U.S. Senators: The song remains the same. *Legislative Studies Quarterly* 25:237-258.

Ceiling unlimited. 1973, September 22. *New York Times*, editorial page.

Changing the abortion law. 1969, November 10. *New York Times*, editorial page.

Cheers. 1969, December 5. *Wall Street Journal*, editorial page.

Cochrane, J. L. 1975. The Johnson administration: Moral suasion goes to war. In *Exhortation and controls*, ed. C. D. Goodwin, 193-293. Washington, DC: Brookings.

Coles, R. L. 2002. Manifest destiny adapted for 1990s' war discourse: Mission and destiny intertwined. *Sociology of Religion* 63:403-426.

Darendorf, R. 1959. *Class and class conflict in industrial society*. Stanford, CA: Stanford University Press.

Dearing, J. W. and E. M. Rogers. 1996. *Agenda-setting*. Thousand Oaks, CA: Sage.

De Marchi, N. 1975. The first Nixon administration: Prelude to controls. In *Exhortation and controls*, ed. C. D. Goodwin, 295-352. Washington, DC: Brookings.

Demise of the guideposts. 1966, August 5. *New York Times*, editorial page.

Devigne, R. 1994. *Recasting conservatism*. New Haven, CT: Yale University Press.

Dilemma is seen in abortion law. 1965, July 28. *New York Times*, editorial page.

Dorrien, G. 1993. *The neoconservative mind*. Philadelphia, PA: Temple University Press.

Farganis, S. 1993. Feminism and postmodernism. In *Postmodernism and social inquiry*, ed. A. Fontana and D. Dickins, 101-126. New York: Guilford Press.

Flanigan, W. H. and N. H. Zingale. 2002. *Political behavior of the American electorate*. 10th ed. Washington, DC: CQ Press.

Garry, P. M. 1992. *Liberalism and American identity*. Kent, OH: Kent State University Press.

Gleiber, D. W. and S. A. Shull. 1992. Presidential influence in the policy making process. *Western Political Quarterly* 45:441-468.

Gold, H. J. 1992. *Hollow mandates*. Boulder, CO: Westview.

Grafton, C. 1975. The creation of federal agencies. *Administration and Society* 7:328-365.

_____. 1991. Public policy for dangerous inventions in Great Britain and the United States. *Policy Sciences* 24:19-39.

Grafton, C. and A. Permaloff. 2001. Public policy for business and the economy: Ideological dissensus, change, and consensus. *Policy Sciences* 34:403-434.

_____. forthcoming. Supplementing Zupan's measurements of the ideological preferences of U.S. presidents. *Public Choice*.

Gray, J. 1995. *Liberalism*. Minneapolis: University of Minnesota Press.

Green, T. H. 1986. Lectures on the principles of political obligation and other writings. P. Harris and J. Morrow, eds. Cambridge: Cambridge University Press.

Guideposts in a storm. 1964, March 3. *Wall Street Journal*, editorial page.

Hamby, A. L. 1973. *Beyond the New Deal: Harry S. Truman and American liberalism*. New York: Columbia University Press.

Hayek, F. A. 1960. *The constitution of liberty*. Chicago: University of Chicago Press.

Heywood, A. 1992. *Political ideologies: An introduction*. New York: St. Martin's.

Hobhouse, L. T. 1911. *Liberalism*. London: Oxford University Press.

Hoover, K. 1987. *Ideology and political life*. Monterrey, CA: Brooks/ Cole.

Incomes policy needed. 1971, February 28. *New York Times*, editorial page.

Iyengar, S. and W. J. McGuire, eds. 1993. *Explorations in political psychology*. Durham, NC: Duke University Press.

Jackson, J. E. and J. W. Kingdon. 1992. Ideology, interest group scores, and legislative votes. *American Journal of Political Science* 25:805-823.

Jacoby, W. 2000. Issue framing and public opinion on government spending. *American Journal of Political Science* 44:750-767.

Janda, K., J. M. Berry, and J. Goldman. 1992. *The challenge of democracy*. Boston: Houghton Mifflin.

Johnston, L. 1996. *Ideologies*. Peterborough, ON, Canada: Broadview.

Jones, S. L. 1975. The lessons of wage and price controls. In *Wage and price controls*, ed. J. Kraft and B. Roberts, 1-10. New York: Praeger.

Kalt, J. and M. A. Zupan. 1984. Capture and ideology in the economic theory of politics. *American Economic Review* 74:279-300.

Kingdon, J. W. 1984. *Agendas, alternatives, and public policies*. Boston:

Little, Brown.

Kosters, M. H. 1975. *Controls and inflation.* Washington, DC: American Enterprise Institute.

Lasswell, H., D. Lerner, and I. D. Pool. 1952. *The comparative study of symbols.* Stanford, CA: Stanford University Press.

Legal abortions proposed in code. 1959, May 22. *New York Times,* editorial page.

Levin-Waldman, O. M. 1996. *Reconceiving liberalism: Dilemmas of contemporary liberal public policy.* Pittsburgh, PA: University of Pittsburgh Press.

Manning, D. J. 1976. *Liberalism.* New York: St. Martin's.

Merton, R. K. 1968. Manifest and latent functions. In *Social theory and social structure,* ed. R. K. Merton. New York: Free Press.

Nossiff, R. 1998. Discourse, party, and policy: The case of abortion, 1965-1972. *Policy Studies Journal* 26:244-256 .

On prices: An unpleasant surprise. 1972, June 9. *Washington Post,* editorial page.

Ornstein, M. and H. M. Stevenson. 1999. *Politics and ideology in Canada.* Montreal: McGill-Queen's University Press.

Parsons, T. 1951. *The social system.* New York: Free Press.

Permaloff, A. and C. Grafton. forthcoming. The behavioral study of political ideology and public policy: Testing the Janda, Berry, and Goldman model. *Journal of Political Ideologies.*

Pohlman, J. E. 1975. *Price controls: Lessons from recent experience.* In *Wage and price controls,* ed. J. Kraft and B. Roberts, 11-21. New York: Praeger.

Rawls, J. 1971. *A theory of justice.* Cambridge, MA: Belknap Press.

Reagan, L. J. 1997. *When abortion was a crime.* Berkeley: University of California Press.

Reichley, A. J. 1981. *Conservatives in an age of change.* Washington, DC: Brookings.

Remembering the basics. 1971, August 18. *Wall Street Journal,* editorial page.

Richardson, L. E. and M. E. Munger. 1990. Shirking, representation, and congressional behavior: Voting on the 1983 amendments to the Social Security Act. *Public Choice* 67:11-33.

Roberts, F. S. 1976. Strategy for the energy crisis: The case of commuter transportation policy. In *Structure of decision,* ed. R. Axelrod, 142-179. Princeton, NJ: Princeton University Press.

Rochefort, D. A. and R. W. Cobb. 1994. *The politics of problem definition.* Lawrence: University of Kansas Press.

Rochon, T. R. 1998. *Culture moves.* Princeton, NJ: Princeton University Press.

Rockoff, H. 1984. *Drastic measures: A history of wage and price controls in the United States.* Cambridge: Cambridge University Press.

Rokeach, M. 1960. *The open and closed mind.* New York: Basic Books.

Rossiter, C. 1995. *Conservatism in America.* New York: Knopf.

Sabatier, P. A. 1991. Toward better theories of the policy process. *PS: Political Science & Politics* 24:147-156.

Saulnier, R. J. 1968. An appraisal of federal fiscal policies: 1961-1967. *Annals of the American Academy of Political and Social Science* 379:63-71.

Small business, big business, and controls. 1972, May 6. *Washington Post*, editorial page.

Snow, D. A., E. B. Rochford Jr., S. K. Worden, and R. D. Benford. 1986. Frame alignment processes, micromobilization, and movement participation. *American Sociological Review* 51:464-481.

Stein, H. 1988. *Presidential economics.* Washington, DC: American Enterprise Institute.

Storm over steel. 1962, April 15. *New York Times*, editorial page.

Success for controls. 1972, August 3. *Wall Street Journal*, editorial page.

Tax debate. 1966, December 19. *New York Times*, editorial page.

Thompson, K. W. 1981. *The president and the public philosophy.* Baton Rouge: Louisiana State University Press.

Too much tax consensus. 1967, August 29. *Wall Street Journal*, editorial page.

Up, steel! 1963, June 7. *National Review*, editorial page.

Truman, D. B. 1960. *The governmental process.* New York: Knopf.

van Dijk, T. A. 1998. *Ideology: A multidisciplinary approach.* London: Sage.

Van Dyke, V. 1995. *Ideology and political choice.* Chatham, NJ: Chatham House.

Weber, A. R. 1975. The continuing courtship: Wage-price policy through five administrations. In *Exhortation and controls*, ed. C. D. Goodwin, 353-384. Washington, DC: Brookings.

Whose job is restraint? 1966, August 26. *New York Times*, editorial page.

Wrightson, M. T. 1976. The documentary coding method. In *Structure of decision*, ed. R. Axelrod, 291-332. Princeton, NJ: Princeton University Press.

Yes, the freeze is unfair. 1971, July 18. *Washington Post*, editorial page.

Young, J. P. 1996. *Reconsidering American liberalism.* Boulder, CO:

Westview.

Young, K. 1977. Values in the policy process. *Policy and Politics* 5:1-22.

Zupan, M. A. 1992. Measuring the ideological preferences of U.S. presidents: A proposed (extremely simple) method. *Public Choice* 73:351-361.

Chapter 9

Measuring the Ideological Preferences of U.S. Presidents: A Proposed (Extremely Simple) Method*

Mark A. Zupan

Introduction

In the political economy literature, a leading explanation for bureau-cratic/regulatory policy outcomes posits congressional dominance (see, for example, Weingast 1984; Weingast and Moran 1983). While acknowledging the potential for slack between congressional-principals and bureaucrat-agents, the congressional dominance theory largely assumes that through instruments such as budget authorization and oversight, hearings, and input over regulatory appointments, congressmen and ultimately congressmen's constituents are able to fully control the actions of bureaucrats.[1] According to the congressional dominance theory, therefore, the seemingly independent behavior of regulators such as Alfred Kahn of the Civil Aeronautics Board and Mark Fowler of the Federal Communications Commission in reality reflects the desires of overseeing legislators and the constituents who elect the legislators.

Initially, the congressional dominance theory was applied to regula-

*Reprinted with permission from *Public Choice* 73 (1992):351-361.

tory agencies such as the Federal Trade and Securities and Exchange Commissions. In the case of the Federal Trade Commission, for example, because a causal link was found in a time series analysis between the caseload mix chosen by commissioners and ratings measuring the liberalness/conservatism of supervising congressional representatives, the congressional dominance theory was taken to be confirmed and the hypothesis/"myth" of a runaway bureaucracy was rejected (Weingast and Moran 1983).[2]

More recently, the congressional dominance theory has been applied to explain the behavior of the Federal Reserve Board (Grier 1990) and even the Supreme Court (Spiller and Gely 1990). In analyzing the determinants of post World War II U.S. Supreme Court labor relations decisions, for instance, Spiller and Gely argue that the Supreme Court, in order to avoid having its decisions statutorily-reversed by Congress, must position itself on the contract curve between the ideal policy points (in terms of a pro-labor/anti-labor, liberal/conservative spectrum) desired by the Senate and House. Any leeway for the Supreme Court to exercise its own, independent policy preferences is confined, consequently, to the ideological distance between the ideal policy points desired by the two chambers of Congress.

The theory of congressional dominance, of course, runs counter to the hypothesis of bureaucratic independence advanced by some earlier researchers (see, for example, Borcherding 1977; Niskanen 1971; Tullock 1965). According to the bureaucratic independence hypothesis, positive policing costs ensure that bureaucratic-agents are only imperfectly monitored by their principals and that bureaucrats thus have some ability to affect regulatory outcomes.

The theory of congressional dominance also does not take into account the influence a president may have on bureaucratic policy outcomes. This may not be appropriate as Moe (1985, 1101) notes in detailing the impressive weapons the president has at his disposal with respect to (in many ways typical) agencies such as the National Labor Relations Board (NLRB):

> Most obviously, he [the president] makes appointments to the Board and can thereby choose individuals whose policy views are consistent with his own; although he cannot remove them from office (they serve fixed, staggered terms of five years), careful selection minimizes the importance of this restriction, as does the fact that many members leave before their terms expire. As part of the appointment power, he chooses his own chair, who in turn plays a central role in controlling internal agency resources and hiring "appropriate" staff at all levels of

the organization. In addition to appointments, the president can rely upon the OMB [Office of Management and Budget] in monitoring the NLRB's performance, shaping its budgets, and screening and modifying its legislative proposals, and he can also rely upon an important intangible resource, presidential leadership: precisely because he occupies the office of the president, many executive employees throughout the government believe he has a legitimate role to play in directing administrative behavior, and, on many issues, has a right to expect their compliance.

Relative to explanations of bureaucratic behavior that leave room for presidential influence and/or the independent preferences of bureaucrats themselves, however, the theory of congressional dominance has one important advantage. Specifically, whereas measures of the ideological preferences of U.S. presidents and bureaucrats are not readily available, ideological ratings for congressional representatives abound. On an annual basis, numerous ideological watchdog groups such as the Americans for Democratic Action (ADA), American Conservative Union (ACU), League of Conservation Voters (LCV), National Taxpayers Union (NTU), and the AFL-CIO's Committee on Political Education (COPE) rate the extent (typically on a 0-100 scale) to which members of the House and Senate cast roll call votes in support of the respective groups' self-defined notions of the good society. Since measures of congressional ideological preferences are so readily available, it is comparatively easy for researchers to obtain empirical support for the congressional dominance theory relative to other, broader models of regulatory outcomes. The question remains, however, whether the empirical support that has been offered recently for congressional dominance (for example, Grier 1990; Spiller and Gely 1990; Weingast 1984; Weingast and Moran 1983) in reality reflects data availability dominance.

As a first step toward testing the explanatory power of the congressional dominance theory relative to other, broader theories of regulatory policymaking, this paper outlines a simple method for measuring the ideological preferences of U.S. presidents. Whereas most ideological watchdog groups such as the ADA, NTU, LCV, COPE, and ACU provide direct ratings of only members of Congress, the direct ratings turn out to provide an indirect means of contemporaneously rating U.S. presidents. The section which follows outlines and employs the proposed methodology to develop a presidential ADA rating. Although the same methodology could also be employed to calculate a presidential NTU, ACU, LCV, and/or COPE rating, the ADA is focused on since previous studies that have provided empirical support in favor of congressional dominance (for example, Grier 1990; Spiller and Gely 1990; Weingast 1984; Weingast and Moran 1983) have all employed ADA ratings to measure the preferences of overseeing legislators.

Developing a Presidential ADA Rating: Data and Methodology

Since 1947, the ADA has published an annual measure of the liberalness/conservatism of members of the House and Senate. For each year, the ADA selects anywhere from 7 to 37 roll-call votes (typically 20 votes in recent years) in each chamber of Congress that it deems to be ideologically-revealing litmus tests. Individual congressional representatives are then positioned on a 0-100 scale based on the percentage of times they vote in favor of the liberal position on the ADA-selected issues.

Paralleling the ADA publication, the *Congressional Quarterly Almanac* (CQ) has provided an annual compilation, since 1945, of all issue-related roll call votes recorded in the House and Senate.[3] In the description of each vote, CQ identifies whether the president took a position on the vote--for the purpose of calculating presidential support scores for individual congressional representatives.[4] The ground rules employed to determine whether the president has taken a position on a vote, as well as the position that the president has taken, are described in CQ (1976, 992):

CQ tries to determine what the president personally, as distinct from other administration officials, does and does not want in the way of legislative action by analyzing his messages to Congress, press conference remarks and other public statements and documents. *Borderline Cases*--By the time an issue reaches a vote, it may differ from the original form on which the President expressed himself. In such cases, CQ analyzes the measure to determine whether, on balance, the features favored by the President outweigh those he opposed or vice versa. Only then is the vote classified. *Some Votes Excluded*--Occasionally, important measures are so extensively amended on the floor that it is impossible to characterize final passage as a victory or defeat for the President. *Procedural Votes*--Votes on motions to recommit, to reconsider or to table often are key tests that govern the legislative outcome. Such votes are necessarily included in the presidential support tabulations. *Appropriations*--Generally, votes on passage of appropriations bills are not included in the tabulation, since it is rarely possible to determine the President's position on the overall revisions Congress almost invariably makes in the sums allowed. Votes on amendments to cut or increase specific funds requested in the President's budget, however, are included. . . . *Changed Positions*--Presidential support is determined by the position of the President at the time of a vote, even though that position may be different from an earlier position, or may have been reversed after the vote was taken.

By matching the ADA-selected issues with the roll call votes on which, according to CQ, the president took a position, it is possible to develop an annual ADA rating for U.S. presidents over the 1947-89 time period. Table 1 lists, by year, the total number (between the House and Senate) of: CQ recorded roll call votes; ADA-selected issues; and ADA-selected issues on which, according to the CQ, the president took a position. Table 2 provides an annual breakdown of the number of pro-ADA and anti-ADA stances taken by each president as well as each president's annual pro-ADA percentage. Table 3 tabulates a cumulative ADA rating for each post-World War II president over their various terms in office.

Observations and Conclusion

Several observations can be made concerning the data presented in the tables. First, as one might expect, not all Democratic or Republican presidents are alike. As shown in Table 3, John Kennedy has a higher cumulative pro-ADA rating than does Lyndon Johnson than does Jimmy Carter. On the Republican side, Dwight Eisenhower comes in at roughly the middle of the ADA liberal/conservative ideological spectrum and considerably to the "left" of both Ronald Reagan and George Bush.

Second, while there appear to be significant differences between the ideological preferences of presidents from the same party, the correlation between a president's annual or cumulative pro-ADA percentage and a dummy variable reflecting the party of the president (Democrats equal unity, Republicans equal zero) is still fairly high. For example, the correlation between the nine post World War II presidents' cumulative pro-ADA percentages (Table 3) and a party dummy variable is 0.93. The correlation between presidents' annual pro-ADA percentages (Table 2) and a party dummy variable is 0.87.[5] Thus, while a dummy variable reflecting the party of a president may not be the most preferred measure of presidents' ideological preferences, such a variable may be a reasonably accurate substitute for the pro-ADA percentages reported in Tables 2 and 3.

Table 1.   Total CQ Recorded Votes, ADA-selected Votes, and ADA-selected
Votes on Which President Took Stance, 1947-1989

Year	CQ Recorded Votes in Congress	ADA-selected Votes	ADA-selected Votes on Which President Took Stance
1947	207	22	22
1948	203	29	17
1949	348	27	17
1950	383	33	21
1951	311	25	10
1952	308	27	20
1953	160	26	14
1954	247	23	16
1955	163	19	9
1956	203	21	9
1957	207	21	17
1958	293	24	15
1959	292	22	12
1960	300	21	14
1961	320	20	16
1962	348	20	17
1963	348	29	24
1964	318	32	21
1965	459	36	21
1966	428	37	24
1967	554	28	18
1968	514	26	19
1969	422	44	17
1970	684	46	22
1971	743	64	20

Table 1. Continued

Year	CQ Recorded Vote Votes in Congress	ADA-selected Votes	ADA-selected Votes on Which President Took Stance
1972	861	36	14
1973	1135	45	18
1974	1081	44	18
1975	1206	37	12
1976	1341	40	10
1977	1341	40	17
1978	1350	40	20
1979	1169	38	18
1980	1135	36	23
1981	836	40	24
1982	924	40	20
1983	904	40	19
1984	683	40	19
1985	820	40	21
1986	842	40	20
1987	931	45	28
1988	944	40	22
1989	691	40	20

Third, as are the ratings of congressional representatives published annually by ideological watchdog groups such as the ADA, the presidential ratings reported in Tables 2 and 3 are sensitive to the issues reaching (or not reaching) a vote on the House/Senate floor. President Bush's low 1989 pro-ADA percentage, for example, may partly reflect the fact that (*Congressional Quarterly Weekly Report* December 30, 1989, 3545): "all the 1989 tests of his [Bush's] clean-air proposal took place in committee." President Johnson's higher pro-ADA percentages in 1964 and 1965 relative to 1966-68 partly reflect the focus of Congress on debate and passage of Johnson's Great Society programs during the early

Table 2. An Annual Presidential ADA Rating, 1947-1989

Year	President	Pro-ADA Stances	Anti-ADA Stance	Pro-ADA Percentage
1947	Truman	21	1	0.95
1948	Truman	16	1	0.94
1949	Truman	17	0	1.00
1950	Truman	21	0	1.00
1951	Truman	10	0	1.00
1952	Truman	20	0	1.00
1953	Eisenhower	7	7	0.50
1954	Eisenhower	6	10	0.38
1955	Eisenhower	6	3	0.67
1956	Eisenhower	6	3	0.67
1957	Eisenhower	11	6	0.65
1958	Eisenhower	8	7	0.53
1959	Eisenhower	3	9	0.25
1960	Eisenhower	5	9	0.36
1961	Kennedy	15	1	0.94
1962	Kennedy	16	1	0.94
1963	Kennedy	22	0	1.00
1963	Johnson	2	0	1.00
1964	Johnson	21	0	1.00
1965	Johnson	20	1	0.95
1966	Johnson	18	6	0.75
1967	Johnson	10	8	0.56
1968	Johnson	17	2	0.89
1969	Nixon	6	11	0.35
1970	Nixon	3	19	0.16
1971	Nixon	2	18	0.10

Table 2. Continued

Year	President	Pro-ADA Stances	Anti-ADA Stance	Pro-ADA Percentage
1972	Nixon	3	11	0.21
1973	Nixon	2	16	0.11
1974	Nixon	4	10	0.29
1974	Ford	0	4	0.00
1975	Ford	2	10	0.17
1976	Ford	0	10	0.00
1977	Carter	13	4	0.76
1978	Carter	15	5	0.75
1979	Carter	13	5	0.72
1980	Carter	17	5	0.77
1981	Reagan	0	24	0.00
1982	Reagan	2	18	0.10
1983	Reagan	1	18	0.05
1984	Reagan	1	18	0.05
1985	Reagan	0	21	0.00
1986	Reagan	1	19	0.05
1987	Reagan	0	28	0.00
1988	Reagan	0	22	0.00
1989	Bush	0	20	0.00

years of his administration.[6]

Finally, the presidential ADA ratings developed in this paper do not appear to evidence a bias toward the middle (i.e., a 0.5 rating) as a function of the percentage of times a president takes a position on the ADA-selected issues.[7] The correlation between a variable reflecting the distance (expressed in absolute value terms) between a president's annual pro-ADA percentage and 0.5 and the percentage of times the president takes a position on the issues selected by the ADA for the same year is 0.06.

Table 3. Cumulative ADA Ratings for Post-World War II U.S. Presidents

President	Total Number of ADA-selected Issues on Which President Took A Position		President's Cumulative Pro-ADA Percentage
	Pro-ADA	Anti-ADA	
Truman	105	2	0.98
Eisenhower	52	54	0.49
Kennedy	55	2	0.96
Johnson	88	17	0.84
Nixon	20	85	0.19
Ford	2	24	0.08
Carter	58	19	0.75
Reagan	5	168	0.03
Bush	0	20	0.00

In conclusion, the methodology and data presented in this paper are intended to be a first step toward testing the explanatory power of the congressional dominance theory relative to other, broader conceptions of bureaucratic/regulatory policy outcomes. After developing measures of the independent ideological preferences of bureaucrats, I plan to examine a specific case of bureaucratic policymaking as a function of the interests of overseeing legislators, the president, relevant interest groups, and bureaucrats themselves.[8] The approach to be taken in analyzing bureaucratic policy outcomes ultimately also may be useful in explaining judicial decisionmaking. For example, on an issue like abortion or civil rights, to what extent do the independent preferences of Supreme Court justices such as Scalia, Brennan, and Warren matter?[9] And to what extent do the positions taken by such justices reflect the interests of overseeing/appointing legislators, presidents, and relevant interest groups?

Appendix

Presidential and average Senate ADA ratings, 1947-1989[a]

Year	President	Presidential Pro-ADA Percentage	Average Senate Pro-ADA Percentage
1947	Truman	0.95	0.44
1948	Truman	0.94	0.49
1949	Truman	1.00	0.45
1950	Truman	1.00	0.46
1951	Truman	1.00	0.43
1952	Truman	1.00	0.49
1953	Eisenhower	0.50	0.43
1954	Eisenhower	0.38	0.43
1955	Eisenhower	0.67	0.37
1956	Eisenhower	0.67	0.47
1957	Eisenhower	0.65	0.51
1958	Eisenhower	0.53	0.47
1959	Eisenhower	0.25	0.47
1960	Eisenhower	0.36	0.51
1961	Kennedy	0.94	0.55
1962	Kennedy	0.94	0.46
1963	Kennedy	1.00	0.54
1963	Johnson	1.00	0.51
1964	Johnson	1.00	0.52
1965	Johnson	0.95	0.51
1966	Johnson	0.75	0.48
1967	Johnson	0.56	0.45
1968	Johnson	0.89	0.43
1969	Nixon	0.35	0.51

Appendix. Continued

Year	President	Presidential Pro-ADA Percentage	Average Senate Pro-ADA Percentage
1970	Nixon	0.16	0.47
1971	Nixon	0.10	0.49
1972	Nixon	0.21	0.45
1973	Nixon	0.11	0.51
1974	Nixon	0.29	0.58
1974	Ford	0.00	0.51
1975	Ford	0.17	0.52
1976	Ford	0.00	0.50
1977	Carter	0.76	0.50
1978	Carter	0.75	0.46
1979	Carter	0.72	0.41
1980	Carter	0.77	0.52
1981	Reagan	0.00	0.41
1982	Reagan	0.10	0.47
1983	Reagan	0.05	0.46
1984	Reagan	0.05	0.43
1985	Reagan	0.00	0.41
1986	Reagan	0.05	0.43
1987	Reagan	0.00	0.54
1988	Reagan	0.00	0.51
1989	Bush	0.00	0.46

[a] Unlike the official ADA ratings, the Senate pro-ADA percentages reported above: do no count abstentions as indicating opposition to the "liberal" position; and account for cases where a senator announces, but does not cast a roll call vote, either in favor of or against the liberal position on an issue.

Notes

1. The congressional dominance theory is also implicit in Stigler's (1971) and Peltzman's (1976) "capture" theory of politics.

2. See Moe (1987) and Muris (1986) for important critiques of the Weingast and Moran (1983) empirical work. Weingast and Moran (1986) is a reply to the Muris (1986) critique.

3. Quorum-check votes, for example, are excluded from the CQA compilations.

4. The CQ has identified whether the president took a position on a vote, by vote, since 1953. Between 1947 and 1952, CQ provided an annual, summary boxscore on how the president fared, in terms of issues supported and opposed, versus Congress. The issues listed in the boxscore can fairly easily be matched with the individual roll call votes listed elsewhere in the almanac for the 1947-52 period.

5. In calculating the annual correlation, President Johnson's 1963 and President Ford's 1974 pro-ADA percentages are included as separate observations (i.e., separate from President Kennedy's 1963 and President Nixon's 1974 pro-ADA records).

6. The extent to which the issues reaching a vote in Congress influence and are influenced by the ideological preferences of the president (at least as the preferences are measured by my proposed methodology) is an important question for future research. The correlation between the Table 2 presidential pro-ADA percentage and the mean (analogously-constructed) pro-ADA percentage for the Senate (see the Appendix) is 0.04.

7. One could argue, for example, that presidents who are less likely to take positions on ADA-selected issues are also less likely to want to be labeled as "extremists" and are thus more likely to position themselves as the middle of the ADA ideological spectrum.

8. In the course of the investigation, I plan to draw on the approach developed in Kalt and Zupan (1984 and 1990) for distinguishing between the independent preferences of legislators and the interests of legislators' constituents in explanations of congressional policy outcomes.

9. By undertaking a content analysis of the editorials in several of the nation's leading newspapers written in response to Supreme Court nominations, Segal and Cover (1989) develop one possible measure of justices' independent ideological values from Earl Warren to Anthony Kennedy (1953-88).

References

ADA Congressional Scorecard/ADA Legislative Newsletter/ADA Today/ ADA World. 1947-1989. Washington, DC: Americans for Democratic Action, Inc., bimonthly/monthly.

Borcherding, T. E. 1977. *Budgets and bureaucrats: The sources of gov-

ernment growth. Durham, NC: Duke University Press.

Congressional Quarterly Almanac. 1945-1989. Washington, DC: Congressional Quarterly, Inc., annual.

Congressional Quarterly Weekly Report. various weeks. Washington, DC: Congressional Quarterly, Inc., weekly.

Grier, K.B. 1990. Congressional influence on U.S. monetary policy: An empirical test. Unpublished paper, Department of Economics, George Mason University.

Kalt, J.P. and M. A. Zupan. 1984. Capture and ideology in the economic theory of politics. *American Economic Review* 74:279-300.

_____. 1990. The apparent ideological behavior of legislators: Testing for principal-agent slack in political institutions. *Journal of Law and Economics* 33:103-131.

Moe, T. M.1985. Control and feedback in economic regulation: The case of the NLRB. *American Political Science Review* 79:1094-1116.

_____. 1987. An assessment of the positive theory of "congressional dominance." *Legislative Studies Quarterly* 12:475-520.

Muris, T. J. 1986. Regulatory policymaking at the Federal Trade Commission: The extent of congressional control. *Journal of Political Economy* 94:884-889.

Niskanen, W. A. 1971. *Bureaucracy and representative government*. Chicago: Aldine-Atherton.

Peltzman, S. 1976. Toward a more general theory of regulation. *Journal of Law and Economics* 19:211-240.

Segal, J. A. and A. D. Cover. 1989. Ideological values and the votes of U.S. Supreme Court justices. *American Political Science Review* 83: 557-565.

Spiller, P. T. and R. Gely. 1990. Congressional control or judicial independence: The determinants of U.S. Supreme Court labor relations decisions 1949/1988. Unpublished manuscript, University of Illinois, Urbana-Champaign.

Stigler, G. J. 1971. The theory of economic regulation. *Bell Journal of Economics and Management Science* 2:3-21.

Tullock, G. 1965. *Politics of bureaucracy*. Washington, DC: Public Affairs Press.

Weingast, B. R. 1984. The congressional bureaucratic system: A principal-agent perspective (with applications to the SEC). *Public Choice* 44:147-191.

Weingast, B. R. and M. J. Moran. 1983. Bureaucratic discretion or congressional control?: Regulatory policymaking by the Federal Trade Commission. *Journal of Political Economy* 91: 765-800.

_____. 1986. Congress and regulatory agency choice: Reply to Muris. *Journal of Political Economy* 94:890-894.

Acknowledgments

Discussions with Linda Cohen, Tom Gilligan, Ken Koford, Pablo Spiller, and Matt Spitzer helped in the development of this paper. Research support has been supplied by the USC School of Business and a Faculy Innovative Research Fund grant.

Chapter 10

Public Policy for Business and the Economy: Ideological Dissensus, Change and Consensus*

Carl Grafton and Anne Permaloff

This study's immediate objectives are to synthesize liberal and conservative policies toward the governance of business and the economy in the years 1961-1998, to determine where liberals and conservatives agreed and where they did not, and to determine whether positions changed over the years studied. A theory is presented that explains why consensus occurs and why dissensus has sometimes been resolved. This period was selected because it spans a time of substantial social, economic, technological, and political change as well as ideological conflict.

We define an ideology as an action oriented model of people and society. Two assumptions serve as foundations for our theory. The first is that ideology sometimes affects public policy as an independent variable. The second assumption is that ideological adherents are capable of learning in the face of a changing world.

The First Assumption: Ideology Affects Policy-Formulation

Among scholars ideology, usually on a liberal-conservative spectrum,

*Reprinted with permission from *Policy Sciences* 34 (2001):403-434.

has been established as a measurable independent variable explaining a wide variety of political decisions (Burden, Caldeira, and Groseclose 2000; Rothenberg and Sanders 2000; Levine, Carmines, and Huckfeldt 1997; Sussman and Daynes 1995; Tatalovich and Schier 1993; Jackson and Kingdon 1992; Dougan and Munger 1989; Stimson 1991, 117-127; Chressanthis 1991; Richardson and Munger 1990; Medoff 1989; Segal, Cameron, and Cover 1992; Jacoby 1991; Bender 1991; Davis and Porter 1989; Nelson and Silverberg 1987; Kalt and Zupan 1984; Schneider 1979). An article by Sam Peltzman (1985) is occasionally cited as supporting something close to a pure economic interpretation of congressional voting, but a careful reading suggests that ideology or at least an unknown variable just the opposite of economic self-interest plays a part. Additional quantitative studies with similar findings could be cited. While Robert Bernstein (1992) does not show that ideology affects public policy, he demonstrates how legislators can get away with ideological deviation from their constituents.   Trying to disentangle ideological voting from bedrock variables such as class, region, and race is no easy matter methodologically, and a widely used indicator of ideological predilection of members of Congress may exaggerate the role of ideology, but overall there seems little doubt that ideology plays an independent part (Jackson and Kingdon 1992; Brunell, et al. 1999; Snyder 1992).

In addition to quantitative-statistical analyses, countless descriptive studies of the political process regard ideology as important (Langston 1992; Reeves 1993, 38-63; Giglio 1991, 59, 97; Milkis 1993, 149-185; Beam, Conlan, and Wrightson 1990).   Studies of public opinion show movement along the liberal-conservative ideological continuum and shifting perceptions of the distance between the voters and such institutions as Congress and the presidency (Flanigan and Zingale 1998). Several studies also show that there is enough ideological thinking among U.S. elites and even voters that policy can be affected (Herrera 1996-97; Frymer 1994).   Virtually any presidential biography or first hand account of presidential decision-making contains convincing examples of the importance of ideology in policy-making (Whitaker 1996).   It is a rare issue of *Congressional Quarterly Weekly Report* that omits at least a reference to decision-makers' places on the conservative-liberal spectrum. This is not to suggest that ideology is the only factor influencing public policy formulation and implementation, but it is clearly an important one (Barber 1988, 7).

Political scientists' first tendency is to explain policy outcomes by bedrock variables which are often seen as affecting legislative or presidential decision-making via interest group pressure or constituent preferences (Wright 1990; Citrin, Green, Muste, and Wong 1997; Stein and Bickers 1994; Alvarez and Saving 1997; Filer, Kenny, and Morton 1993; Bickers and Stein 1996; Ferejohn 1974). Most of the studies cited in the preceding two paragraphs show that bedrock variables are important but that ideology sometimes adds a great deal to explanations of outcomes. Some of these studies speculate about the reasons ideology can sometimes be important, but they do not go far beyond the notion that some individuals enter public life to make a difference based on belief structures that in the United States center on the standard liberal-conservative spectrum. We assume that ideology in some circumstances in some actors can be treated as an independent variable explaining public policy outcomes.

The Second Assumption:
Ideological Adherents Are Capable of Learning

Just because ideological adherents can affect public policy does not mean that ideologies change over time. Indeed, one of the major criticisms of ideology by some political theorists and practitioners is that ideologues hold to a ridged belief system that is unaffected by reality. Napoleon Bonaparte, responding in part to the inventor of the term ideology, maintained that to formulate laws, instead of relying on the "cloudy metaphysics" of ideology, society should derive "laws from knowledge of the human heart and from the lessons of history. . . ." (McLellan 1995, 5) British parliamentarian Edmund Burke stressed the importance of history, experience, and specific circumstances in making judgments about public policy (in Bate 1960, 19). For Burke the rigid formulas offered by ideology were useless and even destructive. Many contemporary thinkers regard ideologies as rigid and unresponsive to changes in the world around them (Shils 1966; Kirk 1993, 4-6).

Ideological change in the face of important events is observable, however. Liberalism underwent significant alteration as it faced first royalist despotism and then the industrial revolution, urban growth, the Great Depression, and post-industrial technological change (Lane 1962, 166). Historians of liberalism and conservatism frequently stress the adaptive nature of and changes in these systems of thought (Hamby 1992; O'Sullivan 1976, 119-153; Muller 1997). This suggests what we treat as an assumption: enough liberal and conservative ideologues are capable of learning to produce changes in these systems of thought. It also points to the possibility of applying learning theory to the study of ideological change.

We picture ideological adherents--liberals and conservatives--capable of learning and modifying policy positions in a changing world but doing so only after some delay. Models of political learning, lesson drawing, social learning, and government learning (the terms differ among authors) come in some variety. Because we do not have sufficient space to consider them in detail, a review of several differences among public policy learning theories by Colin J. Bennett and Michael Howlett (1992) will be used.

One difference among political learning theories concerns who is learning. In our case the answer is simple--liberal and conservative ideologues are (at least sometimes) learning, and they pass lessons learned along to their allies and the world at large with the idea of affecting public policy--changing it or defending the status quo. By liberal and conservative ideologues we mean the community of people who identify themselves as liberals or conservatives and who earn a living by maintaining, updating, and promoting their ideological perspectives or devote substantial personal financial resources to maintaining, updating, and promoting their ideological perspectives (e.g., William F. Buckley, Jr.). They include the editorial writers of liberal and conservative publications, members of many interest groups such as Americans for Democratic Action, most political party activists, and many others. Most members of the U.S. political elite including party leaders, legislators and executive branch officials think of themselves as liberals, conservatives, or some moderate mixture of the two, e.g., conservative fiscally but liberal socially. Ideological changes, which often occur in response to exogenous social, economic, or technological change, become known to members of the political elite who, to the degree that they make public policy ideologically and not according to other considerations (e.g., economic self-interest or race) change their positions.

There are a variety of reasons why learning occurs. For example, Bennett and Howlett (1992, 276) cite Peter A. Hall as "arguing that learning serves the object of better goal attainment by governments." Among ideological adherents better goal attainment might translate into avoiding irrelevance or more positively making a difference in the world. Ideologues who believe that they can do good in the world via the intelligent application of their ideological system must learn the lessons the world teaches as interpreted by the ideology or the community of ideologues. Refusal to learn such lessons must mean less than optimal effectiveness in doing good. Our sense of how the national communities of liberals and conservatives learn and change follows the Bennett and Howlett observation that: "organizational theorists share notions of organizational adaptation and behavior change due to knowledge accumulation and value-change within institutions and their members." (277; also see March and Simon 1958, 178-193; Polsby 1984, 165-166).

In addition to examining who is learning and why, Bennett and Howlett review political learning theories in terms of how learning occurs. The conception that seems to best fit ideological adherents is that developed by Richard Rose. Bennett and Howlett's rendition of Rose is as follows: "in any effort to reduce dissatisfaction with existing policies, policymakers have three alternatives: to turn to their national past; to speculate about the future; or to seek lessons from current experience in other places." (284) All three approaches are common to ideologues.

The phrase "reduce dissatisfaction with existing policies" in the above quotation raises an issue that Bennett and Howlett do not discuss head on, and that is dissatisfaction in terms of what? Again, our concentration on ideologues instead of the government officials studied by most political learning theorists makes our task easier. One overly simple response would be that ideologues are dissatisfied with existing policies by the standards of their ideology. A stark example is liberal and conservative attitudes toward the minimum wage. Liberals, who in some sense can be said to value equality more highly than do conservatives, observe that some employees are paid at levels so low that they cannot support a family. As time passes since the last increase in the minimum wage and as inflation erodes the value of the currency, liberals become increasingly dissatisfied with the existing situation and begin pushing for another increase. Conservatives, viewing the same situation, see not low paid heads of families, but unskilled workers and teens new to the job market and worth no more than what the market allows.

This type of reduction of dissatisfaction is simply an application of the existing ideology to circumstances; it does not result in change in the ideology. Change in the ideology itself is more interesting. Here social, economic, or technological change would lead ideological adherents to become dissatisfied with their own position. This is an important part of the analysis and theory presented here.

Learning theory and the related field of systems analysis offer potentially rich avenues to studying ideological change (Hilgard and Bower 1975; Horton and Turnage 1976; Steinbruner 1974). However, given the fact that our topic is ideological change in the realm of business and the economy, we are probably on safer ground in this early stage of our work concentrating on the most direct source of dissatisfaction with existing policies and/or policy prescriptions. That source of dissatisfaction is most likely to be market failure or its opposite, non-market or government failure.

Theories of Market and Non-Market Failure

Charles Wolf, Jr. (1979) presents an especially clear rendition of the theories of market and non-market failure. The theory of market failure is that the market system optimally manages the production and distribution of private goods, but that in some circumstances it does not work. Those circumstances involve public goods, negative externalities, high capital investment activities such as hydroelectric dams, natural monopolies, and distributional inequity. When market failure occurs, government intervention is required.

The theory of non-market failure amounts to a theory of government failure. Government programs fail for the following reasons: lack of accountability caused by absence of a bottom line; lack of competition in the public sector; a reward structure for elected government officials who promote solutions to market problems without assuming responsibility for the cost or even functionality of those solutions; a reward structure for administrators that rewards budget growth; dysfunctional control games; unanticipated side effects of government programs; and/or distributional inequities.

It is the conventional wisdom that liberals are more sensitive to market failure than conservatives and conservatives more sensitive to government failure than liberals. These differences might explain disagreements between liberals and conservatives with regard to public policies toward business and the economy. It is also conventional wisdom that an economic class component explains at least some differences. Liberals are commonly seen as more sensitive to the needs of lower classes than are conservatives. But neither of these differences by themselves appears to offer an explanation of ideological change.

We can speculate that conservatives would accept the status quo regarding situation X. Liberals regard situation X as a case of market failure for any of the reasons listed above; so, liberals propose expansion or enactment of a government program to resolve situation X. Conservatives oppose the liberal plan. If the liberal plan is passed and works, it is conceivable that conservatives will be convinced of the error of their ways and change their position. Similarly, if the program is not enacted and situation X persists, conservatives might come to regard their original opposition to the liberal plan as mistaken, and change their position. A mirror image of this scenario would have the liberal program enacted and failing. Here liberals would recognize their mistake and move to cancel or alter their program. Both scenarios and other permutations and combinations are possible.

The Content of Liberalism and Conservatism

Authors describing or participating in the formulation of American liberalism and conservatism over the last forty years present widely varying images of these ideologies including denials in some instances that they are ideologies. Intellectual currents and political trends begin and end abruptly, twist, fade, shift, and occasionally reappear. Allies become opponents; opponents become allies. Which currents and trends are important or have ended, and which authors and politicians have accomplished what is difficult, if not impossible, to discern from the vast and growing literatures produced by theorists and historians.

One example illustrates the problem. In *The Conservative Tradition in America* Charles W. Dunn and J. David Woodard (1996, 16-17) display a table comparing the dominant tendencies of liberalism and conservatism. The table is divided into three categories: government, the economy, and cultural and religious values. Under government the individual is listed as the "primary focus" for liberals. For conservatives it is the community. But many self-described liberals whose works were published well before the Dunn and Woodard study are trying to shift the primary focus of government away from the individual toward the community.[1] And, while Burkean, cultural, or religious conservatives have the community as their primary focus, Chamber of Commerce conservatives and classical liberals regard the individual as paramount. We could continue this exercise with the entire Dunn and Woodard list, but there seems little reason to do so. Their interpretation of what constitutes conservatism and liberalism in 1996 often conflicts with contemporary political behavior and the work of many liberal and conservative theorists. Many treatments of contemporary liberalism or conservatism that attempt to be comprehensive can be disassembled in a similar manner.

Theorists and historians provide little information on the relationship between ideology and public policy. It is surprising how many pages and even chapters of these works one can read without seeing a reference to a public policy issue except as an occasional example to make a theoretical point.[2] Benjamin Barber (1988, 8-9) captured the spirit of many theorists when he observed that they were "philosophers first . . . and students of or participants in politics per se only in some remote, tertiary sense." He added: "Readers will search in vain . . . for signs of salient historical interests, sociological artifacts, or political practices." Any attempt to relate liberalism and conservatism to public policy must locate other vehicles for ideological content (Geise 1991; Honig 1993; Gerencser 1995; Downing and Thigpen 1993).

Measuring Liberalism and Conservatism

Many empirically oriented students of ideology use the ideological rating systems provided by interest groups such as Americans for Democratic Action and the National Rifle Association. Most rating systems result in a single number that summarizes a member of Congress' ideological position for a given time period and allows a ranking from most to least supportive of the group's philosophy. This sort of reduction by its nature misses important strands of ideology and ideological change. Another drawback with interest group ratings is that they represent only those matters that reach the floor of the House or Senate. For quantitative studies this may be acceptable, but one point made repeatedly by ideological theorists of all stripes is that there is a difference between the realms of ideological purity and political practicality.

We believe that newspaper editorials offer a way past these difficulties.[3] Editorials include all policy areas on or near the public agenda and a wide range of current issues. At the same time, the institutional nature of the publishing organization constrains the eccentricities of individual authors. Lasswell, Lerner and Pool (1952, 17) endorsed this use of editorials:

> Newspapers appear regularly and frequently, in uniform formats. Also, they have a more or less explicit point of view. The press is mainly an information medium rather than an entertainment medium; and the most significant category on which the press regularly presents news and views is the political, including the ideological.

They also tell us that the "press is . . . rich in the vocabulary of political ideology current among the elite of any given time."(17)

To further restrict temporary personal foibles, we tried to select two conservative and two liberal national newspapers. The newspapers had to be national in scope and consistent in ideological perspective. On the right those standards narrowed the field to the *Wall Street Journal*. The *Journal* labels itself conservative and is so regarded by competing publications and the conservative and liberal political communities.

Selection of a second conservative newspaper represented a bigger problem. No other conservative newspaper is comparable to the *Journal* in circulation, prestige, and recognized conservative leadership. That realization forced us to turn to journals of opinion, and having done so the automatic choice was *National Review*. Few would argue that it has been consistently conservative, and most regard it as having been more responsible than any other single publication including the *Journal* for shaping contemporary conservatism. Using two rather different kinds of publications, a daily newspaper (except weekends) and a journal of opinion, as gauges of ideological sentiment does not represent a methodological problem. When, for example, the *Journal* and *National Review* declare themselves opposed to the minimum wage the format and frequency of publication is of no import. What matters is the position taken.

In selecting two representatives of liberalism, it occurred to us to stay with one newspaper and one journal of opinion, but we were unable to find a consistent representative of liberalism that would serve as a counterpart to *National Review*. So, we returned to two newspapers. The criteria narrowed the field to the *Washington Post* and the *New York Times*, two of the nation's most prestigious newspapers.

Editorials analyzed in the present study were selected by simple random sampling of publication days in the years 1961-1998--1,377 days for the newspapers and 326 issues for the biweekly *National Review*. All editorials appearing on those days were read and coded. This came to 4,673 editorials in the *Washington Post*, 4,901 in the *New York Times*, 1,939 in the *Wall Street Journal*, and 2,314 in *National Review*. The variations in numbers of editorials results from the fact that: the *Post* and *Times* publish daily while the *Journal* does not; *National Review* publishes biweekly; and the number of editorials per issue varies within and among the publications.

A comparison of one aspect of the editorials of these four publications with the Americans for Democratic Action (ADA) standard provides fairly convincing support for their liberal and conservative standing. With a different purpose in mind, Mark A. Zupan (1992) translated ADA ratings of members of Congress into ratings of presidents from Harry Truman through George Bush. Zupan matched ADA roll call votes to those roll call votes on which *Congressional Quarterly* identified the president as personally taking a position and determined whether the president supported or opposed the ADA position. The number of pro-ADA stances taken by a president divided by the total number of ADA-selected votes on which that president took a stance generated Zupan's Pro-ADA score. Zupan calculated the figures for each year in the 1947-1989 period as well as cumulative scores for each president (351-352). His results for Kennedy through Bush (much of the time period covered in the present study) are included in Table 1. The number of Zupan-ADA stances is comparable to the number of *Journal* and *National Review* editorials and substantially lower than the number in the *Post* and *Times*.

The highest ADA score (1.0) represents total support for liberal ADA positions. A score of 0.5 is midway while 0.0 indicates total lack of support for ADA policy preferences. Most of the presidential Zupan-ADA ratings are roughly predictable based on an intuitive sense of how the ADA regarded the particular presidents. For example, Kennedy and Johnson scored high except that Johnson's ratings deteriorated as foreign policy (Vietnam) replaced domestic reform as the central focus of his administration. A link between the Zupan-ADA ratings and editorials can be established for those editorials that take a direct position for or against a presidential policy. We calculated presidential support scores for each publication by dividing the number of editorials explicitly supporting a stated presidential position by the total number of editorials taking a stand on a presidential position. These scores are also reported in Table 1.[4]

Strong relationships exist between all four publications and the Zupan-ADA ratings: WSJ-Zupan-ADA $r^2 = .74$; NR-Zupan-ADA $r^2 = .62$; WP-Zupan-ADA $r^2 = .71$; NYT-Zupan-ADA $r^2 = .76$. In all cases probabilities of statistical significance are far beyond the .001 level. The Zupan-ADA scores are negatively related to the *Journal* and *National Review* scores but positively related to scores for the *Times* and *Post*. Time series plots (not included here) also strongly suggest that the presidential ratings of these editorials and the Zupan-ADA rating are measuring the same phenomenon, and that there is a clear ideological separation between the *Times* and *Post* on one hand and the *Journal* and *National Review* on the other.

Coding Editorials

The unit of analysis was the editorial in its entirety. For our purposes this unit yielded the best representation of the symbolic meaning or semantic coherence (Weber 1990). Each editorial was read and coded based on 18 detailed coding fields. Three code fields were used in this article: the major subjects of the editorial; presidential support; and whether the editorial advocates an increase, decrease, or no change in federal power over business.

One set of fields identified the editorial: newspaper name; date of publication; editorial title; and editorial number. A second focused on whether specific elements of traditional liberal-conservative ideological debate were discussed in the editorial. These fields focused on federal power over the individual; federal power over business; orientation toward government spending; the free market model; state and local government power over the individual; and state and local government power over business. If a theme was coded as present, a secondary code

Table 1: Presidential Agreement Scores Compared to Zupan ADA Scores

President	Year	Zupan ADA Scores	Presidential Agreement Scores			
			N.Y. Times	Wash. Post	Wall St. Journal	Nat. Review
Kennedy	1961	0.94	1.00	0.86	0.23	0.00
	1962	0.94	0.89	0.90	0.15	0.05
	1963	1.00	0.89	0.84	0.27	0.00
Johnson	1964	1.00	0.67	0.90	0.15	0.00
	1965	0.95	0.64	0.97	0.17	0.12
	1966	0.75	0.77	0.88	0.00	0.06
	1967	0.56	0.71	0.93	0.14	0.06
	1968	0.89	0.69	0.90	0.00	0.20
Nixon	1969	0.35	0.38	0.63	1.00	0.55
	1970	0.16	0.40	0.23	0.79	0.78
	1971	0.10	0.47	0.52	0.54	0.75
	1972	0.21	0.37	0.52	0.33	1.00
	1973	0.11	0.16	0.28	0.73	0.58
Ford	1974	0.14	0.41	0.44	0.50	0.40
	1975	0.17	0.44	0.71	0.65	0.36
	1976	0.00	0.21	0.61	0.80	0.00
Carter	1977	0.76	0.78	0.82	0.18	0.17
	1978	0.75	0.67	0.83	0.08	0.00
	1979	0.72	0.68	0.56	0.00	0.06
	1980	0.77	0.79	0.61	0.00	0.20
Reagan	1981	0.00	0.21	0.32	0.93	1.00
	1982	0.10	0.27	0.45	0.76	0.78
	1983	0.05	0.24	0.39	0.68	0.86
	1984	0.05	0.39	0.26	0.71	0.60
	1985	0.00	0.36	0.26	1.00	0.92
	1986	0.05	0.30	0.28	0.75	0.70
	1987	0.00	0.24	0.51	0.69	0.59
	1988	0.00	0.47	0.50	0.82	0.67

Table 1. Continued

President	Year	Zupan ADA Scores	Presidential Agreement Scores			
			N.Y. Times	Wash. Post	Wall St. Journal	Nat. Review
Bush	1989	0.00	0.61	0.53	0.71	0.44
	1990		0.58	0.52	0.50	0.37
	1991		0.37	0.69	0.63	0.53
	1992		0.28	0.45	0.80	0.36
Clinton	1993		0.74	0.92	0.15	0.14
	1994		0.58	0.79	0.16	0.06
	1995		0.71	0.63	0.07	0.00
	1996		0.67	0.47	0.00	0.04
	1997		0.25	0.40	0.08	0.06
	1998		0.42	0.38	0.00	0.00

then focused on the editorial's orientation toward that theme. For example, whether it supported an increase or decrease in federal power over business or specifically defended the status quo. These secondary codes were adapted in appropriate form for each of the primary coding categories.

A modification of the work of Kenneth Janda, Jeffrey M. Berry, and Jerry Goldman (1992, 175) served as the basis for an order-equality field. They based their effort on conservative and liberal theory and empirical analyses of responses to public opinion questions. By their reckoning, a liberal tends to favor equality over order, and a conservative tends to favor order over freedom. Roughly speaking, this conception of liberalism and conservatism is consistent with most general characterizations of these ideologies. In addition, one would expect to observe liberals favoring a relatively vigorous government pursuit of equality and conservatives more accepting of inequality as a fact of life and favoring fewer government policies in pursuit of equality (Van Dyke 1992, 85, 224-229). Codes available for the field were order, equality, both, and neither.

Three fields were reserved for the specific subject with which the editorial dealt. Subject 1 represented 18 major policy areas: economics; defense or foreign policy; the environment, energy, and transportation;

protection of physical safety (not crime related); labor relations; civil rights--affirmative action and discrimination related to business; civil rights--voting rights and other basic rights; crime; education; urban issues; science and technology; the media; the arts; government operations; politics; local government; Washington, DC; and other. Subjects 2 and 3 then subdivided the broader category into more specific areas of policy concern. For example, under operation of the economy, these fields included: agriculture; economic growth or inflation issues; deprecation allowance; general discussion of the federal tax code; progressivity of the federal tax code; economic planning; economic development; the minimum wage; and government regulation of financial institutions. Most editorials focused on just one policy area but occasionally a second policy area might appear in the same editorial and would be recorded.

The presidential support field focused on whether the editorial took a position on a policy which the editorial writer identified as one upon which the president had taken a position. A blank code in the field indicated that the editorial identified no presidential position; a yes meant an identified presidential position was supported in the editorial; and a no meant that the editorial did not support the presidential position.

Two free form fields also were used. One was for a short summary of the editorial; the other was a memo field.

Separate coding of a sample of editorials yielded an intercoder reliability level over .90 depending on the complexity of a field. Coding was performed by the authors and disagreements were resolved by discussion.

Each editorial identified as dealing with business and the economy was reread and examined for its full content. Here we looked for consistency in positions taken over time and breaks in patterns. For example, the *New York Times* year after year and decade after decade favored unrestricted free international trade. Any *Times* editorial that appeared to represent a change in position was carefully reread and the nature of the change recorded. Reading of subsequent editorials focused on whether a long term or temporary change had occurred. Also, differences between the two liberal and two conservative newspapers required extra consideration. The most notable (rare) differences of this sort were between the liberal newspapers from the 1960s-1970s regarding agricultural subsidies and among all four publications regarding immigration. In the case of immigration the positions of the liberal publications were confused (not confusing, but confused) and the conservatives completely disagreed with each other. We therefore located and read all *Post* and *Times* editorials for the years in which immigration was an active issue.

One concern was whether the sample size was sufficiently large and representative. Ideologies are relatively stable bodies of ideas. We would expect to see some stability in the percentage of editorials devoted to each policy category from year to year, but this percentage would be unlikely to remain constant from year to year even with the full universe of editorials because editorials and ideologies respond to changing conditions.

Table 2 shows percentage shares and standard deviations for the five major policy areas that received the most editorial coverage in all of the four publications examined. The similarity of means and their associated standard deviations for the liberal publications compared to the conservative publications suggest the relative stability combined with occasional ups and downs to be expected with these data. Not surprisingly, coverage of the economy is greatest in the *Journal.* Year to year changes in policy area coverage also make sense. For example, civil rights editorials in the *Times* and *Post* took an above average share throughout the 1960s during the height of the civil rights struggles in the South. The subject matter of ideology probably renders our data relatively insensitive to the number of editorials sampled.

Federal Government Power Over Business and the Economy

Most liberals or conservatives would agree that they are sharply separated by differences regarding the desirability of increased federal government power over business and the economy. The federal government exercises power over business and the economy primarily via regulations and taxes. The conventional view is that the *Post* and the *Times* favored increased federal government power over business and the economy, and that *National Review* and the *Journal* took the opposite view.

For a majority of years in the 1961-1998 range of this study all four publications followed patterns suggested by the conventional image. Figure 1 displays plots of the percentages of combined *Times/Post* and *Journal/National Review* editorials that favored increasing federal power over business as a percentage of the number of editorials that took a position on increasing or decreasing federal power over business.

Table 2. Percentage of Editorials Devoted to Major Policy Areas, 1961-1998

		N.Y. Times	Wash. Post	Wall St. Journal	Nat. Review
Defense and Foreign Policy	Max	39.7	33.7	44.4	51.0
	Min	18.3	14.3	4.2	17.6
	Mean	29.0	23.6	21.9	33.8
	S.D.	4.9	3.8	9.9	8.2
Civil Rights	Max	14.6	12.5	10.4	16.7
	Min	0.0	1.1	0.0	1.9
	Mean	5.7	6.4	4.0	7.7
	S.D.	3.1	3.3	2.8	3.8
Crime	Max	12.4	16.5	10.4	14.7
	Min	0.9	0.7	0.0	0.0
	Mean	5.8	7.3	2.8	3.0
	S.D.	3.2	3.5	2.5	3.3
Environment and Energy	Max	13.9	25.0	17.0	8.3
	Min	1.2	0.8	0.0	0.0
	Mean	7.3	7.4	5.4	2.7
	S.D.	3.5	5.8	3.8	2.6
The Economy	Max	16.0	18.4	46.0	25.3
	Min	4.2	3.5	11.5	4.0
	Mean	8.9	9.1	27.3	9.4
	S.D.	3.1	3.6	9.4	4.5

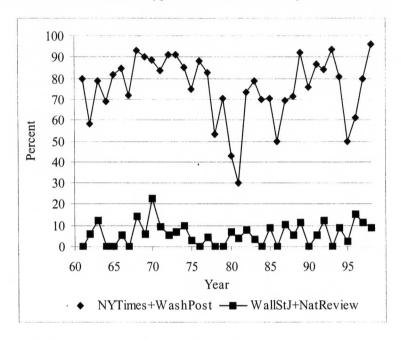

Figure 1. Washington Post + New York Times and Wall Street Journal + Na
tional Review Editorials Favoring Increase in Federal Power Over Business and
the Economy.

The mid 1970s through the mid 1980s appear to constitute a valley in
Post and *Times* support for increasing federal power over business. The
mid 1990s were another briefer and more shallow valley. The *Journal*
and *National Review* do not show a counterpart to the valleys seen in the
Times and *Post*. Both conservative publications are consistently unenthusiastic about the application of federal power over business and the
economy. Even in 1981 when the liberal and conservative positions were
at their closest more than 25 percentage points separated them.

A Broad Characterization of Editorials

Figure 1 suggests that the two ideologies share few if any common
opinions regarding the application of federal power to business and the
economy. However, beyond the apparent chasm between liberals and
conservatives were nuances and change little appreciated by either side as
they are represented in the four publications or among their advocates

elsewhere. Analysis of editorial content indicates that throughout the time period studied all four publications shared a considerably wider range of theories and values than one might suppose after viewing Figure 1. To test whether reality and expectation coincide, we combined all editorials that dealt with the economy or business into one business and economics grouping. For example, editorials placed in this grouping when the issue discussed explicitly had implications for business or the economy included: economics; environment, energy, and transportation editorials focusing on such issues as pollution, endangered species and energy shortages; civil rights editorials dealing with business related age, sex, racial or other forms of discrimination; labor relations; and so on. Patterns both of dissensus and emerging consensus were discovered.

Dissensus

Dissensus follows a pattern suggested by the conventional wisdom. That is, when liberals and conservatives rigidly disagree, liberals nearly always favor greater federal power and larger centralized bureaucracies and have less confidence in the market to do the right thing than do conservatives. Closely related to these observations, conservatives regard market forces as having a greater affect on human behavior than do liberals. These differences seem attributable to basic value disagreements.

The environment

With regard to the environment, despite some exceptions to be discussed later, there is a tendency among liberals to discount tradeoffs between environmental protection and economic development and to push for a return to or maintenance of a pristine environment.[5] In the 1990s this was especially notable with regard to wet lands and endangered species. For example, a 1992 *Post* editorial on Pacific Northwest logging approved the invocation of the Endangered Species Act to protect the northern spotted owl, arguing that the owl, while not inherently important was "a proxy for its old-growth habitat, a priceless and disappearing resource."[6] The *Post* editorial also rejected the idea that the Northwest faced a choice between owls and jobs:

> If heavy logging continues on the public lands, in not too many years there will be neither owls nor jobs; the resource will be depleted. . .
> Conservationists say that here is not a case in which the environment

can be saved only at the economy's expense; rather they argue that in the long run it will be good for the economy and environment alike if the region shifts from timbering toward other sources of employment.

The difference in tendency between liberals and conservatives in this area seems permanent. Conservatives are inclined to look at a forest and see a crop not fundamentally different from a field of corn. The *Journal* believed that the Endangered Species Act should be:

> amended so that factors such as job losses and social costs are considered. The law shouldn't make absolute protection a form of worship if the same animals are found elsewhere [which was the case with the spotted owl], have many subspecies or can be relocated.[7]

Despite the rigid differences in *tendency* between liberals and conservatives in this area, we will see later that there has been considerable convergence with movements of liberals toward conservatism and vice versa.

Economic policy

Several areas of economic policy are also characterized by distinct and rigid differences. For example, the liberal newspapers consistently supported proposals to increase the minimum wage; the conservative publications just as consistently opposed its very existence. Conservatives argued that an increase in the minimum wage caused businesses to not hire marginal, low skilled workers or to fire such workers after acquiring labor saving equipment made cost-effective by the minium wage increase.[8] Liberals denied that such a relationship existed and argued that low skilled workers could only earn a living wage via federal legislation. The liberal-conservative split on the minium wage was constant throughout the time period studied and showed no sign of convergence.

The minimum wage issue exposes another conservative-liberal schism, this in the realm of economic theory. Liberals regard the minium wage law as effective; they believe that the minimum wage enhances the economic well being of the entire pool of low wage workers. At the very least they believe that a minimum wage raises the incomes of currently employed low wage workers. Most conservatives believe that an increase in the minimum wage causes employers to fire or to stop hiring some low wage workers if the new minimum wage exceeds the lowest wages established by the market. Machinery is a common alternative to low wage workers. Conservatives would add that after workers are replaced by equipment unemployment compensation pays for those put out of work and acts as a disincentive for new job searches and/or skills development. Tax policy is another area of clear liberal-conservative difference. With some exceptions found mainly in the early 1960s, liberals favored tax increases or defended existing tax levels while conservatives showed a strong tendency to reduce taxes. The basic *National Review* and *Journal* formula for economic growth is the minimization of the public sector. This approach is rejected by the *Times* and *Post*.[9]

In the late 1970s conservatives discovered supply side economics and its basic premise that other things being equal a tax increase inhibits the activity being taxed. If the tax in question is the income tax, a tax increase diminishes income earning activities by reducing the incentive to work. Incremental movements in the tax rate will increase revenues, but at some point that will differ among economies and cultures and probably differ in time, additional tax rate increments will produce smaller and smaller marginal increases in revenue collected as workers choose leisure time or tax avoidance strategies such as in-kind trades over taxable work effort. At some point another tax increase will produce a reduction in revenue. If the tax system has moved beyond that point (a very difficult thing to measure), a tax reduction will both stimulate the economy and generate revenue increases.[10]

The logic of the disputes over supply side economics and the minimum wage are essentially the same. Conservatives hold that changes in money flows change behavior and that the market, not government should generate changes in money flow. Liberals argue that government generated money flow changes are both more efficient and effective in changing behavior in desired directions.

Dynamic analysis, an approach to forecasting the impact of tax cuts or increases, was related to supply side economics. This approach factors behavior changes into a forecast of revenue changes resulting from changes in tax incentives. An example is the argument that a one percent tax reduction will produce less than a one percent reduction in revenue (and perhaps even a positive change in revenue) because people will be motivated to earn more taxable income.[11] Static analysis on the other hand assumes that changes in revenue will be in direct proportion to a tax change: a one percent tax reduction will produce a one percent revenue reduction. During the past two decades liberals, including the *Times* and *Post*, and Republican deficit hawks favored static analysis. Conservatives again defended the position that changes in money flows change behavior while liberals essentially held that changes in taxes do not affect behavior.

Liberals and conservatives have differed consistently on the issue of tax progressivity.[12] Liberals favored some measure of progressivity and conservatives advocated a constant (flat) tax rate. The central argument for progressivity is fairness: for a given year the last dollar earned by a millionaire is less valuable to him or her than the last dollar earned by someone with an average salary. Thus, it is fair to apply the higher tax rate to the millionaire; the rates between the two taxpayers will be different but the level of pain will be comparable. Conservatives rarely address this argument directly except to observe that interpersonal comparisons are impossible. They focus on inherent negative incentives to work in a progressive tax, following a logic similar to that used in defense of supply side economics. Conservatives also argue that a flat or single rate can be made much simpler to administer than often complex progressive taxes.[13]

A variant of the progressive tax versus flat or proportional tax divide is a fairly constant dispute regarding income versus consumption (e.g., sales) taxes. Liberals tend to favor the former partly because they can so easily be made progressive; they tend to oppose the latter as regressive. Conservatives tend to favor consumption taxes which are flat rate taxes that can be made proportional with exemptions for necessities such as food and prescription drugs. They also argue that taxing consumption encourages people to spend less and save and invest more. Conservative opposition to income taxes is based on the fact that such taxes can be made progressive.

Taxation of corporate income represents another area of rigid liberal-conservative difference. Throughout the time period studied the federal government taxed corporate profits with the tax collected directly from the corporations. If corporations distribute some or all of the remaining profits to stockholders in the form of dividends, those monies are subject to an individual income tax. Conservatives regard this as a form of double taxation. They have no objection to one or the other, but they regard both as inequitable.[14]

Conservatives and liberals have also shown a consistent split regarding certain kinds of energy profits. When the *Times* and *Post* called for elimination of price controls over petroleum and natural gas, (see below) they concluded that resulting price increases would lead to high profits that oil companies would not be able to invest efficiently because of the sheer volume of those profits. Their solution was an excess profits tax (also known as a windfall profits tax). The *Journal* and *National Review* emphatically rejected this position To conservatives the market was rewarding risk takers who should be free to allocate those rewards any way they saw fit. The spike in energy prices in 2000 may bring a return of this debate along similar lines.

Worker rights

Liberals were also substantially more inclined than conservatives to favor federal legislation to protect worker rights. For example, liberals favored the Family and Medical Leave Act while conservatives tended to oppose it. The debate followed contours similar to those of the minimum wage argument.

Health care

Liberals tend to favor centralized, bureaucratically controlled health insurance systems little different from the original Medicare/Medicaid models.[15] Liberals recognize the merit of conservative criticisms that these system have increased health care costs, are rife with fraud and overburdened with bureaucracy, but they choose to continue with or expand them. However, liberals were unwilling to endorse the proposal formulated by Hillary Clinton which all four publications characterized as closer to a Rube Goldberg machine than a true health plan.[16]

Conservatives favor less bureaucratic and more market oriented solutions such as medical savings accounts. They argue that such devices stimulate savings and thereby aid investment and place the decision making in the hands of the consumer. Liberals reject the conservative medical saving account. They have little faith in the consumer's ability to evaluate information developed and distributed by health care businesses competing for their dollars particularly when the consumer is especially vulnerable. They want a government role in the process; they also argue that medical savings accounts favor those with more income and therefore greater ability to save. The fact that tax cuts are often tied to such plans bothers them as well. We will see below that, somewhat like the environment, the rigid differences in tendency between liberals and conservatives in the field of health care have diminished. In this case the movement is only in the direction of a conservative shift to liberal positions.

Summary

Each of the differences discussed above seem to represent hard core value disagreements between liberals and conservatives. There are also differences with regard to policy implementation that were observed in several policy areas. Both types of differences center on market failure and economic class (which to liberals appears to represent a form of market failure) in ways that differ little if at all from conventional views regarding differences between liberals and conservatives. Table 3 focuses on long standing dissensus between liberals and conservatives. With regard to the minimum wage the positions on both sides appear to be entirely fixed. However, we will see that with some of the other policy areas in Table 3 while the differences remain, they are differences in moving positions by both liberals and conservatives. The differences remain, but they are differences between different positions. We will also see that while both liberals and conservatives are capable of shifting positions in the face of changing circumstances, long standing differences remain.

Table 3. Long Standing Liberal-Conservative Dissensus

Policy Area	Conservatives More Trusting of Market Mechanisms?	Class Differences Important?
The Environment	Yes	NA
Minimum Wage	Yes	Yes
Tax Policy	Yes	Yes
Health Care	Yes	Yes
Worker Rights	Yes	Yes

Explaining Consensus and Movement Toward Consensus

A partial explanation of the liberal-conservative consensus that spanned the time period of the study follows together with an explanation of why initial disagreements narrowed in the directions they did in later years. The explanation is suggested by Figure 2 which portrays all of the positions taken by the four publications regarding business and the economy that included consensus or movement. Figure 2 depends upon a spectrum that characterizes markets as operating successfully (column 1) and market breakdown at the opposite end (column 3). This is a variant on the theory of market failure.

Our theory is that liberal-conservative consensus exists in situations where the market functions successfully (column 1), liberal-conservative dissensus is followed by liberal movement in the conservative direction in situations characterized by what we call market misbehavior (column 2), and liberal-conservative dissensus is followed by conservative movement in the liberal direction in situations characterized market breakdown-- complete or partial breakdown (column 3).

Market functions roughly as per Adam Smith

Column 1 concerns the production and distribution of private goods. The market was at the center of the thinking of all four publications' editors when they discussed economics and business.[17] This broad area of consensus is based on the shared liberal and conservative observation that the market system is demonstrably more successful at production and fairer at distribution than any competing arrangements especially the centralized planning approaches attempted by Marxist and socialist countries. Command economies are the subject of decades of withering criticism from all four publications throughout the time period of the study except toward the end where the failure of command economies was self evident and required no more comment.

Market misbehavior, partial functioning/breakdown, and complete breakdown

Columns 2-3 in Figure 2 refer to market misbehavior and market breakdown whether complete or partial. Although the term market failure has been adequate up to this point, its usefulness has come to an end because it is used in too many different ways to avoid confusion. To select just one example, David L. Weimer and Aidan R. Vining (1999, 74) define market failure as "situations in which decentralized behavior does not lead to Pareto efficiency." By this extraordinarily broad defini- tion, it would be difficult to locate any sector of the market not character- ized by some degree of market failure. It is our sense that most writers do not use this definition, but it is not our purpose to debate the matter. (See Rhoads 1993, 6.)

It is easiest to explain the concepts contained in columns 2-3 by beginning with the extreme case of market breakdown. Complete market breakdown means that the market cannot function theoretically and in fact does not function. The reasons for market breakdown are the same as the standard list of reasons for market failure presented earlier. Some areas of public policy are characterized by mixtures of market breakdown and successful market operation. We label this partial market breakdown. For example, the market model has some applicability in the health care

	Efficient Market
Liberal-Conservative Consensus	*Intellectual foundation for all four publications' views about economics and business. Major components: (1) The market results in higher production of and fairer distribution of private goods than any other economic system. (2) Anything that interferes with free international trade such as tariffs hurts everyone in the long run. (3) The market is the best arbiter of the use of technology in the workplace. (4) Business subsides increase taxes unnecessarily and distort markets.*
Liberal Movement Toward the Conservative Position	
Conservative Movement Toward the Liberal Position	

Figure 2. A Theory of Ideological Change
*Perfect adherence to the model would result only in cells shown in italics.

Market Misbehavior	Market Breakdown
	Partial: Labor Relations--Accept idea that labor-management power should be balanced so that each side can do roughly equal damage to the other. [If the sample had focused on the 1930s, labor relations would be in the 3rd row below.] Complete: None
Wage and price controls favored by liberals in the early Nixon years are abandoned. Energy price controls and rationing favored by liberals after the Arab oil embargo are abandoned. Many economic regulations adopted by liberals in and before the New Deal are reduced drastically. The market is viewed as managing such operations as trucking and railroads better than government. Agricultural subsidies, price supports, etc. no longer could be justified. These devices distort markets.	Partial: Environment -- In some ways liberals come to accept the impossibility of creating a pristine environment and recognize the need for trade-offs. Complete: None
	Partial: Health Care -- Conservatives adopt liberal position that coverage of unprotected people is needed. *Partial: Consumer Protection --Conservatives adopt most basic liberal views.* *Complete: Environmental Protection-- Conservatives adopt most basic liberal positions.*

field: doctors, hospitals, and pharmaceutical manufacturing companies offer their services or products and customers buy them.   But, there are several problems with the market model which historically have led to deviations from classic buyer-seller relationships.   A major deviation from the market model is that customer judgements are often impaired by their physical condition (the reason they are in the market).   Second, in some instances the customer cannot afford medical care, and society is unwilling to turn its back on such people.   If the health care field does not represent complete market breakdown, it is far from a fully functioning market even as viewed by conservatives.   Areas of public policy characterized by mixtures of successful market operation and market breakdown require government intervention as surely as areas of public policy characterized by complete market breakdown.   The only difference is that public policy may work around and take advantage of successful market operations.

Market misbehavior (column 2) is distinguished from a fully operational market (column 1) only in short term results of market operation. Even extreme advocates of laissez faire capitalism understand that sometimes the market moves in ways that produce widespread unhappiness (e.g., recessions and stock market downturns).   By definition no elements of market breakdown are present when market misbehavior occurs, but the unhappiness caused by the misbehavior can produce the illusion of breakdown.

Liberal-conservative consensus

Beyond the virtually identical market-oriented manner in which the editors of the four publications think about economics and their hostility toward and contempt for command economies, specific areas of consensus include the need for completely free international trade; the importance of allowing the marketplace to mold the use of technology in the workplace; opposition to business subsidies; and the need for a labor-management balance of power.   With regard to international trade, the four publications agreed that a free market provides optimum coordination of international trade.   In the long run anything that interferes with the market's free operation such as tariffs or quotas hurts everyone by diminishing output and increasing prices.[18]   All four also agreed that the market is the best arbiter of the use of technology in the workplace.[19]   For example, all were hostile to union work stoppages protesting the introduction of automation, and all agreed that business subsidies should not be granted because subsidies increase tax burdens unnecessarily, distort the market, assist inefficient operations, and unjustly hurt businesses that could otherwise stand on their own.[20]

Consensus also existed that labor-management power should be balanced so that each side can do roughly equal damage to the other.[21] Labor relations involves too much government authority for labor relations to fit in column 1, and labor relations does not exactly fit the opposite extreme of complete market breakdown either. Government authority was required to force businesses to recognize the legitimacy of labor unions, but prior to that time businesses had for decades used government authority to constrain union activity. The closest existing theoretical fit for the four publications' thought regarding their desired labor-management balance of power is John Kenneth Galbraith's notion of countervailing power in *American Capitalism* (1952). *National Review* and the *Wall Street Journal* would have been loath to cite this grandee of liberalism as an authority, but he provides the closest theoretical version of their thinking. In any event, what they wanted was a competitive arena, if not a market. Labor-management power was placed in the partial breakdown category in column 3 on a preliminary basis. We will see below that this location, which might appear to violate our theory, may instead support it.

Liberal movement toward conservative positions: Market misbehavior

When liberals and conservatives disagreed and liberals moved toward the conservative position, it was due primarily to market misbehavior. Wage and price controls were favored by liberals in the early years of the Nixon administration when inflation appeared to resist normal monetary and fiscal remedies. Wage and price controls were almost always opposed by conservatives.[22] Liberals abandoned support for wage and price controls, finding that the controls were virtually impossible to administer fairly or effectively.[23] They also advocated energy price controls and rationing after the Arab oil embargo; these policies were always opposed by conservatives.[24] The liberal position became impossible to defend partly because of the difficulty of administering controls and partly because increased oil prices reduced oil consumption (an objective of rationing) which would reduce U.S. dependence on imported oil and also reduce pollution (both of which were liberal goals).[25]

Around 1900 and during the Great Depression progressives and liberals championed economic regulations (especially for trucking and railroads) that liberals reflexively defended probably beyond the time they were needed. By the 1970s liberals concluded that these regulations should be drastically reduced.[26] The market could do a better job of managing these systems than could government.[27]

Liberals (especially the *Post*) initially regarded agribusiness as a special case in terms of the need for subsidies, price supports, and tariff protection.[28] Eventually, the *Times* and later the *Post* concluded that most such devices should be eliminated because they increase tax burdens unnecessarily and distort the market by assisting inefficient operations and hurting businesses that could otherwise stand on their own.[29]

The only instance in which liberals moved to the conservative position that could not be placed in column 2 was liberal acceptance of the impossibility of creating a pristine environment and recognition of the need for trade-offs. Here the original liberal position came close to assuming that no costs were associated with environmentalism--an economically untenable position. Controlling pollution will always be a matter of trade-offs represented by the logic of benefit-cost analysis.[30] Liberals had to bow to the economic reality of opportunity cost. This was not so much a matter of market operations as it was simple reality--every choice means that the best available alternative is foregone. Trying to achieve a pristine environment with perfectly clean water or air means that any action that would cause slightly dirty air or water could not be taken.

Liberals, as their views are reflected in the *New York Times* and *Washington Post*, want to reverse unhappy events or at least ameliorate their effects with quickly applied, direct governmental action. Conservatives tend to favor riding out the events, believing that nothing but the market can correct market misbehavior and that government action usually does more harm than good. Conservatives also believe that direct governmental assistance to those vulnerable members of society most hurt by market movements is often unintentionally destructive.

In the policy areas characterized by market misbehavior, the market produced or appeared to produce undesirable results. Liberal prescriptions for intervention lacked a clear and consistent theory of market breakdown (failure) tied to how the interventions would improve the situation (Weimer and Vining 1999, 74-126; Wolf 1979). For example, farmers endured market ups and downs, but liberals never made clear why farmers deserved more assistance than other businesses or whether that help was cost-effective. Perhaps the strongest case for market breakdown was that of the Arab oil embargo, but even here elements of the embargo strengthened the liberal position in the area of environmental protection. In any event, the embargo proved temporary.

In all of the areas in column 2 liberals came to the realization that government programs could not correct market misbehavior. The best government could do was to aid especially hard hit victims of market movements. This conclusion led to an abandonment or a drastic reduction in levels of programs that sought to intervene in market movements.

Conservative movement toward liberal positions: Partial or complete market breakdown

Full or partial market breakdown appears to have driven ideological movement in the areas of the basic need to protect the environment, health care, and consumer protection. In these instances the movement was by conservatives toward liberal positions. Conservatives adopted most basic liberal positions with regard to environmental protection although conservatives continued to oppose most new liberal initiatives in this area. In other words, conservatives moved toward a moving target.[31] They also adopted the liberal position that improvements in the nation's coverage of unprotected people in the health care system are needed. This change was signaled by the conservative embrace of medical savings accounts.[32] Conservatives and liberals continue to disagree over the means to achieve the goal of universal coverage. Conservatives also adopted most basic liberal attitudes with regard to consumer protection. Product recalls, clearer labeling, and most standard consumer protection techniques became part of the ideological consensus. Somewhat like environmental protection,[33] conservatives have moved toward a moving target. So, there continues to be a gap.

In practice when a new policy problem arises, the distinction between misbehaving markets and partial or complete market breakdown can easily be obscured. This is why liberals sometimes interpret market misbehavior as market breakdown and call for government action to rectify the problem. The movement of liberals to the conservative position is explained by liberal realization that market breakdown did not occur, that government intervention did not help and may have caused harm, and that the market's invisible hand resolved the problem. Under conditions of partial or full market breakdown the movement of conservatives to the liberal position is occasioned by the conservative realization that market breakdown did occur, and that government intervention is a necessity.[34]

The pattern of conservative adoption of liberal positions was quite clear with regard to environmental problems. Although the conservative publications alluded to market solutions to environmental problems, they did not propose anything substantive and workable. As increasingly rigorous environmental legislation and regulations were enacted and enforced, conservatives highlighted weaknesses and produced compromises, but they essentially migrated in the liberal direction even as liberals continued to move toward the application of increasing federal power to enforce higher standards. None of the four publications studied is inclined to admit that positions held in an earlier time were incorrect; so, to some degree a shift in position must be detected by the secession of criticism of a given policy. Neither the *Journal* nor *National Review* has proposed anything like a wholesale retreat to the era of the early 1960s.[35]

Conservative movement toward liberal positions with regard to pollution, wetlands protection, and endangered species protection is not just different in direction from the opposite ideological movement with regard to energy resources where the major liberal nonmarket solutions (price controls and rationing) failed. The key difference is that energy can be treated as a private good. When it is treated as a private good, the market produces and distributes efficiently and fairly according to both liberals and conservatives. Market misbehavior or political interference in market operations such as those of OPEC are best corrected by the market perhaps supplemented by federally sponsored research. Environmental degradation on the other hand is an externality that the market cannot prevent.

Although there remains a decided difference between liberals and conservatives in the area of health care, conservatives have moved toward liberals in that all recognize the need for a universal health insurance program.[36] Originally, conservatives seemed content to ignore the problem. After passage of Medicare and Medicaid, which conservatives opposed, conservatives blamed rising health care costs on these programs and private health insurance policies because these third party providers separated consumer from provider. This diagnosis was accurate up to a point, but it ignored expensive technological advances, and it did not help those in need of health insurance. When conservatives proposed medical savings accounts, a quasi-governmental/market solution, they admitted that the need for some sort of protection existed, and in so doing moved part way toward the liberals.[37] However, a substantial divide remains. Liberals tend to favor centralized federal health care programs encompassing as much of the population as possible. Arguing that such third party payer programs drive up health care costs, conservatives have adhered to market models of which the medical savings account is the ultimate expression. The conservative argument receives some support from the fact that the health care system contains substantial market components.

With regard to consumer protection, Adam Smith's market model assumed that all participants had perfect knowledge, i.e., the kind of knowledge one has in a chess match. Chess players know where all the pieces are; the only secret is the opponent's strategy. In practice, knowledge in the marketplace is often incomplete--closer to the kind of knowledge one has in a poker game. Incomplete knowledge or information asymmetry has become an increasingly important problem for consumers as products have become more and more sophisticated and sometimes dangerous (Grafton 1991; Weimer and Vining 1999, 107-115). For example, chemicals used in agriculture and food processing can produce fatalities, and invisible flaws in the design of home appliances, automobiles, and toys cause fatalities. Critical information is hidden from the consumer.

Despite the clear danger of information asymmetry in consumer protection, the market model still applies to a considerable degree. In many areas consumers can protect themselves by being attentive and utilizing such private sector solutions as consumer magazines that evaluate products. Furthermore, as even the *Times* and *Post* observed through the years, statutory-bureaucratic solutions do not always protect the consumer; they can narrow choices and force prices higher than they otherwise would be. In this area liberals have sometimes shifted rightward as they recognize the limits of government action and the functionality of the market. For conservatives most of the movement has been in the direction of recognizing market breakdown.

Here too, *National Review* and the *Journal* do not highlight past mistakes, but they show no indication of wanting to return to the levels of consumer protection that the country had in the early 1960s. Product recall requirements, clearer labeling, increased attention to safe design, and a regulatory structure to protect consumers and the environment are part of the ideological consensus.[38] Once again, the two sides differ over an ideological divide that has moved in the direction of greater federal power over the business community.

In the field of labor relations a liberal-conservative consensus centered uncharacteristically in an area that falls far short of full market functioning. We placed it in column 3, row 1 of Figure 2. The row location was because of the liberal-conservative consensus in the years 1961-1996 that labor-management power should be balanced. However, if the time period examined had extended back to the 1920s and 1930s, this would be another case of conservative movement in the liberal direction which would place labor relations in the third row instead of the first thus providing a better fit with our theory. When labor unions first appeared, conservatives opposed them until their legitimacy (if not desirability) was grudgingly accepted at some point in the 1930s. The placement of labor relations in the first row is merely an artifact of selecting 1961 as the starting point of this study.

Cross-cutting Issue Areas

Two issue areas find liberals and conservatives in disarray. One is immigration policy. Here the *Times* and *Post,* whose positions are ill defined, fall roughly between *National Review* which favors strict limitations on immigration and the *Journal* which takes the most open--one might almost say liberal--approach.[39] Several *Times* and *Post* editorials observed that liberals in Congress and liberal interest groups were split along the same lines as conservatives.[40] Some liberal members wanted tight restrictions on immigration while other liberals advocated a fairly open immigration policy.

The second cross-cutting issue area concerns transportation. Liberals in what appears to be an almost random pattern have been far from abandoning the market to solve transportation problems except in extreme urban situations. Conservatives also apparently responding to issues in an entirely ad hoc issue-by-issue manner have shown themselves willing to use governmental power in managing the nation's transportation system or to manipulate taxes to reduce auto traffic in cities.[41]

Conclusions

As Lasswell, Lerner, and Pool suggested, editorials provide an aerial view of ideology. And unlike the work of historians and theorists, editorials tie liberalism and conservatism to public policy positions and allow us to focus on relatively recent years. The complex and subtle twists and turns of debate among theorists in the recent past are little evident in editorials. For close students of ideology this is a drawback, but for those more interested in the public policy implications of ideology it is an advantage.

This study did not directly address the first central assumption on which it was based: that ideological adherents and ideological thinking have an independent impact on public policy formulation. All that can be claimed is that much energy goes into ideological thinking, and that changes in public policy often follow changes in ideological thought. Substantially more support is provided for the second assumption that ideological adherents are capable of learning. Responses to economic circumstances follow clear patterns. The connection between learning and systems theory and ideological change deserves deeper exploration. Our analysis of editorials shows that the common image of permanent and wide separation between liberals and conservatives has some basis in reality. Some divisions have not changed significantly in the 38 years we have analyzed, and political histories prior to 1961 and observation since 1998 suggest that the actual time span is much longer. This is especially true with regard to the minimum wage and tax policy. We have also seen little movement with regard to worker rights, but we may have missed a small number of conservative editorials moving slightly leftward in this area. The other areas of long term dissensus listed in Figure 2, the environment and health care, have been marked by leftward movement of both liberals and conservatives that has maintained the distance between them.

The years 1961-1998 have also seen liberal-conservative consensus and movements by both sides toward the other. Much of the long term consensus and movements toward consensus with regard to federal power over business and the economy can be explained using an amended theory of market failure. Long term liberal-conservative consensus centers on agreement that the market economy provides the best system for the production and distribution of private goods domestically and internationally. Initial liberal-conservative dissensus in the face of market misbehavior is often caused by a liberal tendency to mistake unpleasant results of market operations for failure or breakdown. Attempts to use government in these circumstances help little. Initial dissensus in the face of market breakdown is frequently caused by a conservative tendency to mistake market breakdown for market misbehavior. Ignoring market breakdown does nothing to help whatever has gone wrong. When conservatives finally identify the problem as a breakdown, they adjust their positions in the liberal direction.

Notes

1. A typical example is Farganis (1993, 6-7).
2. Examples include: Kautz (1994); Young (1994), and O'Sullivan (1976).
3. A few studies since then have used editorials as a barometer for ideology, but these studies focused narrowly on ideological predilections of U.S. Supreme Court nominees or members (Segal, et al. 1995; Cameron, Cover, and Segal 1990).
4. Many editorials dealt with issues on which the president had acted, but the editorial writer chose not to take an overt pro or con position vis-a-vis the president's stance. While such editorials were excluded from Table 1, examination shows their inclusion would not have changed the results significantly.

5. See *Wall Street Journal*–A species of extremism, May 23, 1990; The Endangered gremlins act, June 3, 1994; Sky falling, Sept. 8, 1994; Playing arctic politics, Nov. 28, 1995; Wetlands, May 26, 1992; *National Review*, Environmentalists aren't, April 11, 1975; *Washington Post*–The owl goes to Congress, May 18, 1992; Hydro vs. the new river, Sept. 3, 1976.

6. *Washington Post*, The owl goes to Congress, May 18, 1992.

7. *Wall Street Journal*, A species of extremism, May 23, 1990.

8. *Wall Street Journal*, Minium debate, Feb. 21, 1995.

9. *Washington Post*–Doctor's advice, Sept. 26, 1982; Who will pay the bill? March 1, 1993; *National Review*–Kemp-Reagan v. Simon-Reagan? April 4, 1980; Kick THEM, Mr. President, Feb. 18, 1983; *Wall Street Journal*–Greenspan bashes Clinton! March 29, 1993; Speed-bump for taxers, April 11, 1996.

10. *National Review*, Counting the gains, July 20, 1998.

11. *National Review*, Reagan's other wound: The budget, May 1, 1981.

12. The exception is basic agreement at the start of the Kennedy years that the progressivity of the income tax had to be reduced. The top marginal rate then exceeded 90 percent.

13. *Wall Street Journal*–Miles to go, Dec. 1, 1995; Very close, Jan. 15, 1996; An "untested" flat tax? Feb. 9, 1996.

14. *National Review*, Kick THEM, Mr. President, Feb. 18, 1983. When Ronald Reagan mentioned that corporate income tax could be eliminated, the media treated this statement as a rude ideological belch. Lester Thurow, a liberal economist, joined Milton Friedman in supporting corporate income tax repeal.

15. *Washington Post*–A CAT in every office, Nov. 28, 1980; Rep. Cooper's plan, Feb. 2, 1994; Accounting for health care. . ., Feb. 9, 1994; As Congress goes home, May 26, 1994.

16. *Washington Post*, Rep. Cooper's plan, Feb. 2, 1994.

17. *Washington Post*, For a tax cut now, July 23, 1962; *New York Times*–Depreciation revised, July 12, 1962; A way to compromise on rents, May 13, 1997.

18. *New York Times*–Risking a trade war, March 5, 1994; Mr. Freeman's mischief, April 3, 1967; Protectionist "Christmas tree" Oct. 17, 1967; *National Review*–Long knives II, April 17, 1981; Staying on track, Nov. 10, 1997; *Washington Post*--Next great debate, Nov. 8, 1961; The trade debate, March 12, 1962; The deal on the trade bill, Dec. 20, 1974; Candy bar politics, Sept. 19, 1995; a rotten tomato deal," Oct. 25, 1996; The fast track fight, Sept. 12, 1997.

19. *Washington Post*–Technology and "unwork," Aug. 29, 1962; Rail truce by mandate, Aug. 23, 1963.

20. *National Review*, Don't count your Chryslers, May 27, 1983.

21. *Washington Post*–The striker replacement issue, March 13, 1995; A ruling on striker replacement, May 15, 1996.

22. *New York Times* –Incomes policy needed, Feb. 28, 1971; Overhauling economic policy, June 23, 1971; Hard line on pay inflation, Dec. 20, 1971; Phase 2, heath-style, Dec. 21, 1973; Zooming prices, Feb. 24, 1974; Fatter food prices, May 18, 1974; A real WIN program, Oct. 17, 1974; Zooming prices, Feb. 24,

1974; *Washington Post*–Is a wage-price policy the answer? Nov. 26, 1970; Yes, the freeze is unfair, July 18, 1971; *Wall Street Journal*–Remembering the basics, Aug. 18, 1971; Less than magic, June 2, 1972; "Success" for controls, Aug. 3, 1972; The learning curve, Jan. 4, 1974.

23. *Washington Post*, Small business, big business, and controls, May 6, 1972; *New York Times*, The wages of inflation, Feb. 3, 1980.

24. *New York Times*–Rationing is fairer, Nov. 15, 1973 and see also After the energy veto, March 8, 1974 and The alternative to gas pump anarchy, June 19, 1979.

25. *Washington Post*–Hard choices on energy, May 22, 1975 and see also A clear and present danger, Jan. 27, 1980; Back to energy policy, Sept. 18, 1990; Energy non-policy, Sept. 28, 1990; *New York Times*–Getting serious about energy, May 25, 1978; Petrified gas policy, May 22, 1980.

26. *New York Times*, Revising bank regulations, Sept. 25, 1962.

27. *New York Times*–Regulatory reform, July 7, 1975; Getting serious about energy, May 25, 1978; A sensible look at the airline "crisis" July 23, 1993; Listening to the radio market, May 14, 1979; *Washington Post*–Criticism of the FPC, Oct. 21, 1976; First decisions for Mr. Reagan, Dec. 28, 1980; The fight over labor regulations, Sept. 26, 1981; Bigness and badness, Jan. 12, 1982; The rush to regulatory reform, Feb. 20, 1995; Misstep on the environment, Jan. 29, 1996; *Wall Street Journal*–Brazen beyond limit? July 7, 1995.

28. *Washington Post*–The coffee agreement, May 25, 1963; Wanted: An international food policy, Sept. 16, 1973; Wheat, corn and milk, March 16, 1975.

29. *New York Times*–Dominican sugar, June 29, 1962; Food for bargaining, April 18, 1963; Wooing the farm bloc, March 3, 1964; *Washington Post*–Uncowed by the politics of milk, May 5, 1971; Senate hayride, May 18, 1990; The forgotten farm cuts, Aug. 13, 1993; Backing off farm reform, Jan. 29, 1996; The farm bill, March 4, 1996.

30. *Washington Post*, The lousewort and the law, April 4, 1977.

31. *Wall Street Journal*–Changing tides, May 10, 1995; Wetlands, May 26, 1992.

32. *Wall Street Journal*, MSA take off, April 9, 1997.

33. *Wall Street Journal*, Consumer power, Sept. 9, 1969.

34. In addition to specific editorials cited in notes below, *National Review* laid out the conservative agenda periodically. Agenda items do not include wholesale roll backs of environmental protection, consumer protection, or federal health care programs. See The national question, Nov. 11, 1996; Newtonian politics, Jan. 23, 1995; After the 100 days, May 1, 1995; Memo to: BC from: [Confidential] May 1, 1995; Zero to forever, Aug. 31, 1995.

35. *Wall Street Journal*–A snail retreat, Dec. 27, 1993; The unspotted sturgeon, Nov. 22, 1993; Risky business, Sept. 15, 1994; Endangered property rights, Sept. 12, 1994; Endangered science, June 30, 1995; The lake effect, Sept. 1, 1995; Matt Ridley, How to smother innovation, June 9, 1993. These are typical examples of acceptance of a basic aspect of environmental protection (the Endangered Species Act) within the context of a critique of what the *Journal*

regarded as an overzealous implementation of that statute; *National Review*–Safety for EPA, March 11, 1996; Clean little secrets, Feb. 6, 1995; A job-free environment, Aug. 28, 1995; Something in the water? May 2, 1994; Second-hand science, July 19, 1993; Clearing the air, March 5, 1990.

36. *Wall Street Journal*–Medical reform simplified, Oct. 18, 1993; Medicare's Gordian knot and Jane M. Orient, A Medicare prescription both, April 24, 1995 (the editorial refers to the Orient article); Peter J. Ferrara, On Medicare: Give the power to the people, Sept. 11, 1995. *National Review*–Off the third rail, Dec. 9, 1996; Disentitlementarianism, March 6, 1995; Medicare reformed? May 29, 1995; 2002--A space odyssey, June 12, 1995; How not to cut, July 31, 1995; Poison pill, Aug. 14, 1995; Mr. Clinton's crisis, Feb. 21, 1994; Accounting for health care, Oct. 4, 1993; Less of some, Oct. 18, 1993; Healthy competition, March 2, 1992.

37. *Wall Street Journal*–Opposed and proud of it, Aug. 9, 1994; Dissecting the uninsured, April 15, 1993. See also the following op-ed page features (not part of sample): Pete Du Pont, The free-market health proposal, July 1, 1994; William Kristol, How to oppose the health plan--and why, Jan. 11, 1994.

38. *Wall Street Journal*–A regulatory wreck, Nov. 28, 1994; Real risk reform, April 18, 1995; Expansion checked, April 27, 1995; *National Review*, untitled, May 10, 1993:8.

39. *New York Times*, Torpedo from the White House, Jan. 24, 1986; *Washington Post* –The fruits of delay, Jan. 28, 1986; Sure, they cost less, May 7, 1986; *National Review*, Importing poverty, Feb. 10, 1997; *Wall Street Journal*, Miami vice? Nov. 26, 1997.

40. *New York Times*, Torpedo from the White House, Jan. 24, 1986; *Washington Post*, The fruits of delay, May 7, 1986.

41. *National Review*, First duty, Sept. 3, 1982.; *Wall Street Journal*–Poor, tired, huddled producers, Oct. 11, 1994; Dangerous sunset provision, March 14, 1996, and Simpson's swan song, April 15, 1996.

References

Alvarez, R. M. and J. L. Saving. 1997. Deficits, Democrats, and distributive benefits: Congressional elections and the pork barrel in the 1980s. *Political Research Quarterly* 50:809-831.

Barber, B. 1988. *The conquest of politics*. Princeton, NJ: Princeton University Press.

Bate, W. J. 1960. *Edmund Burke: Selected works*. New York: Modern Library.

Beam, D. R., T. J. Conlan, and M. T. Wrightson. 1990. Solving the riddle of tax reform: Party competition and the politics of ideas. *Political Science Quarterly* 105:193-217.

Bender, B. 1991. The influence of ideology on congressional voting. *Economic Inquiry* 24:416-428.

Bennett, C. J. and M. Howlett. 1992. The lessons of learning: Reconciling theories of policy learning and policy change. *Policy Sciences* 25:275-294.

Bernstein, R. A. 1992. Limited ideological accountability in House races: The conditioning effect of party. *American Politics Quarterly* 20: 192-204.

Bickers, K. N. and R. M. Stein. 1996. The electoral dynamics of the federal pork barrel. *American Journal of Political Science* 40:1300-1326.

Brunnell, T. L., W. Koetzle, J. Dinardo, B. Grofman, and S. L. Feld. 1999. The R^2 = .93: Where then do they differ? Comparing liberal and conservative interest group ratings. *Legislative Studies Quarterly* 24:87-101.

Burden, B.C., A. C. Gregory, and T. Groseclose. 2000. Measuring the ideologies of U.S. Senators: The song remains the same. *Legislative Studies Quarterly* 25:237-258.

Cameron, C. M., A. D. Cover, and J. A. Segal. 1990. Senate voting on Supreme Court nominees: A neoinstitutional model. *American Political Science Review* 84: 525-534.

Chressanthis, G. A., K. S. Gilbert, and P. W. Grimes. 1991. Ideology, constituent interests, and senatorial voting: The case of abortion. *Social Science Quarterly* 72:588-600.

Citrin, J., D. P. Green, C. Muste, and C. Wong. 1997. Public opinion toward immigration: The role of economic motivations. *Journal of Politics* 59:858-881.

Davis, M. L. and P. K. Porter. 1989. A test for pure or apparent ideology in congressional voting. *Public Choice* 60:101-111.

Dougan, W. R. and M. C. Munger. 1989. The rationality of ideology. *Journal of Law and Economics* 32:119-142.

Downing, L. A. and R. B. Thigpen. 1993. Virtue and the common good in liberal theory. *Journal of Politics* 55:1046-1059.

Dunn, C. W. and J. D. Woodard. 1996. *The conservative tradition in America.* Lanham, MA: Rowman and Littlefield.

Farganis, S. 1993. Feminism and postmodernism. In *Postmodernism and social inquiry*, ed. A. Fontana and D. Dickins. New York: Guilford Press.

Ferejohn, J. A. 1974. *Pork barrel politics: Rivers and harbors legislation, 1947-1968.* Stanford, CA: Stanford University Press.

Filer, J. E., L. W. Kenny, and R. B. Morton. 1993. Redistribution, income, and voting. *American Journal of Political Science* 37:63-87.

Flanigan, W. H. and N. H. Zingale. 1999. *Political behavior of the Ameri-*

can electorate. 9th ed. Washington, DC: CQ Press.

Frymer, P. 1994. Ideological consensus within divided party government. *Political Science Quarterly* 109:287-311.

Galbraith, J. K. 1952. *American capitalism: Countervailing power.* Boston: Houghton Mifflin.

Geise, J. P. 1991. In defense of liberalism. *Western Political Quarterly* 44:583-604.

Gerencser, S. A. 1995. Voices in conversation: Philosophy and politics in the work of Michael Oakeshott. *Journal of Politics* 57:724-742.

Giglio, J.N. 1991. *The presidency of John F. Kennedy.* Lawrence: University Press of Kansas.

Gold, H. J. 1992. *Hollow mandates.* Boulder, CO: Westview Press.

Grafton, C. 1991. Government policy for dangerous inventions in the United States and Great Britain. *Policy Sciences* 24:19-39.

Hamby, A. 1992. *Liberalism and its challengers.* New York: Oxford University Press.

Herrera, R. 1996-97. Understanding the language of politics: A study of elites and masses. *Political Science Quarterly* 111:619-637.

Hilgard, E. R. and G. H. Bower. 1975. *Theories of learning.* Englewood Cliffs, NJ: Prentice-Hall.

Honig, B. 1993. Rawls on politics and punishment. *Western Political Quarterly* 46:99-125.

Hoover, K. R. 1987. *Ideology and political life.* Monterey, CA: Brooks/ Cole.

Horton, D. L. and T. W. Turnage. 1976. *Human learning.* Englewood Cliffs, NJ: Prentice-Hall.

Jackson, J. E. and J. W. Kingdon. 1992. Ideology, interest group scores, and legislative votes. *American Journal of Political Science* 36:805-823.

Jacoby, W. G. 1991. Ideological identification and issue attitudes. *American Journal of Political Science* 35:178-205.

Janda, Kenneth, J. M. Berry, and J. Goldman. 1992. *The challenge of democracy.* Boston: Houghton Mifflin.

Johnston, D. 1994. *The idea of a liberal theory.* Princeton, NJ: Princeton University Press.

Kalt, J. P. and M. A. Zupan. 1984. Capture and ideology in the economic theory of politics. *American Economic Review* 74:279-300.

Kautz, S. 1995. *Liberalism and community.* Ithaca, NY: Cornell University Press.

Kirk, R. 1993. *The politics of prudence.* Bryn Mawr, PA: Intercollegiate Studies Institute.

Lane, R. 1962. *Political man.* New York: Free Press.

Langston, T. S. 1992. *Ideologues and presidents.* Baltimore: Johns Hopkins University Press.

Lasswell, H., D. Lerner, and I. D. S. Pool. 1952. *The comparative study of symbols.* Stanford, CA: Stanford University Press, 1952.

Levine, J., E. G. Carmines, and R. Huckfeldt. 1997. The rise of ideology in the post-New Deal party system, 1972-1992. *American Politics Quarterly* 25:19-34.

March, J. G. and H. A. Simon. 1958. *Organizations.* New York: John Wiley and Sons.

McLellan, D. 1995. *Ideology.* Minneapolis: University of Minnesota Press.

Medoff, M. H. 1989. Constituencies, ideology, and the demand for abortion legislation. *Public Choice* 60:185-191.

Milkis, S. M. 1993. *The president and the parties.* New York: Oxford University Press.

Nelson, D. and E. Silberberg. 1987. Ideology and legislative shirking. *Economic Inquiry* 25:15-25.

O'Sullivan, N. K. 1976. *Conservatism.* New York: St. Martin's Press.

Peltzman, S. 1985. An economic interpretation of the history of congressional voting in the Twentieth Century. *American Economic Review* 75:656-675.

Polsby, N. W. 1984. *Political innovation in America.* New Haven, CT: Yale University Press.

Rhoads, S. E. 1993. *The economist's view of the world.* Cambridge: Cambridge University Press.

Reeves, R. 1993. *President Kennedy.* New York: Simon & Schuster.

Richardson, L. E. Jr., and M. C. Munger. 1990. Shirking, representation, and congressional behavior: Voting on the 1983 amendments to the Social Security Act. *Public Choice* 67:11-33.

Rothenberg, L. S. and M. S. Sanders. 2000. Severing the electoral connection: Shirking in the contemporary Congress. *American Journal of Political Science* 44:310-319.

Schneider, J. E. 1979. *Ideological coalitions in Congress.* Westport, CT: Greenwood Press.

Segal, J. A., C. M. Cameron, and A. D. Cover. 1992. A spatial model of roll call voting: Senators, constituents, presidents, and interest groups in Supreme Court confirmations. *American Journal of Political Science* 36:96-121.

Segal, J. A., L. Epstein, C. M. Cameron, and H. J. Spaeth. 1995. Ideological values and the votes of U.S. Supreme Court justices revisited. *Journal of Politics* 57:812-23.

Shils, E. 1968. The concept and function of ideology. *International Encyclopaedia of the Social Sciences* 7:66-76.

Snyder, J. M. 1992. Artificial extremism in interest group ratings. *Legislative Studies Quarterly* 17:319-345.

Stein, R. M. and K. N. Bicker. 1994. Congressional elections and the pork barrel. *Journal of Politics* 56:377-399.

Steinbruner, J. D. 1974. *The cybernetic theory of decision.* Princeton, NJ: Princeton University Press.

Stimson, J. A. 1991. *Public opinion in America: Moods, cycles, and swings.* Boulder, CO: Westview.

Sussman, G. and B. W. Daynes. 1995. The impact of political ideology on congressional support for presidential policy making authority: The case of the fast track. *Congress and the Presidency* 22:141-153.

Tatalovich, R. and D. Schier. 1993. The persistence of ideological cleavage in voting on abortion legislation in the House of Representatives, 1973-1988. *American Politics Quarterly* 21:125-139.

Van Dyke, V. 1995. *Ideology and political choice.* Chatham, MA: Chatham House Publishers.

Weber, R. P. 1990. *Basic content analysis.* Thousand Oaks, CA: Sage Publications.

Weimer, D. L. and A. R. Vining. 1999. *Policy analysis.* Upper Saddle River, NJ: Prentice-Hall.

Whitaker, J. C. 1996. Nixon's domestic policy: Both liberal and bold in retrospect. *Presidential Studies Quarterly* 26:131-153.

Wolf, C. Jr. 1979. A theory of non-market failure. *Public Interest* 55:114-133.

Young, J. P. 1994. *Reconsidering American liberalism.* Boulder, CO: Westview.

Zupan, M. A. 1992. Measuring the ideological preferences of U. S. presidents: A proposed (extremely simple) method. *Public Choice* 73: 351-361.

Chapter 11

Nixon's Domestic Policy:
Both Liberal and Bold in Retrospect*

John C. Whitaker

It was the morning after John Lindsay crushed William Buckley, the intellectual guru of the conservative wing of the Republican party in the 1965 race for mayor of New York. Richard Nixon and I were seated side-by-side sharing the front page of *The New York Times* reading about Buckley's political demise as we taxied toward take-off at LaGuardia. We were headed toward yet one more of those endless Republican fund raising dinners that Nixon hoped would yield still more IOUs from the party regulars as he pushed toward his goal, the presidency in 1968.

I asked Nixon what he thought would be the impact of Buckley's defeat on the conservative wing of the GOP. "The trouble with far right conservatives like Buckley," Nixon said, "is that they really don't give a damn about people and the voters sense that. Yet any Republican presidential candidate can't stray too far from the right wingers because they can dominate a primary and are even important in a close general election. Remember John," Nixon lectured me, "the far right kooks are just like the nuts on the left, they're door bell ringers and balloon blowers but

*Reprinted with permission from *Presidential Studies Quarterly* 26, 1 (1996):131-153.

they turn out to vote. There is only one thing as bad as a far left liberal and that's a damn right wing conservative." Shoving the *Times* aside, Nixon snapped open his brief case, pulled out a yellow pad and started scribbling one liners for the next fund raising dinner, signaling that our conversation had ended.

Around the same period, flying to still another fund raiser, Nixon's seat mate was John Sears, then a young lawyer in the Nixon law firm. Sears recalled that Nixon was talking about the Republican party's attitude toward the poor. "The GOP is basically made up of two groups," Nixon told Sears, "the Goldwater wing who don't like poor people and the Rockefeller wing who are glad to give them some money as long as they don't have to be seen with them."

Now, almost thirty years later, these two conversations still seem to define Nixon's visceral tilt toward the moderate/liberal side when dealing with domestic legislation, coupled with his respect (maybe fear is a better word) for the political clout of the right wing, so necessary to win national elections.[1]

Throughout his career, Nixon's liberal instincts were held on a tight leash by his conservative constituency and this political reality constantly led to seemingly contradictory actions throughout his presidency. For example, he proposed a bold welfare reform program which left the congressional liberals gasping, yet Nixon's fear of the political clout of the conservatives convinced him to abandon his plan as the 1972 election neared. Again he outflanked the liberals with a sweeping environmental program yet complained privately to conservative business leaders that "we made the mistake of going overboard on the environment." He was proud of his record of peaceful integration of the southern public school system but also careful not to sermonize to southern conservatives about civil rights and busing. He was the first president to index Social Security with cost of living increases. Typically Nixonian, years later at a dinner party at his home in Saddle River, New Jersey, he told a group of fiscally conservative businessmen who had generously donated to his Library, that indexing Social Security (which was a major contributing factor in subsequent years to the soaring cost of entitlement programs) "was the greatest mistake of my presidency."

Some refuse to recognize the moderate to liberal tilt to Nixon's domestic policy. For many it is more comfortable to accept his stereotype image as a hard line anti-communist assuming he was just as conservative on domestic issues. Actually the record supports that Nixon was more liberal than such Republican presidents as Eisenhower, Ford, Reagan, or Bush. At the same time, Nixon's domestic record seems more conservative than recent Democrat presidents such as FDR, Truman, Kennedy,

Johnson, Carter and Clinton, putting Nixon squarely in the middle of the political spectrum of modern presidents.

Liberal to many means sympathetic to the needs of the poor and the handicapped, and minority rights. Nixon's record supports that view. For example, when Nixon left office, more funds were being spent on entitlements than on defense. To others, liberal means responsibly progressive, a reformer in the sense that Theodore Roosevelt is described as a liberal. Even liberal *New York Times* columnist Tom Wicker called Nixon a reformer. To still others, the liberal litmus test is a firm conviction that government action is the best way to solve social problems, a pro-federal regulatory mindset. Nixon was not a liberal in that sense, although some of Nixon's policies (welfare reform, increased spending on human resources, and wage and price controls) are distinctly liberal by this definition.

Nixon came to power following thirty years of escalating centralization and growth of the federal government, just after the guns and butter era of Lyndon Johnson's War on Poverty, which seemed to be the nadir of Franklin Roosevelt's New Deal. His efforts put him on a direct collision course with those who had a vested interest in retaining "inside the beltway" government. Yet, in spite of the stain of Watergate, the clear liberal bias of the large majority of historians and his unquestioned role as a world leader, which many see as the centerpiece of his presidency, a strong case can be made that Nixon's domestic policy was equally innovative and bold and deserves closer examination. Among other things, Nixon had some remarkably innovative "firsts." The first president to appoint a special committee to consider the question of population growth;[2] the first president to create an Office of Child Development;[3] and propose a program for "The First Five Years of Life";[4] and the first president to send to Congress a message entirely devoted to energy policy.[5]

While Nixon unquestionably supplied the inspiration and leadership for his administration's domestic legislation, credit should be given to many key advisers who helped shape the Nixon domestic agenda. And, perhaps more an influence on policy than most realized, "Patricia" Catherine Thelma Ryan Nixon quietly weighed in--on the moderate to liberal side.

The Liberal Spender

Although Nixon's budgets (FY 1970-1975) reflect expansion of entitlement programs initiated in the 1960s, his spending priorities and the large increases he allotted to domestic programs clearly place him politically left of center. Of course all succeeding presidents spent even more on domestic programs than Nixon did, but this was due to inflation and the growth of built-in entitlements, not a conscious decision to shift priorities toward more domestic spending as Nixon had done.

The Nixon years saw military spending decline while domestic spending rose to the point that for the first time since World War II, domestic exceeded defense. Social welfare programs used up fully one-third of the total budget. His FY 1974 budget proposed spending nearly 60 percent more on social programs than Johnson had in FY 1968. He extended the food stamp program nationwide, the first program to provide help for all the poor. The number of people receiving federal food assistance jumped from 6.9 million in 1969 to 15 million by 1973.

Nixon increased spending for the poor, aged, and handicapped, nearly doubled the Johnson Indian budget, started a special program with a $60 million budget to encourage minority businesses, increased college student loans, put $100 million in research for his "war on cancer," doubled the budget for environmental clean-up and new park land acquisition, and proposed $1.5 billion to help school districts meet problems related to court ordered desegregation.

Nixon proposed general revenue sharing, a straight cash transfer to the states to be used at the state's discretion. On top of that, he proposed special revenue sharing, converting narrowly focused special purpose grants into six broad purposes--urban development, rural development, education, transportation, job training, and law enforcement--with the states and localities making their own priority spending decisions. The total $16 billion proposal for both general and special revenue sharing would have increased federal aid to the states and localities by 25 percent.[6]

In a decision that fueled the growth of entitlement programs, Nixon indexed social security to the cost of living adjustments (COLAs) and politicians ever since have considered "messing with social security COLAs" as untouchable--the deadly "third rail" of politics. Although his welfare reform program failed, a part of this program, a guaranteed payment for the elderly, the blind, and disabled, survive to this day. However, liberals should not take too much comfort in Nixon's move to index social security with cost of living adjustments. Instead, Nixon instituted COLAs as a means of stopping Congress from playing the politically popular bidding game of raising social security benefits before every election.

Nixon critics dismiss this record of "liberal spending" emphasizing instead his single minded efforts to dismantle much of Lyndon Johnson's anti-poverty programs, especially the Job Corps, Office of Economic Opportunity, and federal funding of day care. However, critics tend to forget that Nixon proposed cash payments in place of social services and the budget impact, had his welfare reform program become law, might well have exceeded the cost of the programs Nixon wanted to cancel; programs that he considered nothing more than a full employment plan for federal social workers and lawyers. Nixon often complained that "too much money sticks to the fingers of the bureaucrats and doesn't get through to the poor."

It's a bit of a stretch to call Nixon's economic policies truly liberal (in FY 1970 he was the last president to propose a balanced budget), but perhaps the closest observer of his philosophy, Herbert Stein, chair of Nixon's Council of Economic Advisers, characterized Nixon and his economic advisers as "conservative men with liberal ideas."[7] Stein wrote:

> By many measures the Nixon years were a period of retrogression from the conservative economic stand point. The increase in government non-defense spending accelerated greatly. The federal deficit grew. Inflation increased. The extent of government regulation increased. The Nixon price and wage controls were an enormous peacetime intervention into the American economy.[8]*

Deficit spending, higher inflation, regulation of the free market system, whether intended or not, is a legacy associated with liberal Democrat presidents to the left of Nixon. At the time of the Nixon presidency, a fundamental struggle was being played out: liberal economic theory was beginning to collide with a rising vogue of conservative economic ideas. Stein told me that Nixon's decisions to back wage and price controls as well as the concept of a "full employment budget," that is, to deliberately run a deficit when unemployment was high ("now I am a Keynesian," Nixon would say with delight), was part of Nixon's "general schizophrenia." Specifically Stein said:

> Nixon felt he ought to be for traditional virtues. He regarded himself a champion of the silent majority. But he wanted to be a "modern man" and recognized as such by intellectuals and liberals. He was impatient with the dull, pedestrian and painful economics of conventional conservatism.

(Nixon did not want to be an old fuddy dud Republican, according to Stein.)[9] "He called that the economics of three yards in a cloud of dust, whereas he yearned for the long bomb."[10]

Instituting wage and price controls certainly fulfilled Nixon's version of the long bomb, fateful as that decision turned out to be. In his memoirs, Nixon called his decision

> politically necessary and immensely popular in the short run. But, in the long run, I believe that it was wrong. The piper must always be paid, and there was an unquestionably high price for tampering with the orthodox economic mechanisms.[11]

Spoken like a true conservative.

Liberal or conservative, Nixon did leave an interesting economic legacy,[12] including a tax cut in 1969 that relieved six million poor from paying any federal taxes at all; a closed gold window which eventually lead to floating exchange rates and free market forces determining the value of the dollar (gold prices moved from $35 per ounce then to nearly $400 per ounce); an accelerating trend toward reduced tariffs and other barriers to international trade; and early progress toward a policy of deregulating airline, railroads, and trucking to the enormous benefit of consumers. Overshadowing everything else, Nixon's two greatest economic legacies were first, the unintended one, that wage and price controls, in the foreseeable future, will be discredited as a means of controlling inflation and second, future presidents will follow Nixon's lead by placing higher priority on non-defense spending.

Government Reorganization: Breaking the Iron Triangle

"You know what Washington is, don't you," Nixon once lectured me. "It's a place where every morning 300,000 people drive to work, have a cup of coffee, then start writing memos to each other. No wonder the damn town won't work." Nixon was talking about the desperate need to reorganize the federal government for both better decision making and more efficient delivery of services to the people, a dull subject but hard work that needed doing.

Reorganization of the federal government has been a concern of modern American presidents, at least through Bill Clinton (although Reagan and Bush proposed very little in this area). Dwight Eisenhower took a group of scattered agencies and formed the Department of Health, Education, and Welfare (HEW). After "Sputnik" had pricked America's pride in its scientific supremacy, he also created the Office of Science and Technology in the Executive Office of the President. John Kennedy gave the chairman of the Civil Service Commission the lead role in establishing government-wide personnel policies. Lyndon Johnson took the fiercely competitive bureaus, offices, and other fiefdoms that had grown up over the years to represent the various modes of transportation and molded them into one Department of Transportation. He drew together another group of agencies to form the Department of Housing and Urban Development and created the Office of Economic Opportunity, the advocacy agency for the poor.

But President Nixon went the furthest. He eliminated the Department of the Post Office, replacing it with a public corporation free of congressional political patronage. He merged the Peace Corps and Vista into one agency called Action. He created the Environmental Protection Agency, the National Oceanic and Atmospheric Administration, the Federal Energy Office, and later the Federal Energy Administration. Finally he proposed that the Atomic Energy Commission be abolished, with most of its functions going to two new agencies, a Nuclear Regulatory Commission and an Energy Research and Development Administration (both were created by law after Mr. Ford became president). In the Executive Office of the President, Nixon revamped the Office of Management and Budget, created first the Urban Affairs Council and then the Domestic Council, the Office of Telecommunications Policy, and the Council on International Economic Policy. Just as important as creating new institutions, he eliminated from the Executive Office of the President the Office of Science and Technology, [14] the National Council on Marine Resources and Engineering Development, the National Aeronautics and Space Council, and the Office of Emergency Preparedness. Nixon also accepted and used effectively a Council on Environmental Quality, which was established in the Executive Office of the President on the initiative of Congress.

But Nixon's most ambitious reorganization plan failed. He proposed that the Departments of State, Defense, Treasury, Justice, and a smaller version of Agriculture be retained,[15] and that the remaining seven departments and several agencies should be combined into four new ones: Community Development, Human Resources, Natural Resources, and Economic Affairs. When Congress failed to act, Nixon moved administratively to appoint four "super cabinet" officers--reflecting the four functional departments he had in mind.[16] He then installed them in the Executive Office Building to serve as his major advisers and, above all, as referees and coordinators of a government that had become so big and complex that it was nearly impossible to run it in the old style.

In trying to fundamentally reorganize the government, Nixon took on a political fight almost impossible to win because he was offending the "iron triangle"--the special interests, select members of Congress, and the bureaucracy--the three power centers that really run the federal government. First of all, the special interest lobbyists do not want change. After all, many have spent their adult lives getting to know the players in the other two corners of the triangle. Nor do the bureaucrats want change. No matter how often they are assured that they will not lose their jobs when they are transferred to some new and strange department, they are bound to worry. Then there is the uncertainty of who their new boss will be. Finally, the members of the congressional committees resist change because the longer they hold their committee assignments, the more influence they can exert on the departments under their jurisdiction. Cabinet officers typically serve three or four years, whereas the ranking senators and congressmen on the authorization and appropriations committees usually work their way up the congressional seniority ladder over a ten- or fifteen-year period. Consequently, if they do their homework they probably know more about a department than its cabinet officer, and their staffs generally know precisely where to go in the department to get the information they want, often before the secretary knows.[17]

Nixon believed government should be organized around functions rather than on the basis of programs heaped on programs, many outmoded and often unconnected. He wanted his cabinet officers to be less the special pleaders, reflecting narrowly based interest groups, and more the broad-based officials setting priorities. This thinking was at odds with the tendency of members of Congress to restrict their thinking only to the narrower issues as defined by the jurisdictional limits of their particular committee assignments. As lawmakers perfect their narrow specialties, the president, acutely aware of the problem of priority setting, is robbed of the balanced advice he should receive from his cabinet officers who, over time, also become captured in the "iron triangle."

Nixon was the last president to try to reorganize the government on a grand scale. The Clinton administration has made vigorous efforts "reinventing government" dealing with cost cutting, reducing the federal payroll and simplifying federal procurement and civil service hiring practices. President Carter, who did sign legislation creating a Department of Energy and the Department of Education, had a task force that did an excellent job of refining Nixon's proposals (there are only so many ways you can shuffle the boxes on an organization chart), but in the end decided it was not worth the political capital to try. Except for modest organizational tinkering, no president has tried since, and the fossilized federal structure that would drive any modern corporation into bankruptcy continues to flourish today growing like a giant amoeba in a science fiction movie.

Welfare Reform: An Idea Before Its Time

In late spring 1969, months before Nixon unveiled his Family Assistance Plan (FAP) on August 6 that promised to bring order out of the chaos of America's welfare programs, Daniel Patrick Moynihan came up the stairs from his White House basement office to visit me in my second floor cubby hole next to John Ehrlichman's spacious corner office. Pat kept trying to flatter me in his Irish way, emphasizing how much better I knew the president than he did and would I have any tips on how he could win Nixon's approval for his welfare plan. Moynihan was already locked in a well-publicized insider Washington battle with presidential counselor Arthur Burns, a friend of Nixon's going back to the Eisenhower years. Moynihan's welfare reform plan required much money and stressed incentives to remove people from the welfare rolls. Burns wanted less money and strong work requirements and really preferred having no new welfare program at all.

My advice to Moynihan: "Just keep working at it," I told Pat, "and remember, the President is intuitively more liberal than you think. You have that going for you and you'll probably win out in the end." Moynihan really did not need my advice and I could see from watching the president and Moynihan interact at both full cabinet and Urban Affairs Council meetings that they got along very well, often taking playful jibes at each other. At one cabinet meeting, former Harvard professor Moynihan told Nixon he had lined up three statistically representative college students to address the cabinet. "By random sample," Pat smiled, "two of them are from Harvard." Nixon shot back, "That's all right, Pat, by random sample, two of them will be drafted [into military service]."[18]

Burns' case was weakened by polls that showed two-thirds of the American people liked the idea of welfare reform. Also, the pipe smoking economist had a pedantic, slow delivery that quickly made Nixon's eyes glaze over, a style of conversation that put Burns at a disadvantage compared to Moynihan who tossed out sparkling one-liners that Nixon loved.

While more relaxed with Moynihan than with Burns, Nixon felt squeezed between the two with Budget Director Robert Mayo and Vice President Spiro Agnew siding with Burns against the program. So Nixon asked John Ehrlichman to run interference with Agnew, Burns, Mayo and Moynihan. Ehrlichman did so well that in the fall of 1969 Nixon appointed him head of the new Domestic Council, a small White House staff dedicated to getting a common, agreed on set of facts before the president, with option papers systematically laid out for the president's decisions. Nixon loved the system. He started checking the boxes beside the options he liked, or scribbling new ideas in the margins, demanding more information and often devising options no one else had thought about. Most of his work was done quietly and reflectively by the fireside in the Lincoln sitting room in the upstairs family residence of the White House. Evening reading, Nixon soon discovered, was a lot better way to run the government. No whining cabinet officers to talk to putting their spin on the facts. In truth, Nixon did not relish meeting with cabinet officers on a one-on-one basis. He did not even like to talk to them on the phone. Once aide Stephen Bull confronted Nixon in the Oval Office strongly recommending that the president take a call from a cabinet officer who was phoning for the fourth time in as many days trying to get through. "No," the president said dead pan, and then with a wink, "tell him you can't find me."

Ehrlichman gamely plowed into the FAP controversy playing the role of referee and honest broker.** HEW Secretary Robert Finch and his Undersecretary John Veneman recommended a floor payment of $1,600 for a family of four, an idea first proposed by conservative economist Milton Friedman, namely, a guaranteed annual income, a direct cash payment replacing social services for the poor. Missing in the Finch/Veneman plan was an incentive for a poor person to get a job, in fact, there was a disincentive because the plan proposed that fifty cents should be deducted from every dollar of additional income the welfare recipient earned above the federal $1,600 dole. Nixon was looking for a combination that would satisfy both the liberals with a generous monthly check and conservatives with a penalty for not working, with an added incentive to work one's way off the welfare rolls. George Shultz ultimately provided the answer.

At cabinet meetings Nixon was beginning to notice his new Secretary of Labor, an economist and former Dean of the University of Chicago School of Business. Nixon had never met Shultz until after the election and he turned out to be a pleasant surprise. Nixon noticed that Shultz had a way of hanging back in cabinet discussions, then at the end neatly packaging the available options, ticking off the pros and cons. Nixon liked Shultz's organized mind and it caught the president's attention when Shultz, at Urban Affairs Council meetings, started emphasizing that while the Moynihan/Finch/Veneman plan helped the unemployed, it lacked any focus to help the working poor. So Nixon asked Shultz to see if he could come up with a proposal that took the best of the Moynihan and Burns plan.

Shultz retained the Moynihan/Finch/Veneman proposal for a $1,600 a year payment to a poor family of four but added two measures to appease the conservatives. First, he proposed stopping federal payments for those who did not take an available job except for mothers with pre-school children, the aged, and the disabled.   Second, if a person on welfare took a job he or she in effect could pocket the first $20-a-week pay by not deducting it when calculating the benefit level--in other words, a good incentive to take a job. "The bottom line," in Nixon's words, "no work, no welfare. The only exception would be the aged, the infirm and the mothers of pre-school children."[19]

At first, Nixon's welfare reform legislation moved quite well in Congress, passing the House in April 1970 by a 243 to 155 vote, but, in the summer, the Senate Finance Committee rejected two drafts of the bill. In 1971, the House again passed the bill and Nixon raised the ante on the annual welfare payment for a family of four from $1,600 to $2,500 to try to satisfy the liberals on the Senate Finance Committee. It still wasn't enough.   Finally, Nixon refused an offer for an even more costly version of the bill (a $3,000 per year payment) proposed by Senator Ribicoff and FAP was dead--"an idea ahead of its time," in Nixon's words.[20]

"Predictably," Nixon later wrote in his memoirs, "conservatives denounced the plan as a mega-dole [while liberals] complained that the dollar amounts weren't enough and the work requirements were repressive. In fact," Nixon wrote,

> FAP would have immediately lifted 60 percent of the people then living in poverty to incomes above that level. This was a real war on poverty; but the liberals would not accept it . . . as Moynihan observed, it was as if they could not tolerate the notion that a conservative Republican President had done what his liberal Democratic predecessors had not been bold enough to do.[21]

Another interpretation is that if Nixon had kept with his liberal impulses to take on the battle of reforming welfare, he just might have pulled it off. Instead, he followed his political instincts, catering to the conservatives as the 1972 presidential election drew closer.[22]

A third interpretation, shared by some welfare specialists, is that sweeping welfare reform is an impossible dream. Martin Anderson, for example, who played a central role in welfare debates in both the Nixon and Reagan White House, pointed out that three basic elements are inextricably linked together in any fundamental welfare reform plan--the benefit level, the marginal tax rate, and the cost to taxpayers, writing:

> When any two of the three basic elements of radical welfare reform are set at politically acceptable levels, the remaining element becomes unacceptable. For example, if both the minimum welfare benefit level and the tax rate are set so they will be acceptable in today's political

context, the cost of radical welfare reform balloons into tens of billions of dollars, adding millions of Americans to the welfare rolls. On the other hand, if the welfare benefit level is set at a politically tolerable level, and the overall cost is held down, the result is a tax rate that approaches confiscatory levels and destroys the financial incentive to work. And, finally, if the cost is acceptable and the tax rate is low enough to create a strong financial incentive to work, the level of welfare benefits in the plan must be reduced to such a low level that the plan would have no chance whatsoever of being enacted. There is no way to achieve all the politically necessary conditions for radical welfare reform at the same time.[23]

President Nixon started something that President Clinton and Congress are still trying to resolve. Since the time of Nixon's FAP legislation, over the years liberals and conservatives seem to be narrowing their differences. Conservatives better understand the huge costs needed to train people to get off the welfare rolls while liberals are learning it makes sense to pressure welfare recipients as well as give them incentives to work.

In 1988, modest progress was made when President Reagan signed a bill drafted by Pat Moynihan with help from Bill Clinton, then leading a governors' task force on welfare reform. The law required each state to set up a program to give incentives and penalties to get welfare mothers off the rolls and the federal government paid part of the costs.[24]

In 1992, Clinton campaigned for president with the catchy phrase, "two-years-and-out." He meant that after two years on welfare, with a few exceptions, the federal check would be cut off if the welfare recipient did not find a job or work in some sort of public service job. Clinton never explained who would pay for these public sector jobs, nor how the rising cost of job training would be paid. Nor did he suggest how someone on welfare was going to find work in the private sector in a sluggish economy that made it even harder to find entry-level jobs. Fundamental welfare reform is much more complicated than Clinton's "two-years-and-out" campaign slogan, but was a start toward finishing the job Nixon initiated.

A Strong Environmental Record Without Demagoguery

When President Nixon and his staff walked into the White House on January 20, 1969, they were totally unprepared for the tidal wave of public opinion in favor of cleaning the nation's environment that was about to engulf them. If the president-to-be showed little interest in the issue, so did the national press corps. In fact, Nixon staff members do not recall even one question put to the candidate about the environment.

During the 1968 presidential campaign, neither the Nixon nor Humphrey campaign gave more than lip service to environmental issues. Nixon's thoughts, like those of his opponent, Hubert Humphrey, focused on the issues of the day--Vietnam, prosperity, the rising crime rate, and inflation. On October 18, 1968, CBS aired a radio address by Nixon about "America's Natural Resources."[25] One radio speech on natural resources and the quality of the environment seemed adequate to cover an issue that stirred little interest among the electorate. Attention was needed for more important issues.

In the Hubert Humphrey camp, things were just as quiet. The vice president dedicated a park in San Antonio, Texas, on August 10, and the John Day Dam in Oregon on September 28, using both occasions to discuss the environment and conservation. Otherwise, Humphrey said nothing on the issue.[26]

It seems hard to believe that only seventeen months after the election, on April 22, 1970, the country would celebrate Earth Day, a national outpouring of concern for cleaning up the environment. Politicians of both parties jumped on the issue. So many politicians were on the stump on Earth Day that Congress was forced to close down. The oratory, one of the wire services observed, was "as thick as smog at rush hour."[27]

When Rachel Carson published *Silent Spring* in 1962, few would have guessed that by the end of the decade the environment would have exploded as an issue. A comparison of White House polls (done by Opinion Research of Princeton, New Jersey) taken in May 1969, and just two years later in May 1971, showed how concern for the environment had leaped to the forefront of our national psyche. In May 1971, fully a quarter of the public thought that protecting the environment was important, yet only 1 percent had thought so just two years earlier. The public's concern over air and water pollution jumped in the Gallup polls from tenth place in the summer of 1969 to fifth place in the summer of 1970, and was perceived by the public at the time as more important than "race," "crime" and "teenage" problems, but not as important as the perennial poll leader's "peace" and "pocketbook" issues.[28]

In the early 1970s, it was clear that the executive branch could not respond to public demand to clean up the environment without first creating an organization to do the job. The status quo was unacceptable. Better coordination of environmental programs in the federal government was clearly needed. At the time forty-four agencies located in nine separate departments had responsibilities for "the environment and natural resources." No single department had enough expertise to take charge. Nixon began by discarding the option of a Department of Environment and Natural Resources (an enlarged Interior Department), as well as several other reorganization plans. In July 1970, he sent Congress his Environmental Protection Agency plan. The sixty-day period for congressional objections expired in September and the new agency came into being on December 2, 1970.

Additionally, Nixon ordered the federal agencies to shed spare federal acreage that would be converted into parks and recreation areas, especially in urban areas. In other words, he told his cabinet, when in doubt, create a park with your spare lands. And, after much bureaucratic wrestling and White House pressure, they did. More than 82,000 acres in all fifty states were converted into 642 parks, the majority of them in or very close to cities, really bringing parks to the people. More money was dedicated to buying wildlife habitat, and Congress passed Nixon's controversial proposal to protect endangered species. Nixon issued executive orders restricting ocean dumping and tightened environmental standards for off-shore oil drilling. To quell the insatiable development instincts of the Army Corps of Engineers he canceled construction of the Cross Florida Barge Canal.

But what Nixon, nor for that matter any president since, was unable to accomplish, was to address the cost of pollution abatement control. How fast should the nation clean up and at what cost? Nixon knew he would pay a political price by not proposing the "toughest" and costliest pollution control standards, but after looking not only at the federal budget, but at the macro-economic impact, he decided on a more moderate course. He often repeated to me, "Because our actions are responsible and not demagogic, we will never receive the credit due us."

Years later, the accomplishments of the Nixon years are plain to see. New clean air, water, solid waste, and pesticide laws, including the great urban parks in New York City and San Francisco harbors. Nixon routinely budgeted at the $300 million level for parkland acquisition in the early 1970s, a strong commitment compared to the eroded value of today's dollar when President Clinton proposed only $209 million for the same purpose in his FY 1994 budget.[29]

At the time Nixon was assailed from both sides: by those who bitterly resented the cost of environmental clean-up, and by those who insisted that the movement take absolute priority over all other considerations. Between these he steered a progressive middle course, establishing the environment as a national priority, but doing so in a way that enabled economic growth to go forward--so that the nation could, in the long term, continue to afford the cost of environmental clean-up together with the rising standard of living that the people demanded.

Major Health Reform Proposals Before Their Time

> In the last twelve months alone, America's medical bills went up 11 percent. . . in the last ten years it has climbed 170 percent. . . . since 1960 medical costs have gone up twice as fast as the cost of living. . . I want America to have the finest health care system in the world. . . and I want every American to be able to get that care when he needs it . . . to ensure that no American family will be prevented from obtaining basic medical care by inability to pay.[30]

These words sound like Bill Clinton, but the quotes are from Richard Nixon's February 18, 1971, Special Message to Congress Proposing a National Health Strategy.

To finance universal medical coverage, like Clinton, Nixon wrestled with the notion of completely cutting out insurance companies, severing the link between employment and health insurance. In the end, again like Clinton, Nixon proposed a program designed to correct–"not by destroying our present insurance system, but by improving it."[31] Nixon proposed a National Health Insurance Standards Act, the first president to propose legislation requiring *all* employers to provide health coverage for their employees. "In the past," Nixon said,

> we have taken similar action to assure workers a minimum wage, to provide them with disability and retirement benefits, and to set occupational health and safety standards. Now we should go one step further and guarantee that all workers will receive adequate health insurance protection.[32]

In his televised address to a joint session of Congress unveiling his universal health care proposal, President Clinton generously credited Nixon's achievement, saying:

> Under this [Clinton's] health care security plan, every employer and every individual will be asked to contribute something to health care. This concept was first conveyed to the Congress about 20 years ago by President Nixon. And today a lot of people agree with the concept of shared responsibility between employers and employees and that the best thing to do is to ask every employer and every employee to share that.[33]

To protect the unemployed, part time employed, and the self-employed, Nixon proposed a $1.2 billion annually federally funded Family Health Insurance Plan to provide health insurance to all poor families with children headed by a self-employed or unemployed person whose income was below a certain level. Like Clinton, Nixon wanted to establish special regional insurance pools to "offer insurance at reasonable group rates to people who did not qualify for other programs: the self-employed, for example, and poor risk individuals who often cannot get insurance."[34]

Nixon asked Congress for programs designed to foster the growth of health maintenance organizations (HMOs). He wanted insurance plans to allow beneficiaries of their plans to purchase membership in HMOs. He asked Congress for federal planning grants to help new HMOs get started, plus federal loan guarantees so that private funds could be raised to cover early deficits during the first year of operation of new HMOs until large enough enrollments were obtained to show profits. By fostering the growth of HMOs Nixon, like Clinton, hoped to see doctors working for HMOs and therefore subject to cost driven managed care guidelines at reduced fees. To meet the needs of rural and inner city areas where there are too few doctors, Nixon proposed a special federal grant program to offset the financial risks of establishing HMOs in these areas and, where necessary, give federal support to outpatient clinics in under-served areas. He wanted new loan forgiveness programs for medical students who agreed to practice in rural and inner city areas and asked Congress for $10 million for a new National Health Service Corps "made up largely of dedicated and public spirited young health professionals who will serve in areas which are now plagued by critical manpower shortages."[35]

Nixon took on the American Medical Association by proposing ways to increase the number of doctors and other health professionals (presumably an increase in medical personnel would create more competition leading to lower fees). He proposed grants to schools of medicine, dentistry, and osteopathy based on their ability to increase the number of graduates (based on the recommendations of a Carnegie Commission on Higher Education). He proposed almost doubling federal scholarship funds for low income medical and dental students as well as making large increases in funds targeted to train physician's and dentist's assistants, nurse pediatric practitioners, and nurse midwives. Finally, Nixon proposed a $100 million war on cancer and made a five-fold budget increase for sickle cell anemia, a childhood disease almost always occurring among blacks.

Peaceful Integration of the Southern Public Schools

In a January 28, 1972, memorandum to John Ehrlichman summarizing his civil rights views, Nixon wrote: "My feeling's on race as you know are if anything ultra liberal." In the same memo, Nixon states, "I am convinced that while legal segregation is totally wrong, forced integration of housing or education is just as wrong. . . . This country is not ready at this time for either forcibly integrated housing or forcibly integrated education."[36]

The average liberal would laugh at Nixon calling himself "ultra liberal" on race because liberals, by almost any litmus test, consider themselves tough, strict and, most importantly, fast acting when it comes to enforcement of civil rights. Perhaps liberals should reflect more on accomplishments when it comes to civil rights. The Kennedy and Johnson years produced highly publicized confrontations but little progress desegregating the public school system of the South. As Nixon pointed out in his memoirs, not much had been accomplished by the Johnson administration on their watch in the almost five years since the Civil Rights Act of 1964 had become law. "When I came to office in January 1969," Nixon wrote, "68 percent of the black children in the South were still going to all-black schools and 78.8 percent were going to schools that were 80 percent or more black."[37]

Nixon's goal was peaceful integration carried out with conciliation and understanding. "No vigilante justice and never rub the Southerners' nose in it," was Nixon's constant admonition to his staff. He was quick to slap down administration officials who showed too much enthusiasm for enforcement. With the almost universal criticism of the liberal media he fired his chief civil rights enforcer at HEW, Leon Panetta (who served later as President Clinton's director of OMB, then as White House chief of staff), and Dr. James E. Allen, Jr., his Commissioner of Education, symbolic moves that sent strong signals to southerners that he would go slow on integration.

When Nixon came to office, federal enforcers were already threatening to cut off federal education funds to southern school districts where, in their view, implementation of busing plans were lagging. Nixon's initial response, again accompanied by outrage from liberals, was simply to delay the cut off of funds, have a cooling-off period, then use gentle behind-the-scenes prodding to proceed with integration plans. By July 1969, Nixon publicly abandoned HEW desegregation guidelines that had been set by the Johnson administration and instead chose a deliberately slower route pushing for integration guidelines spelled out by court orders through the Justice Department.

By October, the Supreme Court overturned Nixon's go-slow approach in their *Alexander v. Holmes County Board of Education* decision that specifically rejected the high court's *Brown v. Topeka, Kansas Board of Education* decision of 1954 that had ruled a more leisurely timetable for integration. The *Alexander* decision held that integration with "all deliberate speed" previously set out in the *Brown* decision was "no longer constitutionally permissible" and called on school districts to immediately integrate.

Nixon's response was to promise to enforce the *Alexander* ruling but not use busing as a tool to promote school integration. He then moved rapidly to earn the grudging trust and cooperation of advisory committees the administration had established in southern states. There was genuine consultation for the first time. The result was the peaceful and almost complete integration of the southern school system without the moralizing rhetoric or coercion that had been so prevalent in the Johnson years. Nixon was justifiably proud of his record. He had moved quietly and in the end with speed unimagined by the liberals. Nixon later noted that "the dramatic success of our Southern school desegregation program is eloquently told by the statistics. By 1974, only 8 percent of black children in the South were attending all-black schools, down from 68 percent in the fall of 1968."[38]

Liberal *New York Times* columnist Tom Wicker, not known for his pro-Nixon sympathies, wrote in a "you have to give the devil his due" tone when he said:

> The indisputable fact is that he got the job done--the dismantling of dual schools--when no one else had been able to do it. Nixon's reliance on persuasion rather than coercion, his willingness to work with Southern whites instead of denouncing them, his insistence that segregation was a national, not just a southern problem, the careful distance he maintained between himself and the "liberal establishment", the huge political credit he earned in the south with his Supreme Court nominations and his other gestures to southern sensibility--particularly local leadership-all resulted in a formula that worked.[39]

Besides virtually eliminating the dual black and white school system in the South, the Nixon record on civil rights and better opportunities for minorities is quite solid.[40] For example, he more than doubled the Johnson administration budget for predominantly black colleges and almost tripled the last Johnson budget for civil rights including a hike in funds for the Equal Employment Opportunity Commission and for enforcing fair housing laws. The Nixon administration increased minority federal hiring at both the civil service and presidential appointment levels. In executive positions with salaries above $20,000 (in 1974 dollars), there was a 37 percent increase in African Americans over the last Johnson administration year, 1968. When Nixon left office, African Americans who constituted roughly 10 to 11 percent of the population held 16 percent of all federal jobs. The administration also implemented the

Philadelphia plan to insure federal contractors met fair minority hiring practices including endorsing "set aside" programs. It created the Office of Minority Business Enterprise. Finally, Nixon promoted self-determination for Indians, for the first time delegating decision making from the Bureau of Indian Affairs to local tribal leaders and he nearly doubled the Johnson budget for Indian services.

A Helping Hand for Minority Businesses

In his 1968 presidential campaign, in two radio talks which he titled "Bridges to Human Dignity," Nixon spelled out the need to focus attention on minority problems and suggested the creation of a federal program for black capitalism. Later, this concept was broadened to include other disadvantaged ethnic groups, Hispanics, Asians, and Native Americans. Remarkably, no such continuing program had ever been put in place by any administration, including those liberal ones of FDR, Truman, Kennedy, and Johnson.

Once in office Nixon acted quickly. In March 1969, he issued an executive order setting up the Office of Minority Business Enterprise (OMBE) in the Department of Commerce and told Commerce Secretary Maurice Stans, "This is something long overdue and I want you to give it a high priority. Politically, I don't think there are any votes in it for us, but we'll do it because it's the right thing to do."[41] The strong budgetary support Nixon gave OMBE has not been backed up by his successors, conservative or liberal. The Nixon FY 1970 budget for OMBE was $60 million, remained about that level in the Ford and Carter years and slid downward in the Reagan and Bush years. President Clinton's FY 1994 budget for OMBE was a meager $38 million, an appalling drop in real dollar value from Nixon's $60 million FY 1970 level.

Nixon's OMBE initiative resulted in a tremendous growth in the number of minority businesses from 322,000 in 1969 to 1,213,750 in the 1987 economic census while during the same period minority business sales grew from $11 billion to $77.84 billion. Federal grants, loans, and guarantees to minority businesses shot up from $200 million in 1969 to $7 billion in 1991. Finally, federal purchases from minority businesses ballooned from a mere $83 million in 1969 to $17 billion in 1991.[42] Just as encouraging, over the years minority businesses have become more professional--often higher technology, wholesaling, and financial institutions--all higher paying business and professional activities than the traditionally "mom-and-pop" service businesses of earlier years.

Major Initiatives for Native Americans

Nixon's record on Native Americans remains outstanding. In the largest Indian claims settlement in American history, legislation proposed by Nixon provided Alaskan natives a cash settlement of $500 million, a 2 percent share up to $500 million in Alaskan oil reserves, and land title to 40 million acres. The legislation was more generous than that proposed by the Johnson administration in 1967--that would have extinguished Alaskan native claims to their lands in exchange for the value of the land in 1867 dollars (the year the U.S. bought Alaska from Russia) and granting trust title to only 10 million acres. It needs to be emphasized that if an equitable settlement with Alaskan natives had not become law, it is very doubtful the Alaska pipeline, which pumps a million barrels of oil daily into America's energy life line, would have ever been built. Instead, it is quite likely that Alaskan native lawsuits would have quite justifiably resulted in court orders halting pipeline construction across Alaskan native lands.

Nixon also pushed to restore Indian ownership of additional federal lands including returning public lands along the rim of the Grand Canyon to the Havasupai Tribe in Arizona and returning 21,000 acres to the Yakima Tribe in Washington state where, incredibly, the U.S. government had lost the official treaty map in its files and had displaced the Yakimas from tribal lands sixty-seven years earlier.[43] In a gesture symbolic of religious and tribal rights to all Indians, Nixon endorsed, had his staff actively lobby Congress and, in a White House ceremony in December 1970, signed legislation returning 48,000 acres of public lands with sacred religious meaning to the Taos Pueblo Indians in the Blue Lake region of New Mexico.[44]

The Nixon years were a time of heightened militant Indian radicalism brought on primarily by the frustration of centuries of injustice combined by the fact that they are America's most deprived minority. "On virtually every scale of measurement--employment, income, education, health--the condition of the Indian people ranks at the bottom," Nixon said.[45] However, their plight in no way justified the dangerous forced takeover of the Bureau of Indian Affairs (BIA) building in Washington, the former Alcatraz prison in San Francisco Bay, or the armed standoff at Wounded Knee on South Dakota's Oglala Sioux Pine Ridge reservation. All these actions brought a clamor from "law and order groups" pressuring the White House to intervene with forcible armed actions if necessary. Instead, Nixon worked quietly behind the scenes ordering patience and negotiations. The final result was to diffuse all three of these confrontations with a minimum of bloodshed. In the seventy-two-day standoff at

Wounded Knee only one Indian was killed and one federal marshal paralyzed from a bullet in his spine. Unfortunate as this was, any of these three confrontations without the restraints Nixon ordered, could have easily turned into another Attica or Waco inferno.

Nixon's greatest legacy was formulating an entirely new approach to Indian affairs that two decades later is still being implemented, often with the begrudging help of the paternalistic and fossilized bureaucracy of the Department of Interior's BIA. First, Nixon rejected the doctrine, so prevalent in the Eisenhower, Kennedy, and Johnson years, of termination of the trust relationship between the federal government and the Indian people. Nixon called his policy "self-determination without termination."[46] The centerpiece of this new program was legislation empowering "a tribe, a group of tribes or any other Indian community to take over the control or operation of federally-funded and administered programs. . . whenever the tribal council or comparable community governing group voted to do so."[47] Underscoring his commitment to end the tragic termination policy of some of his predecessors, Nixon signed the act restoring the Menominee Tribe to federal trust status.[48] Over the years since Nixon made the proposal, the BIA and Indian Health Services have been reluctant to relinquish the administrative strings that had accompanied turning over funds directly to local Indian governments. In fairness, however, it needs to be said that many Indian tribal leaders like to continue the rhetoric of "BIA bashing" instead of assuming the responsibilities of self-government. To foster further self-determination, Nixon proposed Indian block grants that packaged together a number of economic and resource development grants so that local tribal governments could pick and choose their own spending priorities.[49]

Nixon also proposed giving Indian governments control, if they choose to accept it, over previously BIA-run Indian schools. He asked Congress to allow funds earmarked for Indian education (under the Johnson-O'Malley Act) in public schools Indians attended, to be directly channeled to Indian tribes so that Indian local governments could decide how these funds were spent to educate Indian children in their public schools.[50] To improve Indian health services, Nixon asked Congress for an additional $10 million with emphasis on training Indians for health service careers,[51] and to promote tribal economic development Nixon proposed increasing the existing revolving loan fund for Indian economic development prospects from $25 million to $75 million. On top of that, he proposed $200 million more to loan guarantees, loan insurance, and interest subsidies to encourage private lenders to loan funds for Indian investment opportunities.[52]

Native Americans owned a significant amount of land--about 50 million acres in the lower forty-eight states alone. Yet the BIA exercised great restraint over the ability of Indian tribes to enter into mining and oil exploration and other commercial opportunities which require leasing of Indian lands over the long term. Tilting clearly toward the side of local Indian control over their tribal lands, Nixon proposed giving tribes the right to lease their lands for up to ninety-nine years for commercial ventures.[53]

At the Department of Interior, the voice for Indian rights and priorities was often overwhelmed by the interests of non-Indian western ranchers whose lands frequently border Indian reservations and where water rights are sometimes usurped by upstream water rights originating on Indian lands. Nixon made two proposals to correct this imbalance. First, he asked Congress to establish an assistant secretary of interior dealing with Indian affairs who reported directly to the secretary. This would replace the old system at the Interior Department when the Commissioner of Indian Affairs views were filtered through an assistant secretary of interior for lands and water, the very officer whose primary constituents were the same western ranchers, often hostile to Indian interests. Second, and even more fundamental, Nixon proposed a new Indian Affairs Trust Council to act as "legal trustee over the land and water rights of Indians . . . to assure independent legal representation for Indians' natural resources rights."[54] The new Trust Council, a three-person board with at least two Indians, would act for legal interests in place of both the Attorney General and the Secretary of Interior, which in many cases, Nixon observed would have, "at the same time both the *national* interest in the case of land and water rights and the *private* interest of Indians in lands which the government holds as trustee." In Nixon's view this put the federal government in a conflict of interest and he noted that "no self-respecting law firm would ever allow itself to represent two opposing clients in one dispute."[55] Today, nearly twenty-five years later, the innovative Nixon Indian policy is still treated with profound respect by the vast majority of tribal leaders who will tell you that Nixon did more for Indians than any president since the Second World War.

The All-Volunteer Armed Force

Americans have never taken kindly to military conscription, accepting it only in times of dire military need. For 366 years, beginning in Colonial times from 1607 until 1973 when Congress responded to Nixon's initiative, the military draft was the law of the land for only thirty-five years, three years during the Civil War and thirty-two years from World War II to 1973.[56] The patriotic call to arms of World War II could not be sustained with the discontent of the Vietnam war and 1968 presidential candidate Richard Nixon seemed to sense this political fact of life. In the 1968 presidential primary, Nixon's GOP contenders, Michigan Governor George Romney and New York Governor Nelson Rockefeller, reacted to the criticism of the inequity of the selective service system by proposing a draft lottery. On the Democrat side, Vice President Hubert Humphrey also supported a lottery, Senator Gene McCarthy focused on alternatives to the draft like volunteer social work, while Senator Robert Kennedy supported a ban on student deferments, and in the 1972 presidential campaign, liberal Democrat George McGovern, like Nixon, supported an all-volunteer military service.

The idea of a volunteer armed force to replace the draft system came to Nixon from Martin Anderson, a young Columbia University professor who had been recruited to the Nixon presidential campaign staff by Nixon's law partner, Leonard Garment. Anderson pushed the idea of an all-volunteer military, an idea he had picked up from reading conservative economist Milton Friedman's 1962 book, *Capitalism and Freedom*,[57] which stressed the violation of personal freedom inherent in the national draft system.

Anderson packaged his argument in a twenty-eight page memo to Nixon[58] arguing that an all-volunteer armed force was moral, fair, increased national security, was economically feasible, and would ultimately produce a more professional and efficient armed force, ending his memo on a moral high note: "We should establish a volunteer armed force that will offer the young people of this country the opportunity to participate in her defense with dignity, with honor, and as free men." Nixon reacted cautiously, seeking the advice of an old Eisenhower administration colleague who generally favored only tinkering and reshaping the draft system and friends like Missouri Congressman Thomas Curtis, an early and vigorous advocate of an all-volunteer military service.

As part of his presidential campaign, Nixon used the technique of a series of radio speeches to frame some rather high brow public policy issues, convinced they appealed to the "intellectual liberal press corps." He decided to make the all-volunteer army the subject of one of these addresses. No doubt Nixon saw a political opening. Humphrey had been plagued by anti-Vietnam hecklers at his campaign rallys and the idea of ending the draft with an all-volunteer armed force was bound to be favorably received by young voters with the prospect of being drafted clouding their future. Also, Humphrey's position was simply to tinker with the present draft system and Nixon clearly seized the high ground by proposing a volunteer system in place of mandatory conscription. On

October 17, 1968, Nixon delivered his radio address, "The All-volunteer Armed Forces."[59] "I've looked at this question very carefully," Nixon said, "and this is my belief: Once our involvement in the Vietnam war is behind us, we move toward an all-volunteer armed force." For moral underpinning, Nixon pointed out, "a system of compulsory service that arbitrarily selects some and not others simply cannot be squared with our whole concept of liberty, justice and equality under the law. It's only justification is compelling necessity."

Once elected, Nixon immediately proved his radio address was not campaign rhetoric. In office only nine days, on January 29, 1969, Nixon sent a memo (drafted by Anderson) to the new secretary of defense, Melvin Laird, asking for a detailed plan to replace the draft with an all-volunteer armed service as the Vietnam war wound down. Wanting Pentagon control, Laird tried to dodge the presidential order by proposing to Nixon a one-year study focused on the pay scales and budgeting impact of an all-volunteer force, to be followed by another Pentagon study on the overall feasibility of an all-volunteer military. Instead, Nixon took control away from Laird by appointing on March 27 a fifteen-person commission reporting directly to him, headed by Thomas Gates, a former secretary of defense in the Eisenhower administration. Nixon directed the commission "to develop a comprehensive plan for eliminating conscription and moving toward an all-volunteer armed force."[60] In other words, the commission was not to decide if a volunteer force was feasible, but instead propose a concrete plan to make it happen.

Four years later, after the Gates Commission's favorable report, delays because of budgetary impact, and long debates in Congress whose leadership in the House and Senate Armed Services Committees generally opted for the status quo favoring the draft, Nixon's leadership eventually carried the day. In June 1973, the military draft formally ended and the following year all-volunteer armed forces became a reality and has produced a more professional and efficient armed force that has worked successfully for two decades.

In an April 17, 1991, commentary in *The Los Angeles Times,* Anderson reviewed the doubts that had lingered about the all-volunteer armed forces.

> Since the United States abolished the military draft almost 20 years ago, we have argued and debated many aspects of the all-volunteer force–the degree to which it represented and mirrored our society, the number of high school graduates in its ranks, its racial composition, the number of women--but the central question, how well would it fight, was rarely raised and remained an unanswered question until

January 16, 1991 (the day Operation Desert Storm started in the Persian Gulf War). The world now knows the answer. The all-volunteer armed force of America is an awesome fighting machine.

Later, after leading the fight to end the draft, Nixon developed strong misgivings about an all-volunteer armed force being able to maintain parity between NATO and the Warsaw Pact nation's nuclear and conventional capabilities. In his 1980 book, *The Real War,* Nixon wrote:

> I considered the end of the draft in 1973 to be one of the major achievements of my administration. Now seven years later, I have reluctantly concluded that we should reintroduce the draft. The need for the United States to project a strong military posture is now urgent, and the volunteer army has failed to provide enough personnel of the caliber we need for our highly sophisticated armaments. Its burden should be shared equally by all strata of society, with random selection and as few deferments as possible. Even so, it will cause hardships, and whatever its form, the draft is inherently unfair; it can only be justified by necessity. But as we look at the 1980s, necessity stares us in the face: we simply cannot risk being without it. To put off that hard decision could prove penny wise and pound foolish; our reluctance to resume the peacetime draft may make us weak enough to invite war, and then we will find ourselves imposing a wartime draft instead.[61]

Nixon modified this view in 1993:

> I had no doubt whatever about the wisdom of going forward with the voluntary army once the Vietnam War was over. By 1980, however, as you will recall, our military forces under Carter had sharply deteriorated in quality. With the global threats which I set forth in detail in *The Real War,* I felt it was essential to improve efficiency and saw no way to do so except by reinstituting the draft. Since then, however, during the Reagan-Bush years, there has been a dramatic improvement in the quality of the men and women who joined the armed forces. Consequently, I endorse the all-volunteer Army approach without qualification today.[62]

Pat Nixon Spoke Quietly

When Pat Nixon died at age 81, many recalled the shy, quiet, politically correct image, forever, it seemed, sitting on a political campaign platform, face upraised with a fixed smile, listening with apparent rapt attention to her husband's speeches, most of which she had probably heard before. Although she shunned the political spotlight, she did not lack convictions and she often dealt, albeit in a quiet way, with policy issues of substance.

In 1972 she was the first First Lady since Eleanor Roosevelt to address a national political convention.[63] She was the first First Lady to call publicly for a woman on the Supreme Court, saying, "our population is more than 50 percent women, so why not?"[64] Apparently confident she was succeeding, in convincing her husband to appoint women to the highest court, she told the press in September 1971, "Don't you worry, I'm talking it up--if we can't get a woman on the Supreme Court this time, there'll be a next time."[65] At a family dinner on October 21, 1971, the day Nixon announced two nominations to the Supreme Court (Lewis F. Powell, Jr. and William H. Rehnquist), Julie Nixon Eisenhower noted that, "mother strongly stated that one of the nominees should have been a woman and gave her reasons. My father, with exaggerated weariness, finally cut off the conversation with the excuse: 'We tried to do the best we could, Pat.'"[66]

Nearly a year later on September 14, 1972, Pat Nixon still lobbied her husband for a woman on the Supreme Court. Interior Secretary Rogers Morton and I happened to be meeting with the President and the First Lady, briefing her on her upcoming trip to Yellowstone National Park where she would make an appearance as part of the centennial anniversary of the U.S. National Park Service. Somehow, the conversation turned to the Supreme Court and Mrs. Nixon said, "Dick, how about a woman?" Then she complained that one of Nixon's recent nominations, then a sitting Supreme Court Justice, was "too old for the job." Trying to humor her and again end the ever on-going argument, Nixon winked and said, "That's okay Pat, as soon as the election is over, I'll get rid of him."

Pat Nixon was the first First Lady to favor the equal rights amendment. "I am for women. I am for equal rights and equal pay for equal work--it was time to formally recognize that women in employment and other areas deserve equal treatment with men."[67] On a visit to then Yugoslavia, she said their parliament, like the U.S. Congress, had too few women.[68] She pressed her husband to appoint more women to high government posts, and Nixon appointed Barbara Franklin (later George Bush's Secretary of Commerce) as the nation's first White House staff member whose specific mission was to recruit women into government,[69] and Ann Armstrong became the first female counselor to any president in January 1972. On civil rights she strongly supported her husband's quiet efforts to integrate the southern public school system. "As a former teacher," Julie Nixon Eisenhower wrote,

> mother hoped that the long cherished system of neighborhood schools
> could be preserved whenever possible, and she heartily supported the

administration's strategy of creating a climate of cooperation in the south toward integration so that the lower courts would not be compelled to resort to rulings such as busing to carry out the higher court's decree.[70]

According to Carl Sferrazza Anthony, Pat Nixon "was a pro-choice advocate, stating 'I think abortion should be a personal decision'-- the first First Lady to voice such an opinion (a view her husband did not share), let alone mention the word abortion."[71] Sensing another early trend, Pat Nixon cautiously opened the door to the possibility of amnesty for Vietnam draft deserters. "I think that those who ran should not be accepted back at the moment. I do feel that if they decide to serve, maybe on a volunteer capacity or something like that, and earn their way back into the country, that would be another thing."[72]

Five times she campaigned with her husband for national office (twice for vice-president in 1952 and 1956 and three times for president in 1960, 1968, and 1972), a record unsurpassed in American history. As the wife of the vice-president, she visited fifty-three nations and by the end of her White House years she had represented the United States in seventy-eight nations, making her the most widely traveled First Lady in history. She did solo missions to Brazil, Venezuela, Peru (to bring aid to earthquake victims), and on visits to Ghana, the Ivory Coast, and Liberia, she privately met with those nation's leaders to discuss Rhodesian and South African policy and the likely impact of the Nixon's forthcoming trip to the People's Republic of China. Helen Thomas, dean of the White House press corps who has covered first ladies back to Mamie Eisenhower, called Pat Nixon "the warmest First Lady I covered and the one who loved people the most."[73]

On her death, obituaries referred to Pat Nixon as the last of the traditional first ladies. In reality she was, along with Lady Bird Johnson, the first of the modern first ladies who dealt with their convictions and with thorny cutting-edge public policy issues. Ignoring all this, Nixon said the day she was buried at the Nixon Library, "when you think of Pat," "I hope you will always remember the sunshine in her smile."[74]

Legacy of Talent for Other Presidents

Nixon left a legacy of highly talented people who went on to serve in the cabinets of later presidents. This extraordinary group includes: two secretaries of state (Alexander Haig and George Shultz); five secretaries of defense (Frank Carlucci, Richard Cheney, Donald Rumsfeld, James Schlesinger, and Caspar Weinberger); three secretaries of interior

(Thomas Kleppe, Donald Hodel, and James Watt); two secretaries of agriculture (Richard Lyng and Clayton Yeutter); a secretary of commerce (Barbara Franklin), energy (James Schlesinger), and labor (Ann McLaughlin); and a secretary of education who also served as governor of Tennessee (Lamar Alexander).[75] Other Nixon alumni stars include two U.S. senators (Pat Moynihan and John Warner); a Supreme Court Chief Justice (William Rehnquist); a chairman of the Federal Reserve (Paul Volker); three administrators of the EPA (Douglas Costle,[76] William Riley, and William Ruckelshaus) and five assistants to the president for national security (Richard Allen, Frank Carlucci, Anthony Lake, Colin Powell, and Brent Scowcroft). So far four Nixon administration alumni have run for president (Lamar Alexander, Pat Buchanan, Al Haig, and Don Rumsfeld). And then there was defeated Texas senatorial candidate George Bush who went on to greater things after solid training in Nixon appointed posts as U.S. Representative to the United Nations and Chairman of the Republican National Committee.

One can quibble over whether Nixon was left of center, middle of the road or a moderate, but his most important contribution was that for the first time he raised bold new domestic policy issues before they had ripened in the national mind-set--issues like revenue sharing, reorganizing the federal government to better deliver services, improving our health delivery system, revamping our welfare system--all issues that still seek resolution today. Nixon's greatest domestic legacy is that he slowed the leftward march of government, opened the door that made possible the Reagan-Bush years and continues to pull Bill Clinton, heir of the Democratic Leadership Council, toward the center of the political spectrum.

Notes

1. In the 1965 New York mayoral race political analysts noticed for the first time that a conservative like Buckley could draw votes away from traditional Democrat Catholic voters in Queens and Brooklyn. It was the beginning of a trend that Nixon, Reagan, and Bush nurtured in their campaigns.

2. Richard Nixon, Special Message to the Congress on the Problems of Population Growth. In *Public papers of the presidents of the United States* (Washington, DC: GPO, July 8, 1969), 521-530.

3. Richard Nixon, Statement Announcing the Establishment of the Office of Child Development. In *Public papers* (Washington, DC: GPO, April 9, 1969), 270-272.

4. Richard Nixon, Special Message to the Congress on Education Reform. In *Public papers* (Washington, DC: GPO, March 3,1970), 228-238.

5. Richard Nixon, Special Message to the Congress on Energy Resources. In *Public papers* (Washington, DC: GPO, June 4, 1971), 703-714.

6. Richard Nixon, Messages to Congress on the State of the Union. In

Public papers (Washington, DC: GPO, January 22, 1971), 54.

7. Herbert Stein, *Presidential economics.* (New York: Simon and Schuster). See chapter 5, Nixon: Conservative men with liberal ideas, 133-208.

8. Ibid., 34.

9. Author's conversation with Herbert Stein, October 1993.

10 . Stein, *Presidential economics,* p. 135.

11. Richard Nixon, *RN the memoirs of Richard Nixon* (New York: Grosset and Dunlop, 1978), 521.

12. For an analysis of the Nixon domestic spending, see Carl Lieberman, Legislative success and failure: The social welfare policies of the Nixon administration, in *Richard M. Nixon: Politician, president, administrator,* ed. Leon Friedman and William F. Levantrosser (Westport, CT: Greenwood Press, 1991), 107-131.

13. However, Johnson was unable to get Congress to move the Maritime Administration into the new Department of Transportation.

14. But in June 1975, President Ford proposed legislation to create a similar organization, the Office of Science and Technology Policy, and on May 11, 1976, he signed the National Science and Technology Policy Organization and Priorities Act of 1976, P.L. 94-282 (90 Stat. 459), thus reversing Nixon's decision.

15. Nixon had originally proposed eliminating the Department of Agriculture, then modified the proposal under constituency political pressure, but still recommended reducing the department's proposed size from 85,600 employees and annual outlays of $8.7 billion to 28,000 employees and annual outlays of $5.2 billion. Today, the department has about 114,000 employees and an annual budget of roughly $62 billion.

16. See Richard Nathan, *The plot that failed* (New York: John Wiley and Sons, 1975) for a good description of Nixon's attempts to use his cabinet members as managers of the broad functions of government.

17. President Nixon appointed thirty-one cabinet officers to the twelve major departments and gave cabinet status to seventeen more advisers. President Truman made twenty-two cabinet appointments, Eisenhower twenty-one, Kennedy thirteen, and Johnson twenty, Ford inherited twelve and eventually appointed twelve more, while Carter named twenty-one, Reagan thirty-three, and Bush twenty.

18. The author's recollection from a September 29, 1969, Urban Affairs Council meeting.

19. Nixon, *RN the memoirs,* 426.

20. Ibid., 428.

21. Ibid., 427.

22. For a detailed history of Nixon's Family Assistance Plan, see John Robert Greene, *The limits of power* (Bloomington and Indianapolis: Indiana University Press, 1992), 47-51; Joan Hoff-Wilson, Outflanking the liberals on welfare, in *Richard M. Nixon: Politician, president, administrator,* ed. L. Friedman and W. F. Levantrosser, 85-106; and Lieberman, Legislative Success and Failure, Ibid., 115-118.

23. Martin Anderson, *Welfare, the political economy of welfare reform in the United States* (Stanford, CA: Hoover Institution, 1978), 143-144.

24. The Family Support Act of 1988 (P.L. 100-485), signed into law October 13, 1988.

25. Richard Nixon, *Nixon speaks out: Major speeches and statements in the*

presidential campaign of 1968 (New York: Nixon-Agnew Committee, October 25, 1968).

26. Democratic National Committee news releases of August 10 and September 28, 1968.

27. *Washington Post,* April 23, 1970, 20.

28. For more polling data on the environment issue in this time period, see John C. Whitaker, *Striking a balance: Environment and natural resources policy in the Nixon Ford years* (Washington, DC: American Enterprise Institute, 1977) 8-16.

29. See Associated Press, Acquisition of park lands to take a hit, April 8, 1993.

30. Richard Nixon, Special Message to the Congress Proposing a National Health Strategy. In *Public papers* (Washington, DC: GPO, February 18, 1971), 170-186.

31. Ibid., 183.

32. Ibid.. 183.

33. President Clinton, Health care remarks, *Congressional record,* Vol. 139, No. 125 (Washington, DC: GPO, September 22, 1993), H6899.

34. Richard Nixon, Special Message to the Congress Proposing a National Health Care Strategy. In *Public papers* (Washington, DC: GPO, February 18, 1971), 185.

35. Ibid., 177.

36. Nixon, *RN the memoirs,* 443-444.

37. Ibid., 439.

38. Ibid., 443.

39. Tom Wicker, *One of us, Richard Nixon and the American dream* (New York: Random House, 1991), 506.

40. Nixon's civil rights record still polarizes historians. For a positive interpretation, see Hoff, *Nixon reconsidered,* 77-114. For a moderate view, see Greene, *The limits of power,* 41-47. For a distinctly unfriendly view of Nixon's record, see Alvy L. King, Richard M. Nixon, Southern strategies, and desegregation of public schools, in *Richard M. Nixon: Politician, president, administrator,* ed. L. Friedman and W. F. Levantrosser, 141-158, and former HEW Secretary Robert Finch's response to King's paper, ibid., 173-175. For a detailed narrative focusing on the political impact on Nixon's southern public school integration policy, see Wicker, *One of us,* 484-507, and H. S. Dent, *The prodigal South returns to power* (New York: John Wiley and Sons, 1978), 119-156.

41. Maurice H. Stans, Nixon's economic policy toward minorities, in *Richard M. Nixon: Politician, president, administrator,* ed. L. Friedman and W. F. Levantrosser, 240.

42. Statistics supplied by Richard Stevens, staff researcher OMBE, U.S. Department of Commerce.

43. Richard Nixon, Statement on Signing Executive Order Providing for Return of Certain Lands to the Yakima Indians. In *Public papers* (Washington, DC: GPO, May 20, 1972), 609.

44. Richard Nixon, Special Message to the Congress on Indian Affairs. In *Public papers* (Washington, DC: GPO, July 8, 1970), 569.

45. Ibid., 564.

46. Ibid., 565.

47. Ibid., 567-568.

48. Richard Nixon, Statement on Signing the Menominee Restoration Act. In *Public papers* (Washington, DC: GPO, December 22, 1973), 1023.

49. Richard Nixon, State of the Union Message to the Congress on Human Resources. In *Public papers* (Washington, DC: GPO, March 1, 1973), 144.

50. Richard Nixon, Special Message to the Congress on Indian Affairs. In *Public papers* (Washington, DC: GPO, July 8, 1970), 570.

51. Ibid., 572.

52. Ibid., 571.

53. Ibid., 571.

54. Ibid., 573.

55. Ibid., 573.

56. See Ralph Pomeroy Witherspoon, "The Military Draft and the All-Volunteer Force: A Case Study of a Shift in Public Policy," PhD diss., Virginia Polytechnic Institute and State University, 1993, for an in-depth review of the history of the draft and a fascinating narrative of Nixon's initiative to end the draft and bring the all-volunteer armed forces to reality.

57. Milton Friedman, *Capitalism and freedom* (Chicago: University of Chicago Press, 1962).

58. The memo is reproduced as appendix B in Witherspoon's thesis.

59. Nixon, *Nixon speaks out*. The radio address is also reproduced as Appendix C in Witherspoon's thesis.

60. Richard Nixon, Statement Announcing Appointment of the President's Commission on an All-Volunteer Armed Force. In *Public papers* (Washington, DC: GPO, March 27, 1969), 258-259.

61. Richard Nixon, *The real war* (New York: Warner Books, 1980), 201.

62. Letter to the author from President Nixon, November 4, 1993.

63. Carl Sferrazza Anthony, *First ladies, Vol. II, The saga of the presidents' wives and their power, 1961-1990* (New York: William Morrow, 1991), 203.

64. Carl Sferrazza Anthony, Pat Nixon, stealth feminist? *Washington Post,* June 27, 1993.

65. Julie Nixon Eisenhower, *Pat Nixon, the untold story* (New York: Simon and Schuster, 1986), 321.

66. Ibid., 321.

67. Anthony, *First ladies,* 194.

68. Anthony, Pat Nixon, stealth feminist?

69. See archives Nixon Library and Birthplace, Yorba Linda, CA, press release by Barbara Hackman Franklin, March 13,1985. "In a two year period (1972-1974), the number of women in appointive jobs increased dramatically, and it should be underscored that many of them were 'firsts'. Women were serving in jobs no woman had ever served before . . . the first woman chairman of the Atomic Energy Commission, the first woman member of the Council of Economic Advisers. There were also dramatic changes in the career service. For example, during this period, the first women became FBI agents, forest rangers and sky marshalls, and the foreign service opened its ranks more completely to women." Also see the White House Fact Sheet, *Women in the federal government,* released August 18, 1972, indicating Nixon nominated the first six women as U.S. Army generals, and the first woman as Navy Rear Admiral.

70. Eisenhower, *Pat Nixon,* 285.

71. Anthony, Pat Nixon, stealth feminist?

72. Ibid., 191-192. [sic]

73. Ibid., 167. [sic]

74. President Nixon's tribute to Pat Nixon, given to family members and friends after her services at the Nixon Library, June 26, 1993.

Notes by *Presidential Studies Quarterly* Editor

*The nation was not at peace when Nixon announced his New Economic Policy on August 15, 1991. For more detail on Nixon's economic policies see the article by Paul W. McCracken in this issue [Vol. 26, 1].

**For an explanation of how FAP fit into Nixon's attempt to redefine federal, state, and local relationships under his "New Federalism," see article by Richard N. Nathan in this issue.

Acknowledgments

Thanks are due to a number of President Nixon's cabinet and White House staff for reviewing the text, adding their recollections, helpful comments and pointing out factual errors: Martin Anderson, Stephen Bull, James Cavanaugh, Kenneth Cole, Jr., Christopher DeMuth, Harry Dent, John Ehrlichman, Richard Fairbanks, Robert Finch, Barbara Franklin, Edwin Harper, Stephen Hess, William Kriegsman, Paul McCracken, Bradley Patterson, Michael Raoul-Duval, Glenn Schleede, John Sears, Roger Semerad, Maurice Stans, and Herbert Stein.

Not surprisingly, some objected to my putting a liberal label on Nixon, whether liberal meant big spender, a pro-government mindset, sympathetic to the poor, or reformer in the tradition of Theodore Roosevelt. After all, what Republican likes to be called a "liberal"? On one major point, there was no disagreement: Nixon's domestic policy was bold and innovative, raising policy issues long before they had ripened in the national mind-set, issues still not resolved today.

Thanks are also due to John Taylor, director of the Richard Nixon Library and Birthplace; Robert Smalley who served as a close confidant of Secretary of Commerce Maurice Stans, and William Lyons, deputy undersecretary of the Department of Interior in the Nixon years. President Nixon offered constructive comments and Julie Nixon Eisenhower verified the factual information in the paper dealing with her mother.

Also, my deep appreciation to Lois Tschirhart who pushed her antiquated word processor through many drafts of this paper.

Finally, like most authors who played a role in just one presidential administration, I may have a tendency to overemphasize presidential initiatives, forgetting that really new fresh ideas in Washington are rare and that every president builds on, to some degree, what went before.

It is unfortunate that neither Arthur Burns nor Bryce Harlow lived to review this paper. I'm sure they could have made significant improvements because they had the rare advantage of serving two presidents (Eisenhower and Nixon), giving them a wiser and more seasoned perspective than most presidential advisers. Often Arthur and Bryce had to cool my enthusiasm for what I thought was a new idea by recounting the history, often over many years, of precisely what had happened to my "new initiative."

Appendix

Basic Regression Analysis

Several of the articles included in this volume use a statistical technique called regression analysis as their major research methodology. In general, statistics attempts to determine whether events are occurring because of chance or cause and effect. Using statistics we can rarely prove the existence of a cause and effect relationship, but we can calculate the probability of an event being the result of a causal factor, and we can also investigate various aspects of the nature of the relationship.

Regression analysis seeks to estimate the value of a dependent variable--the behavior we are trying to understand or explain--based on the behavior of one or more independent variables believed to be impacting the dependent variable's behavior. The estimate is based on past behavior patterns of the variables used in the analysis.

Many of the articles assume that ideology is an independent variable that affects another variable's behavior. One example is found in Chapter 2 where Levine, Carmines and Huckfeldt examine the impact of ideology (independent variable) on partisanship (dependent variable). When only one independent variable is used in regression analysis, simple regression is being performed. When two or more independent variables are examined, the analysis is know as multiple regression.

Regression analysis tries to model the change in the dependent variable as a function of the change in the independent variable. The simplest model used for such estimation is a straight line. The equation that represents a straight line when there is only one independent variable is:

$$y = a + bx$$

where y is the value of the dependent variable; x is the value of the independent variable; a is the value of y when x is equal to zero (a is also called the y-intercept or the constant in the equation); and b is the slope of the line or the change in y divided by one unit change in x (b is called the coefficient of x). In addition there is always an error factor which is assumed to be random.

In their Table 1 Levine, Carmines, and Huckfeldt show the results of six different regression analyses. The data came from survey research results. In each analysis ideology is the independent variable (x) and partisanship is the dependent variable (y). For 1972 they report a constant (a) equal to 2.08 and a b or coefficient value equal to 0.79. The lack of a minus sign before each number indicates that these are positive numbers. If values of a and b are substituted into the equation, we get:

$$y = 2.08 + 0.79x \quad \text{or} \quad \text{Partisanship} = 2.08 + 0.79*\text{Ideology}$$

When the value of x (Ideology) is zero, the value of y (Partisanship) is 2.08. The 0.79 value for b tells us that as the value of x increases by 1, y increases by 0.79. Because the number is positive, an increase in the value of x results in an increase in the value of y. If the number had been negative, an increase in the value of x would have resulted in a decline in the value of y. Regression analysis done on data collected in 1967, 1980, 1984, 1988 and 1992 results in different estimates for y because both the constant (a) and the slope (b) of the line change.

The same table reports two other values. The first is R^2, commonly known as variance explained. R^2 is the percent of the variance in the dependent variable (y) explained by the independent variable (x). An R^2 value of 1.0 would mean that all the variance (changes) in the dependent variable values can be explained by the independent variable. For 1972, the table reports an R^2 of 0.10, meaning about 10 percent of the time changes in partisanship (their y) can be explained by the changes occurring in ideology (their x). This means that 90 percent of the time changes in partisanship are related to other variables that are not part of the analysis or random error. By comparing the R^2 values in each of the six years of analysis, the authors point out that in each successive year examined, ideology explains more of the variance or change occurring in partisanship, but note that in 1992 the R^2 value is still relatively low, 0.18.

The second value reported is the t-score associated with the value of each regression coefficient (*b*). *T*-scores are used to test the null hypothesis that the value of the coefficient equals zero. If the coefficient equaled zero, the value of the dependent variable would equal *a* (the *y*-intercept), meaning changing values of the independent variable would be having no impact on the dependent variable and R^2 would be zero. Researchers are interested in *t*-scores that are significant at the .05 confidence level, meaning that fewer than 95 times out of 100 it would be a mistake to reject the null hypothesis. Levine, Carmines, and Huckfeldt do not give the statistical significance of the *t*-scores in their table, but most of the tables reported throughout this volume provide that information.

Multiple Regression

In multiple regression, $y = a + b_1x_1 + b_2 x_2 + b_3x_3 \ldots + b_nx_n$ would represent the straight line equation with each *x*, a different independent variable. The coefficient associated with each independent variable indicates the change in *y* divided by one unit change in *x* while all other independent variables are being held constant. Each of these regression coefficients may also be called a partial regression coefficient.

Table 2 in Chapter 2 presents the result of a multiple regression. Again, partisanship is the dependent variable. Model 1 in the table has nine independent variables: education, income, region, race, class, union, urban, Jewish, and Catholic. The regression coefficients that appear in bold type represent those coefficients that are statistically significant based on the calculated *t*-score values. Again, a separate regression was run on data collected for each of the six years depicted in the table. Only four independent variables (race, union, Jewish and Catholic) were statistically significant in all six years, meaning that it is safe to reject the hypothesis that there is no relationship between the variable and partisanship when the other eight variables are held constant. In multiple regression analysis the statistically non significant independent variables are often dropped from the analysis and a new regression equation computed.

Note that Table 2 presents R^2 values for each analysis. Now this value represents the variance or change in *y* that may be explain by all the independent variables working together. Overall, the variance explained by the nine independent variables is small, ranging from a low of 13 percent to a high of 19 percent.

When the authors add ideology as a tenth independent variable (model 2), the added variable is in a statistically significant relationship with partisanship in each of the six years, and the variance explained by the ten independent variables ranges from a low of .21 to a high of .31

with the R^2 value higher in each year in model 2 compared to the same year using model 1. The authors use this change in R^2 as an important piece of evidence that ideology impacts partisanship.

Adjusted R^2

At times a value known as adjusted R^2 is reported along with R^2. Adjusted R^2 is usually reported when there are a large number of independent variables being used in the analysis. In such cases adjusted R^2 will be lower than R^2. Adjusted R^2 corrects for the fact that the chance variations associated with each independent variable have more and more impact on the dependent variable when the number of independent variables increases. In effect the impact of these chance variations is reduced.

Standard error

Several tables in this volume also display a value representing standard error also known as the standard error of estimate. Like R^2, this is a measure of the spread of data points around the regression line. It reflects the difference between predicted values (i.e., values predicted on the basis of the regression line) and actual values. The focus of this statistic is on variation in y unaccounted for by x. The standard error is the standard deviation of the points from the regression line.

The standard deviation is a measure of dispersion. If a data set is distributed normally, 68.27 percent of cases are included between the boundaries of the mean plus or minus the standard deviation, 95.45 percent of cases are included between the boundaries of the mean plus or minus twice the standard deviation, and 99.73 percent of cases are included between the boundaries of the mean plus or minus three times the standard deviation.

Whenever the standard error of a coefficient is larger than the coefficient itself, the reliability of the coefficient is in doubt.

Beta weights

Another value often reported for each independent variable in a multiple regression analysis is a beta weight or beta (also known as the coefficient of multiple determination). Beta weights are regression coefficients for standardized data, data translated to a common scale based on the standard deviation of the data. A beta weight is the average amount of increase in the dependent variable when the independent variable increases by one standard deviation unit and the other independent variables are held constant. Beta weights may be positive or negative. When they are used by most of the authors in this volume, they are reported as positive or negative, but in many other articles only the absolute value of the beta weight is reported. In such instances the unstandardized coefficient also is reported. The positive or negative sign associated with each unstandardized coefficient also applies to the beta weight.

Because the beta weights are based on standardized data, their values (unlike the values of unstandardized coefficients) may be compared. The higher the absolute value of the beta weight, the more impact that independent variable has on the dependent variable relative to the impact of the other independent variables. For example, a beta of .50 indicates that an independent variable has twice as much impact as an independent variable with a beta value of .25.

Major Assumptions of Linear Regression

Regression analysis requires that the data included in the analysis meet several criteria, and there are specific statistical tests that may be applied in the analysis phase to test for whether these conditions have been met. The tests will not be discussed here due to space limitations, but they are described in the recommended works listed at the end of the Appendix.

Some of the major assumptions required for a sound regression analysis are listed below. The list is only partial and emphasizes the assumption directly addressed by various authors in this volume.

(1) Data are measured at the interval or ratio level (continuous data). Despite this requirement, ordinal data, especially 5- and 7-point scales, often are used in analysis. And, because many variables of interest to the social scientist are measured nominally (for example, race, region, and party control of the House or Senate), these variables are converted into "dummy" variables. A dummy variable indicates the presence or absence of a condition with 1 normally representing the presence of the condition and 0 representing its absence. For example, Democratic control of the House = 1 and Republican control (or not Democratic) = 0. Special regression techniques (LOGIT and PROBIT) have been developed to deal with nominal and ordinal data.

(2) Multicollinearity levels are relatively low. Multicollinearity exists when two or more independent variables in a multiple regression

are highly correlated with each other. As a result their separate impacts are difficult to determine, and their presence will increase the standard errors associated with the regression coefficients. An example would be trying to estimate the dependent variable income, when the independent variables are race and education.

(3) Linearity of the data. Some data may in fact represent curvilinear relationships (for example, follow a parabola instead of a straight line) and require other analysis approaches.

(4) No systematic measurement error, only random error.

(5) No outliers or extreme cases exist. Extreme cases will distort results and are often excluded from analysis. Another approach for dealing with their presence is to transform or alter the data structure through various means such as converting the data to logarithmic values.

Recommended Readings on Regression

There is a large literature on regression analysis. The works listed here are sources especially useful to those who are looking for a basic understanding of the technique and its appropriate applications. More specialized materials may be found in the Sage Publications series, Quantitative Applications in the Social Science which includes works by two authors (Edward G. Carmines and William G. Jacoby) whose articles appear in this volume.

Berk, R. A. 2003. *Regression analysis: A constructive critique.* Newbury Park, CA: Sage Publications, Inc.

Kahane, L. H. 2001. *Regression basics.* Newbury Park, CA: Sage Publi-cations, Inc.

Vogt, W. P. 1998. *Dictionary of statistics and methodology: A nontechnical guide for the social sciences,* 2nd ed. Newbury Park, CA: Sage Publications, Inc.

G. David Garson's *PA 765 Statnotes: An Online Textbook* (available at http://ww2.chass.ncsu.edu/garson/pa765/statnote.htm) is a very useful guide to a variety of statistics. Should you have difficulty entering the site directly simply use a search engine, inputting the author's name and/or the name of the text. The general site has useful links to other online materials related to statistics.

List of Contributors

BARRY C. BURDEN is Associate Professor of Government at Harvard University. He received his Ph.D. from Ohio State University. His research and teaching are based in American politics, with an emphasis on electoral politics and representation. He is co-author of *Why Americans Split Their Tickets: Campaigns, Competition, and Divided Government* and editor of *Uncertainty in American Politics*. He has published articles in the *American Political Science Review*, *American Journal of Political Science*, *British Journal of Political Science*, *Legislative Studies Quarterly*, *Political Science Quarterly*, *Electoral Studies*, and elsewhere.

GREGORY A. CALDEIRA is Distinguished University Professor and University Chaired Professor of Political Science at Ohio State University. He received his Ph.D. from Princeton University. His fields of specialization are public law and judicial politics, American political institutions, organized interest groups, and comparative law and courts. His research has appeared in such journals as the *British Journal of Political Science*, *American Journal of Political Science*, *Journal of Politics*, *Political Analysis*, *Legislative Studies Quarterly*, *American Political Science Review*, *International Social Science Journal*, *Law & Society Review*, and in many anthologies.

EDWARD G. CARMINES is Professor of Political Science at Indiana University. He received his Ph.D. from SUNY Buffalo. His major teaching and research interests are in the areas of American politics, political behavior, and research methodology. He is co-author of *Statistical Analysis of Social Data*; *Reliability and Validity Assessment*; *Mea-*

surement in the Social Sciences; Unidimensional Scaling; Issue Evolution: Race and the Transformation of American Politics; and *Reaching Beyond Race.* In addition, he has published numerous chapters in edited books and articles appearing in such journals as the *American Political Science Review, Journal of Politics,* and *American Journal of Political Science.*

ROGER W. COBB is Professor of Political Science at Brown University. He received his Ph.D. from Northwestern University. Among other books, he has co-authored or co-edited *Cultural Strategies of Agenda Denial: Avoidance, Attack, and Redefinition; Participation in American Politics: The Dynamics of Agenda-Building; Political Uses of Symbols;* and *Politics of Problem Definition: Shaping the Policy Agenda.* Some of his articles have appeared in the *Policy Studies Journal, Journal of Aging and Social Policy,* and *Journal of Aging Studies.*

CARL GRAFTON is Professor of Political Science and Public Administration at Auburn University Montgomery. He received his Ph.D. from Purdue University. Co-author of *Big Mules and Branchheads: James E. Folsom and Political Power in Alabama* and *Political Power in Alabama: The More Things Change . . . .* and co-editor of *The Uneasy Partnership,* he has published numerous articles and book chapters on computer applications in political science and public administration, federal agency creation and reorganization, public policy for dangerous inventions, public budgeting, and the behavioral study of ideology and public policy. Some of his work has appeared in *Policy Sciences, Administration and Society, PS: Political Science and Politics, Public Choice, Journal of Political Ideologies, Social Science Journal* (forthcoming), the *Southeastern Political Review* (now *Politics & Policy*) and *Public Productivity Review.* He is book review editor for the *Social Science Computer Review.*

TIM GROSECLOSE is Associate Professor of Political Economy and Associate Professor of Political Science at Stanford University. He received his Ph.D. from Stanford University. His research interests are vote-buying models, elections, and measuring the ideology of politicians. His research has appeared in such journals as the *American Journal of Political Science* and the *American Political Science Review.*

ROBERT HUCKFELDT is Professor of Political Science at the University of California at Davis. He received his Ph.D. from Washington

University St. Louis. His interests lie in the areas of political participation, public opinion, communication, and voting. He has written or co-authored *The Dynamics of Political Mobilization, II: Deductive Consequences and Empirical Application of the Model*; *Dynamic Modeling: An Introduction*; *Politics in Context: Assimilation and Conflict in Urban Neighborhoods*; *Race and the Decline of Class in American Politics*; and *Citizens, Politics, and Social Communication: Information and Influence in an Election Campaign*. His research has also appeared in such journals as the *American Journal of Political Science*, *Political Behavior*, *American Journal of Sociology*, *American Politics Quarterly*, *Journal of Theoretical Politics*, *Journal of Politics*, *American Political Science Review*, *Political Psychology*, and in many anthologies.

WILLIAM G. JACOBY is a professor in the Department of Political Science at Michigan State University. He received his Ph.D. from the University of North Carolina at Chapel Hill. His areas of interest include public opinion, voting behavior, state politics, and quantitative methodology. He is editor of *The Journal of Politics*. His books include three monographs in the Sage series Quantitative Applications in the Social Sciences including *Statistical Graphics for Visualizing Multivariate Data*. His recent research has appeared in such journals as the *American Journal of Political Science*, *Public Administration Review*, and *Journal of Public Administration Research and Theory*.

JOSEPH P. KALT is the Ford Foundation Professor of International Political Economy, John F. Kennedy School of Government, Harvard University. He also serves as faculty chair of the Harvard University Native American Program (HUNAP) and co-director of the Harvard Project on American Indian Economic Development. He received his Ph.D. from the University of California at Los Angeles. He has published widely in the area of natural resources economics and policy. He is the author or co-author of *The Economics and Politics of Oil Price Regulation*; *Federal Policy in the Post-Embargo Era*; *Drawing the Line on Natural Gas Regulation*; and *What Can Tribes Do? Strategies and Institutions in American Indian Economic Development*. His work has also appeared in many journals including the *American Economic Review* and *Natural Resources Journal*.

JONATHAN KNUCKEY is an assistant professor in the Department of Political Science, University of Central Florida. He received his Ph.D. from the University of New Orleans. His research and teaching interests include voting behavior, southern politics, political parties, campaigns and elections, and research methods. His research has appeared in *Party Politics*, *American Review of Politics*, *Polity*, *Politics & Policy*, and *Social Science Quarterly*. He has also co-authored chapters in *Louisiana: Laissez les bon temps rouler!* and *The 2000 Presidential Election in the South*.

JEFFREY LEVINE is a Managing Director at Westhill Consulting, a division of Westhill Partners. He received his Ph.D. from Indiana University. He focuses on developing positioning campaigns for corporate clients and organizing electoral research and strategy for political campaigns--including the 2004 presidential bid of Richard Gephardt. His research interests include public opinion, political behavior, and public opinion. His publications have appeared in such journals as *Public Opinion Quarterly*, *American Political Science Review*, and *American Politics Quarterly*. In addition, he has conducted political analysis for the International Brotherhood of Teamsters and ABC's Sunday morning program "This Week," and he has appeared on MSNBC and Fox News.

ANNE PERMALOFF is Professor of Political Science and Public Administration at Auburn University Montgomery. She received her Ph.D. from the University of Minnesota. Her articles and book chapters focus on state public administration, constitutional reform in Alabama, computer applications in political science and public administration, public budgeting, and the behavioral study of ideology and public policy. Some of her articles have appeared in *Policy Sciences*, *PS: Political Science and Politics*, *Public Choice*, *Social Science Journal* (forthcoming), *State and Local Government Review*, *Southeastern Political Review* (now *Politics & Policy*), *Public Productivity Review*, *Cumberland Law Review*, and *Journal of Political Ideologies*. She is co-author of two books--*Big Mules and Branchheads: James E. Folsom and Political Power in Alabama* and *Political Power in Alabama: The More Things Change . . . .*

DAVID A. ROCHEFORT is Professor of Political Science at Northeastern University. He earned his Ph.D. from Brown University. His areas of study include public policy, health and mental health care, social welfare, and methodology. Among other books, he has written or co-edited *The New Politics of Health Policy*; *From Poorhouses to Homelessness: Policy Analysis and Mental Health Care*; *The Politics of Problem Definition: Shaping the Policy Agenda*; and *American Social Welfare Policy*.

His research has appeared in such journals as the *Public Administration Review*, *Health Affairs*, and *Policy Studies Journal*.

RAYMOND TATALOVICH is Professor of Political Science at Loyola University Chicago. He received his Ph.D. from the University of Chicago. His primary research areas are public policy analysis, focused specifically on moral conflicts, as well as the presidency and Canadian politics. Included among the eleven books that he has authored or co-authored are *The Modern Presidency and Economic Policy*; *Nativism Reborn? The Official English Language Movement and the American States*; *Cultures at War: Moral Conflict in Western Democracies*; and *The Presidency and Political Science: Two Hundred Years of Constitutional Debate*. His scholarly works have also appeared in such journals as the *Journal of Politics, Political Research Quarterly, Social Sciences Quarterly, Polity, Presidential Studies Quarterly, White House Studies, American Review of Canadian Studies*.

MARK WATTIER is Professor of Political Science at Murray State University. He holds a Ph.D. from the University of Tennessee. His research and teaching interests include political behavior, political parties, and campaigns and elections. His scholarly works have appeared in such journals as *Women & Politics, American Review of Politics, Southeastern Political Review* (now *Politics & Policy*), *Journal of Business Communication, Operant Subjectivity, Journal of Politics, American Politics Quarterly*, and *Campaigns & Elections*.

JOHN C. WHITAKER received his Ph.D. in geology from Johns Hopkins University. He coordinated Nixon White House policy for natural resources including the president's messages to Congress dealing with the environment, energy, rural development, and farm policy. Between 1973 and 1975 he was Undersecretary of Interior under Presidents Nixon and Ford. He is author of *Striking a Balance: Environment and Natural Resources Policy in the Nixon Ford Years*.

MARK ZUPAN is Dean and Professor of Economics and Public Policy, William E. Simon School of Business at the University of Rochester. He received his Ph.D. from the Massachusetts Institute of Technology. His research interests include the political behavior of voters and elected officials, water policy, industrial organization, and regulation and political economy. He is the co-author of *Microeconomic Theory and Applications* and *Microeconomic Cases and Applications*. His research has appeared in such journals as the *American Economic Review, Journal of Law and Economics, Rand Journal of Economics, Public Choice,* and *Journal of Regulatory Economics.* His opinion pieces have appeared in the *Wall Street Journal, New York Times,* and *Los Angeles Times,* among other newspapers.

Index